ROBERT ALDRICH

INTERVIEWS

CONVERSATIONS WITH FILMMAKERS SERIES
PETER BRUNETTE, GENERAL EDITOR

Photo credit: Photofest

ROBERT
ALDRICH
INTERVIEWS

EDITED BY EUGENE L. MILLER, JR.
AND EDWIN T. ARNOLD

UNIVERSITY PRESS OF MISSISSIPPI / JACKSON

www.upress.state.ms.us

The University Press of Mississippi is a member of the Association of American University Presses.

Copyright © 2004 by University Press of Mississippi
All rights reserved
Manufactured in the United States of America

11   10   09   08   07   06   05   04   03   4   3   2   1
∞

Library of Congress Cataloging-in-Publication Data

Aldrich, Robert, 1918–
    Robert Aldrich : interviews / edited by Edwin T. Arnold and Eugene L. Miller.
        p.   cm. — (Conversations with filmmakers series)
    Includes index.
    ISBN 1-57806-602-6 (cloth : alk. paper) — ISBN 1-57806-603-4 (pbk. : alk. paper)
    1. Aldrich, Robert, 1918——Interviews.   2. Motion picture producers and
directors—United States—Interviews.   I. Arnold, Edwin T.   II. Miller,
Eugene L., 1945–   III. Title.   IV. Series.

PN1998.3.A44A5   2003
791.43'0233'092—dc21   2003050161

British Library Cataloging-in-Publication Data available

CONTENTS

INTRODUCTION

ROBERT ALDRICH WAS AMONG the last of an old breed of Hollywood filmmakers. Although he came from wealth and power—the Aldrich family in Rhode Island were political and social leaders in the state, and he was first cousin to Nelson Rockefeller, with those politics he firmly disagreed—Aldrich worked his way up through the ranks of the film industry. He tells this story many times in his interviews, how in 1941 he went to work at RKO (through, it should be said, the influence of an uncle), "did everything from production clerk to clapper boy, and then . . . got some second assistant director jobs," as he explained to George Addison in 1962. He was extremely fortunate in his training both at RKO and afterwards. As a first assistant director, he worked with many of the greats from Old Hollywood—such as Lewis Milestone, William Wellman, and Charles Chaplin—as well as a number of the younger directors who were bringing a new, often socially-aware approach to film, figures like Joseph Losey, Robert Rossen, and Abraham Polonsky. He was at the center of the idealistic post-war experiment in independent filmmaking that resulted in Enterprise Studios. From 1946–48, Enterprise, as Aldrich recalled to Joel Greenberg, was "a really brilliant idea of a communal way to make films. It was a brand new departure, the first time I can remember that independent filmmakers had all the money they needed." There he worked on such major films as *Body and Soul* and *Force of Evil*, movies that he constantly used as moral and artistic touchstones for his own later work. After a stint in the early television industry, where he both wrote and directed, Aldrich was ready to helm his own films. By this time he had a clear sense of the business and of his place in it, both as a professional filmmaker and as an artist of conscience.

This highminded description might at first seem unlikely and even misleading for the maker of such hard, violent, sometimes cynical and even vulgar films like *The Dirty Dozen, The Longest Yard, The Grissom Gang,* and *The Choirboys.* No other major director of his times was slammed as fiercely as Aldrich was by outraged critics for the brutality and mean humor of his pictures. But this was a part of his volatile personality. He was a big man and often an angry one, someone who would "come across the table at you" when pushed beyond his limits. He had a simple but deeply-held view of the world. He believed that existence was conflict, that power inevitably corrupts, and that the honest man was bound to lose no matter how "right" or "moral" his intentions. Nevertheless, even though the cards were stacked against you, he believed that you had an almost existential obligation to hold to your basic principles. Compromise was another word for betrayal. His films illustrated this belief again and again, and his professional life was an unusually rocky one, filled with great successes and unmitigated disasters, in large part because of his adherence to this standard. He was, as Peter Bogdanovich called him, "a true maverick." Even near the end of his life, when he had very little influence in Hollywood after a series of box office failures, he could not play the game. In 1981, for example, he told Roderick Mann of a "rough meeting" with studio heads where keeping his temper was imperative if he wanted a job. "Well, I'll never do it again," he said. "They were not right. Sitting there I got so frustrated I nearly had a heart attack. Usually if someone treats me badly I tell them—and that's that. So I've made another enemy. Yet, here I was trying to stay in control and be charming—charming? No, I'm never charming—be convivial and nearly having a heart attack when I should have been throwing the guy out of the window."

In simplest terms this response reflected the heart of Aldrich's professionalism, which never changed. As a young director he spoke of his "personal style [that] must be based on a high moral standard and a sincere and constructive concern for the progress of fellow beings. . . ." As the tired and battered but unyielding old pro, it was still a matter of what was "right." The line, almost a mantra, that he lived by came from his film version of Clifford Odets's play about Hollywood corruption, *The Big Knife:* "Struggle, Charlie, you may still win a blessing." To Aldrich, "struggle" best described life and a man's courageous response to it. "I think it's the manner in which you strug-

gle that entitles you to that blessing," he told David Sterritt in 1976, realisti-
cally adding, "if there is a blessing."

The other side of Aldrich's personality was the funny and compassionate
and even sentimental man who gathered about him a "family" of actors,
composers, cinematographers, screenwriters, and other members of the film
crews that he knew he could trust. He was aware that some among them
might not always be the best choice for a specific film, but he believed in
loyalty, and if they did their best, he would be there for them whenever he
could. Thus, the same names appeared over and over in the credits to his
films. He could be demanding and even abusive if his passion ran high
enough—Aldrich was never one to back away from a fight, even a physical
one—and he butted heads with most of the people he worked with, including tough guys like Jack Palance, Burt Lancaster, Robert Mitchum, Lee Marvin, and Burt Reynolds. But he admired people who stood up for their beliefs,
no matter how explosive the situations might become, and his regret at no
longer being able to work with Palance or Mitchum or Reynolds was genuine. The distinction he made between Bette Davis and Joan Crawford while
filming *What Ever Happened to Baby Jane?* exemplified his appreciation and
respect for the professional ethic. Both women were hard to please and both
made demands on him as a director that he sometimes felt went beyond his
obligations, but Davis, he believed, made demands for the good of the performance, while Crawford's motives were more selfish. He spoke well of
both, for he tried to be a gentleman, but he was quick to replace Crawford
and keep Davis when he made his "sequel" to this film, *Hush . . . Hush, Sweet
Charlotte.*

Aldrich's independent streak earned him enemies in the business, and his
liberal politics sometimes bled over into a righteous outrage that some critics
misread as nihilism. His films did explore the seduction of violence, and in
works like *The Dirty Dozen* or *The Grissom Gang,* anarchy might well seem the
final and only answer. When the New York Film Society of Lincoln Center
held a retrospective of his movies in 1994, they acknowledged this, titling
their program *Apocalypse Anytime!* But imbedded in this anger was also a
fierce exuberance and dark humor that celebrated as well as deplored the
insanity of life. Both critics and viewers too often missed the outrageous
thread of black comedy that ran through Aldrich's films. And there was also
a gentleness, a sadness hidden in works like *Baby Jane* and *The Killing of Sister
George* and especially his last film, *. . . All the Marbles,* that revealed a man of

sensitivity and deep feeling, traits not often associated with Aldrich. He was not always discriminating or tasteful, and he could be guilty of coarseness and even cruelty in his life and in his films, but there was never any question that he was someone who held strong beliefs and desires and was willing to risk everything to accomplish them. As Peter Bogdanovich has correctly noted, "Most of his failed pictures are more compelling than a lot of people's successes."

Nevertheless, it seems safe to say that Aldrich is not well remembered by many filmgoers today, although they might recall *What Ever Happened to Baby Jane?* or *The Dirty Dozen* or *The Longest Yard,* all of which have had long lives through television and remakes or sequels done by other people. Film buffs, who are not as likely to confuse Robert Aldrich with Robert Altman (and what does *M*A*S*H* owe to *The Dirty Dozen* [besides Donald Sutherland], and what, for that matter, does *The Longest Yard* owe to *M*A*S*H?*), will know of Aldrich's remarkable series of movies in the 1950s such as *Apache, Vera Cruz, The Big Knife, Attack,* and especially *Kiss Me Deadly,* original films all that are still fresh, audacious, and masterful reconsiderations of traditional movie genres. Working with actors like Lancaster, Palance, Marvin, and Mitchum, Aldrich was developing a deeply masculine film style, one that recognized and accepted violence and betrayal as essential parts of the human condition without completely denying the possibility of redemption. After a relatively fallow (though still interesting) period abroad, he returned to the United States to make the Gothic horror comedies *What Ever Happened to Baby Jane?* and *Hush . . . Hush, Sweet Charlotte,* and to perfect the all-male "patrol picture"—"It's X number of men trying to get from here to there and back, or from here to there and survive," he explained to Harry Ringel—in such films as *The Flight of the Phoenix* (with James Stewart, Ernest Borgnine, and Richard Attenborough), *The Dirty Dozen* (with Marvin, Charles Bronson, and John Cassavetes), and *The Longest Yard* (with Burt Reynolds and Eddie Albert). Interspersed among these popular films—Aldrich helped to create the concept of the "blockbuster" movie with *The Dirty Dozen* and *The Longest Yard*—were smaller, more personal and perhaps more thoughtful works like *Ulzana's Raid,* a Burt Lancaster western that spoke directly to American involvement in Vietnam; *Hustle,* a Burt Reynolds police drama whose apparent cynicism hides a deep regret for the loss of American innocence; and . . . *All the Marbles,* his last film, a broad remake of *Body and Soul* with Peter Falk as the manager of a pair of female wrestlers. Despite the

seeming crassness of the storyline, it was a final return to the political idealism of his Enterprise days and one last protest against thoughtless capitalism
embodied now by the policies of Ronald Reagan.

Robert Aldrich certainly made his share of bad or even throwaway pictures
(4 for Texas), although he never took on a job with the intention of doing
less than his best. Films like The Angry Hills, Too Late the Hero, or perhaps
even The Choirboys he called "gorilla pictures," using the phrase given him
by Robert Mitchum. These were movies that you wanted to work, labored
hard to make work, but knew all along would never work no matter what
you did. Others were noble failures, films that demanded more than the
makers or the audience could give them, projects like The Legend of Lylah
Clare, The Killing of Sister George, Emperor of the North, and Twilight's Last
Gleaming. These are fascinating attempts to do something new, to challenge
viewer expectation. Aldrich never apologized for any of his films, even when
he acknowledged their lack of success. "You make the pictures that you want
to make," he told David Sterritt. "Sometimes you make it well, sometimes
you make it badly. Nobody does a picture to make it unsuccessful, because X
number of flops will eventually put you out of the game. And nobody looks
forward to that."

Aldrich was never afraid to risk failure; indeed, he sometimes seemed to
court it. His need for independence and desire to control his career led to
one great, even audacious experiment. After the enormous success of The
Dirty Dozen in 1967, Aldrich, anticipating Francis Ford Coppola and George
Lucas, used his profits to buy his own studio. In one sense he was returning
to the Enterprise Studios experiment, the desire to make and distribute his
films without having to compromise for commercial or political reasons. It
was, he told James Powers in 1978, "a marvelous little studio. . . . It was a
sensational operation. We only needed around sixty-five production days a
year to break even." The dream, however, was destined to fail. "Then I followed that classy act by making four dogs in a row," he said. "Nobody is
going to finance you after four dogs." Aldrich's response to this setback was
typically pragmatic: "You jump on a bottle of whiskey for about six months,
and then you've got to go back to work. How? You cut your price, and you
take pictures you wouldn't have taken before."

Aldrich also had very strong political feelings about the rights and respon-
sibilities of directors and of the film industry in general. He had joined the
Directors Guild as a junior assistant in 1942 and served as both vice-president

and then president of the Assistant Director's Council. As a director, he served as first national vice-president of the Guild from 1971 to 1975, and then as president from 1975 to 1979. At the DGA Memorial Service for Aldrich in 1983, fellow director Franklin Shaffner described Aldrich's leadership style as follows: "His was a Jeffersonian concept of the Guild, Lincolnian in passion and with more than a little of Teddy Roosevelt in representing the Guild." Aldrich himself said of his tenure, "I consider myself a political president. The other ones have been very loyal, helpful, dedicated men, but they have not thought of the guild as a political instrument for the betterment of its members." He was later credited with bringing about, in Shaffner's words, "the most remarkable gains to the membership in dollars, residuals and creative rights . . . melding an economic and creative impact which affected the texture and the substance of our working lives as never before."

Robert Aldrich's career, as shown in these interviews, was always a mixture of entertainment, social awareness, professional survival, political savvy, and righteous indignation. In the first interview in this collection, concerning his first film, *The Big Leaguer,* Aldrich said of the characters, "There'll be no traditional makeup for any of the players. . . . They'll look human and natural, instead of like china dolls." He never lost sight of those "human and natural" aspects of his characters, those strengths and flaws that could turn his people into heroes and monsters, occasionally at the same time. He felt that his pictures could handle such complexity, and he argued for what he called "adult" pictures. He was incensed, for example, when his film *The Killing of Sister George* received an "X" rating, the first major American film to be so ranked. He brought suit against Jack Valenti and the Motion Picture Association of America's rating board (among others), arguing that "X-films could be serious instead of dirty." He lost and had to pay $43,000 in court fees, but Aldrich was always willing to take on these battles.

What runs throughout the interviews, as throughout his films, is the need for courage and honesty. Aldrich could be brutal in his observations, but he could also be funny and forgiving. Although, for example, he stood firmly against the Hollywood Blacklist and inveighed against the House Committee on Un-American Activities that took down so many of his early colleagues and friends, he could later say of Elia Kazan, "[he] is a favorite person of mine and, I think, an absolutely tremendous director. It was reported that he made a mistake in the fifties in going before the House Committee on Un-American Activities. People who didn't go before the committee obvi-

ously felt very strongly about it." Aldrich knew that people have their breaking points; all he asked was that they did the best they could for as long as
they could. That was also what he demanded of himself, in both his professional and private life. In his last major interview, Aldrich was asked, "What
would the people you've worked with say about you?" His answer is typically
tough and understanding: "They'd say: He's too set in his ways and he can
be a pretty nasty guy, but if you understand how he works, he's easy to work
with. If you make a mistake and tell him, there's no problem; but if he
catches you in a lie, it's the devil to pay!"

The loyalty that Aldrich inspired in his people proved that many were
willing to accept his conditions because he worked himself harder than anyone else. In 1973, he told John Calendo that he feared losing the energy and
concentration necessary to be a good director. Calendo protested that "an
artist is someone who uses his brain more than his body," to which Aldrich
replied, "No, that's not true. . . . It's not true of the guy who gets to the set
at 6:30 in the morning . . . and then leaves the set at 9 o'clock at night. That's
not true of the director. That's bullshit! He doesn't sit in the goddam trailer
and say, 'Let me know when you're ready, Mr. De Mille!' You know, you're
talking about the *auteur,* the guy who makes the movie, and he's got to run
out of gas sooner than the guy sitting under the umbrella, drinking lemon-
ade. A director is the first guy there and the last guy home. He works harder
and longer and physically more is taken out of him. Now, that's what a director who *is* a director is!"

Robert Aldrich *was* such a director.

In keeping with the conventions of the Conversations with Filmmakers
series, the following interviews are presented chronologically and repro-
duced in their entirety. We have silently edited minor errors but otherwise
have allowed the interviews to read as they were first published. There is
obviously some repetition in the subjects, questions, and answers, but Robert
Aldrich was a forceful, plainspoken man whose words cut through pretense,
and we find his responses, even when they repeat themselves, entertaining
and perceptive. He could tell stories with the best of them.

We would like to thank all of the interviewers and publishers who have
allowed us to reprint these interviews. We especially thank Peter Brunette,
general editor of the series, and Seetha Srinivasan and her associates at the
University Press of Mississippi for accepting Aldrich as a subject. We also owe

a tremendous debt to Alain Silver, whose own work on Aldrich is indispens-
able and who generously shared his research and his knowledge with us. Our
appreciation also goes to Bruce Malloy for helping us track down the interview in *Reid's Film Index* (Australia); Brenda Fernandes at *Sight and Sound*,
Andrew Lockett of the British Film Institute, and Caroline Sisneros of the
Louis B. Mayer Library at the American Film Institute for their assistance; our
colleague Bill Griffin for translating the final interview in this collection; and
director Robert M. Young, who proved a wonderful friend in Los Angeles. We
would also like to thank Dr. Daniel Hurley, former chair of the English
Department, Dr. David Haney, present chair of the English Department, and
Dr. Linda Bennett, Dean of the College of Arts and Sciences at Appalachian
State University, for their support of this project; and our student assistants
Joe Boykin, John Tedder, and especially Cassie Robinson for their skillful
contributions to this volume.

CHRONOLOGY

1918   Born on August 9, in Cranston, Rhode Island, into prominent
              political and social family; his uncle is John D. Rockefeller, first
              cousin is Nelson Rockefeller

1933–37   Attends private Moses Brown School, Providence, Rhode Island

1937–41   Attends the University of Virginia but departs after four years with-
              out a degree and moves to Hollywood to enter film business via
              family connections; takes first film job as production clerk at RKO
              Studios

1944–52   Apprenticeship and internship with some of the film industry's
              most famous directors and writers, including Jean Renoir, William
              Wellman, Lewis Milestone, Joseph Losey, Charles Chaplin, Robert
              Rossen, and Abraham Polonsky; works at experimental Enterprise
              Studios from 1946–48.

1952–53   Television experience in New York City and California; directs epi-
              sodes of *The Doctor, China Smith,* and *Four Star Playhouse*

1953   Directs first feature-length film, *The Big Leaguer*

1954   Directs *World for Ransom,* first of many collaborations with cine-
              matographer Joseph Biroc, editor Michael Luciano, art director
              William Glasgow, and musical director Frank DeVol

1954   Directs *Apache* for Hecht-Lancaster productions, one of the first "pro-Indian" films; follows with *Vera Cruz,* also for Hecht-Lancaster, his first commercially-successful film

1955   Directs *Kiss Me Deadly,* based loosely on the Mickey Spillane novel; quintessential *film noir* receives critical acclaim from Francois Truffaut in *Cahiers du cinéma* and establishes Aldrich's reputation in Europe (film placed in National Film Registry in 1999)

1955   Forms his own production company, The Associates and Aldrich, and directs *The Big Knife,* adapted from the Clifford Odets's play; film wins the Golden Lion Directorial Award at the Venice Film Festival

1956   Directs "woman's picture" *Autumn Leaves,* an Associates and Aldrich production; film wins Silver Bear Award for Best Direction at Berlin Film Festival; directs anti-war combat film *Attack,* which wins Italian Film Critics award at Venice Film Festival, although American Ambassador walks out in protest

1957   Fired as director of *The Garment Jungle* by Columbia Studio head Harry Cohn; replaced by Vincent Sherman during last days of filming; begins four-year period of working in Europe and Mexico

1959   Aldrich in exile; directs *Ten Seconds to Hell* at UFA Studios in West Berlin; directs *The Angry Hills,* based on Leon Uris novel, on location in Greece

1961   Directs Freudian western *The Last Sunset* (screenplay by blacklisted Dalton Trumbo) in Mexico; directs biblical epic *Sodom and Gomorrah* (screenplay by blacklisted Hugo Butler) in Italy and Morocco but film not released in America until 1963

1962   Returns to America and directs Bette Davis and Joan Crawford in *What Ever Happened to Baby Jane?,* his biggest commercial success since *Vera Cruz,* grossing more than $12 million in its first year of release; film is nominated for five Academy Awards including Davis for best actress and Victor Buono for best supporting actor

1963   Directs *4 for Texas,* comic western with Frank Sinatra and Dean Martin; a critical and commercial failure

1965   Directs Gothic horror *Hush . . . Hush, Sweet Charlotte,* a successful follow up to *Baby Jane;* nominated for seven Academy Awards including Agnes Moorehead for best supporting actress

1966   Directs *The Flight of the Phoenix,* based on the novel by Elleston Trevor; film is nominated for two Academy Awards: Ian Bannon for best supporting actor and Michael Luciano for best editing

1967   Directs *The Dirty Dozen,* Aldrich's most commercially successful film, earning $18 million in its first year of release and becoming the number one box office hit of the year; film receives four Academy Award nominations including John Cassavetes for best supporting actor; Aldrich named Director of the Year by the National Association of Theater Owners

1968   Uses profits from *The Dirty Dozen* to purchase his own private studio, the Aldrich Studios; plans, ambitiously, to produce between eight and sixteen films in five years; directs *The Legend of Lylah Clare,* a film about Hollywood, and *The Killing of Sister George* (both Aldrich Studios productions); because of its controversial lesbian love scene, *Sister George* receives an X-rating from the Motion Picture Association of America; Aldrich goes to court to argue that X-ratings should not be interpreted to mean pornographic material but loses

1969   Produces *Whatever Happened to Aunt Alice?* and directs a twenty minute "mini-movie" *The Greatest Mother of 'Em All,* an experiment in finding potential backers for the full-length film. *Alice* is moderately successful but *Mother* is unmitigated disaster

1970   Directs the war film *Too Late the Hero* (the third film produced by Aldrich Studios), shot on location in the Philippines; film is a critical and commercial failure

1971   Directs *The Grissom Gang,* a gangster film based on sensational novel *No Orchids for Miss Blandish* by James Hadley Chase; film is criticized for its explicit violence; this fourth consecutive box-office failure leads to loss of Aldrich Studios, which is eventually sold in 1973

1972   Working now for other studios, Aldrich directs *Ulzana's Raid* for
          Universal; film is thematically connected to earlier *Apache* in its
          view of Native Americans but also comments on the war in Viet-
          nam; proves to be one of Aldrich's most critically acclaimed films

1973   Directs *Emperor of the North* for 20th Century-Fox, a story of hobos
          riding the rails during the Depression; another commercial disap-
          pointment

1974   Directs *The Longest Yard* for Paramount; football/prison film
          becomes biggest box office hit since *The Dirty Dozen;* wins Golden
          Globe as best comedy film of the year

1975   Directs *Hustle,* his second collaboration with Burt Reynolds after
          The Longest Yard; their company Ro-Burt Productions is dissolved
          after film is completed because of tensions between the two men;
          Aldrich is elected to first of two consecutive two-year terms as pres-
          ident of Directors Guild of America; through tough bargaining
          wins unprecedented benefits for Guild membership.

1977   Directs *Twilight's Last Gleaming* for Lorimar; ambitious drama con-
          cerning nuclear terrorism is shot in Munich and West Germany
          but fails at box office; also directs police drama *The Choirboys* for
          Lorimar, based on novel by Joseph Wambaugh who filed suit
          demanding removal of his name from the finished film; subject
          matter earns "Condemned" rating from Catholic Legion of
          Decency

1979   Directs *The Frisco Kid* for Warner Brothers; comic western fails with
          fans and critics despite appearance of Gene Wilder and young Har-
          rison Ford

1981   Directs . . . *All the Marbles* for MGM; his final film is in part a protest
          of the Reagan administration and fails at the box office

1983   Aldrich dies on December 5 at his home in Los Angeles after com-
          plications following surgery; at DGA memorial service two days
          later Abraham Polonsky, Robert Wise, Franklin Shaffner, A. I. Bez-
          zerides, and other members of Aldrich's filmmaking family speak
          of his enormous presence in, and contributions to, the film
          industry.

FILMOGRAPHY

1953
THE BIG LEAGUER
Producer: Matthew Rapf
Director: **Robert Aldrich**
Screenplay: Herbert Baker, based on story by John McNulty and Louis Morheim
Music: Alberto Colombo
Cast: Edward G. Robinson (John B. Lambert), Vera-Ellen (Christy), Jeff Richards (Adam Polachuk), Richard Jaeckel (Bobby Bronson), William Campbell (Julie Davis), Carl Hubble (himself), Paul Langton (Brian McLennan), Lalo Rios (Chuy Aguilar), Bill Crandall (Tippy Mitchell)
Length: 71 minutes

1954
WORLD FOR RANSOM
Production Company: Allied Artists
Producers: **Robert Aldrich** and Bernard Tabakin
Director: **Robert Aldrich**
Screenplay: Lindsay Hardy and Hugo Butler [uncredited]
Cinematographer: Joseph Biroc
Editor: Michael Luciano
Art Direction: William Glasgow
Music: Frank DeVol
Cast: Dan Duryea (Mike Callahan), Gene Lockhart (Alexis Pederas), Patric

Knowles (Julian March), Reginald Denny (Major Bone), Nigel Bruce (Governor Coutts), Marian Carr (Frennessey), Arthur Shields (Sean O'Conner)
Length: 82 minutes

1954
APACHE
Production Company: Released by United Artists [Hecht-Lancaster Productions]
Producer: Harold Hecht
Director: **Robert Aldrich**
Screenplay: James R. Webb, based on novel *Bronco Apache* by Paul I. Wellman
Cinematographer: Ernest Laszlo
Editor: Alan Crosland, Jr.
Art Direction: Nicolai Remisoff
Music: David Raksin
Cast: Burt Lancaster (Massai), Jean Peters (Nalinle), John McIntire (Al Sieber), Charles Buchinsky (Bronson) (Hondo), John Dehner (Weddle), Paul Guilfoyle (Santos), Morris Ankrum (Dawson), Monte Blue (Geronimo)
Length: 91 minutes

1954
VERA CRUZ
Production Company: United Artists [Hecht-Lancaster Productions]
Producer: James Hill
Director: **Robert Aldrich**
Screenplay: Roland Kibbee and James R. Webb, based on story by Borden Chase
Cinematographer: Ernest Laszlo
Editor: Alan Crosland, Jr.
Music: Hugo Friedhofer
Cast: Gary Cooper (Ben Trane), Burt Lancaster (Joe Erin), Denise Darcel (the Countess), Cesar Romero (the Marquis), Sarita Montiel (Nina), George Macready (Maximilian), Ernest Borgnine (Danette), Jack Elam (Tex), Charles Horvath (Reno)
Length: 94 minutes

1955
KISS ME DEADLY
Production Company: Released by United Artists [Parklane Productions]

Producer-Director: **Robert Aldrich**
Screenplay: A. I. Bezzerides, based on novel, *Kiss Me, Deadly* by Mickey Spillane
Cinematographer: Ernest Laszlo
Editor: Michael Luciano
Art Direction: William Glasgow
Music: Frank DeVol
Cast: Ralph Meeker (Mike Hammer), Albert Dekker (Dr. Soberin), Paul Stewart (Carl Evello), Wesley Addy (Pat), Marian Carr (Friday), Maxine Cooper (Velda), Cloris Leachman (Christina), Gaby Rodgers (Lily Carver/Gabrielle), Nick Dennis (Nick), Jack Lambert (Sugar), Jack Elam (Charlie Max), Percy Helton (Morgue Doctor), Juano Hernandez (Eddie Yeager)
Length: 106 minutes

1955
THE BIG KNIFE
Production Company: Released by United Artists [Associates and Aldrich Production]
Producer-Director: **Robert Aldrich**
Screenplay: James Poe, based on play *The Big Knife* by Clifford Odets
Cinematographer: Ernest Laszlo
Editor: Michael Luciano
Art Direction: William Glasgow
Music: Frank DeVol
Cast: Jack Palance (Charlie Castle), Ida Lupino (Marion Castle), Wendell Corey (Smiley Coy), Shelley Winters (Dixie Evans), Jean Hagen (Connie Bliss), Rod Steiger (Stanley Hoff), Ilka Chase (Patty Benedict), Everett Sloane (Nat Danziger), Wesley Addy (Hank Teagle), Paul Langton (Buddy Bliss), Nick Dennis (Nick)
Length: 111 minutes

1956
AUTUMN LEAVES
Production Company: Released by Columbia Studios [William Goetz Productions]
Producer: William Goetz
Director: **Robert Aldrich**

Screenplay: Jack Jevne, Lewis Meltzer, and Robert Blees
Cinematographer: Charles Lang, Jr.
Editor: Michael Luciano
Art Direction: William Glasgow
Music: Hans Salter
Cast: Joan Crawford (Millicent Weatherby), Cliff Robertson (Burt Hanson), Vera Miles (Virginia), Lorne Greene (Mr. Hanson), Ruth Donnelly (Liz), Maxine Cooper (Nurse Evans)
Length: 107 minutes

1956
ATTACK
Production Company: Released by United Artists [Associates and Aldrich Productions]
Producer-Director: **Robert Aldrich**
Screenplay: James Poe, based on play *Fragile Fox* by Norman Brooks
Cinematographer: Joseph Biroc
Editor: Michael Luciano
Art Direction: William Glasgow
Music: Frank DeVol
Cast: Jack Palance (Lt. Joe Costa), Eddie Albert (Capt. Erskine Cooney), Lee Marvin (Col. Clyde Bartlett), William Smithers (Lt. Woodruff), Robert Strauss (Pfc. Bernstein), Richard Jaeckel (Pfc. Snowden), Buddy Ebsen (Sgt. Tolliver), Peter Van Eyck (German officer)
Length: 107 minutes

1957
THE GARMENT JUNGLE
Production Company: Released by Columbia Studios [Harry Kleiner Production]
Producer: Harry Kleiner
Director: **Robert Aldrich** replaced by Vincent Sherman during filming
Screenplay: Harry Kleiner, based on articles "Gangsters in the Dress Business" by Lester Velie
Cinematographer: Joseph Biroc
Editor: William Lyon
Art Direction: Robert A. Peterson

Music: Leith Stevens
Cast: Lee J. Cobb (Walter Mitchell), Kerwin Mathews (Alan Mitchell), Gia Scala (Theresa Renata), Richard Boone (Artie Ravidge), Valerie French (Lee Hackett), Robert Loggia (Tulio Renata), Joseph Wiseman (Kovan), Harold J. Stone (Tony), Wesley Addy (Mr. Paul)
Length: 88 minutes

1959
TEN SECONDS TO HELL
Production Company: Released by United Artists [Seven Arts-Hammer Production]
Producer: Michael Carreras
Director: **Robert Aldrich**
Screenplay: **Robert Aldrich** and Teddi Sherman, based on novel *The Phoenix* by Laurence P. Bachmann
Cinematographer: Ernest Laszlo
Editor: Harry Richardson
Art Direction: Ken Adams
Music: Kenneth V. Jones
Cast: Jack Palance (Eric Koertner), Jeff Chandler (Loeffler), Dave Willock (Tillig), Wesley Addy (Sulke), Jimmy Goodwin (Globke)
Length: 93 minutes

1959
THE ANGRY HILLS
Production Company: Released by MGM [Raymond Stross Productions]
Producer: Raymond Stross
Director: **Robert Aldrich**
Screenplay: A. I. Bezzerides, based on novel *The Angry Hills* by Leon Uris
Cinematographer: Stephen Dade
Editor: Peter Tanner
Art Direction: Ken Adam
Music: Richard Bennett
Cast: Robert Mitchum (Michael Morrison), Elisabeth Mueller (Lisa), Stanley Baker (Konrad Heisler), Gia Scala (Eleftheria), Theodore Bikel (Tassos), Sebastian Cabot (Chesney), Peter Illing (Leonidas), Leslie Phillips (Ray Taylor), Donald Wolfit (Dr. Stergiou)
Length: 105 minutes

1961

THE LAST SUNSET

Production Company: Released by Universal-International [Brynaprod S.A.]

Producers: Eugene Frenke and Edward Lewis

Director: **Robert Aldrich**

Screenplay: Dalton Trumbo, based on novel *Sundown at Crazy Horse* by Howard Rigsby

Cinematographer: Ernest Laszlo

Editor: Michael Luciano

Art Direction: Alexander Golitzen and Alfred Sweeney

Music: Ernest Gold

Cast: Rock Hudson (Dana Stribling), Kirk Douglas (Brendan O'Malley), Dorothy Malone (Belle Breckenridge), Joseph Cotton (John Breckenridge), Carol Lynley (Missy Breckenridge), Neville Brand (Frank Hobbs), Jack Elam (Ed Hobbs)

Length: 112 minutes

1961

SODOM AND GOMORRAH

Production Company: Released by 20th Century-Fox [Titanus Production] (Filmed in 1961, released in 1963)

Producer: Goffredo Lombardo

Director: **Robert Aldrich**

Screenplay: Hugo Butler and Giorgio Prosperi

Cinematographer: Silvio Ippolitti, Mario Montuori, and Cyril Knowles

Editor: Peter Tanner

Art Direction: Ken Adam and Giovanni D'Andrea

Music: Milkos Rozsa

Cast: Steward Granger (Lot), Pier Angeli (Ildith), Stanley Baker (Astaroth), Rossana Podesta (Sheeah), Anouk Aimee (Bera)

Length: 154 minutes

1962

WHAT EVER HAPPENED TO BABY JANE?

Production Company: Released by Warner Brothers [Associates and Aldrich–Seven Arts Production]

Producer-Director: **Robert Aldrich**

Screenplay: Lukas Heller, based on novel *Whatever Happened to Baby Jane?* by Henry Farrell
Cinematographer: Ernest Haller
Editor: Michael Luciano
Art Direction: William Glasgow
Music: Frank DeVol
Cast: Bette Davis (Jane Hudson), Joan Crawford (Blanche Hudson), Victor Buono (Edwin Flagg), Marjorie Bennett (Della Flagg), Maidie Norman (Elvira Stitt), Anna Lee (Mrs. Bates), Barbara Merrill (Liza Bates), Dave Willock (Ray Hudson)
Length: 134 minutes

1963
4 FOR TEXAS
Production Company: Released by Warner Brothers [The S.A.M. Company and Associates and Aldrich Production]
Producer-Director: **Robert Aldrich**
Screenplay: Teddie Sherman and **Robert Aldrich,** from original story by **Robert Aldrich**
Cinematographer: Ernest Laszlo
Editor: Michael Luciano
Art Direction: William Glasgow
Music: Nelson Riddle
Cast: Frank Sinatra (Zack Thomas), Dean Martin (Joe Jarrett), Anita Ekberg (Elya Carlson), Ursula Andress (Maxine Richter), Charles Bronson (Matson), Victor Buono (Harvey Burden), Edric Conner (Prince George), Nick Dennis (Angel), Richard Jaeckel (Mancini), Mike Mazurki (Chad), Wesley Addy (Trowbridge), Jack Elam (Dobie), Margorie Bennett (Miss Emmaline)
Length: 124 minutes

1964
HUSH . . . HUSH SWEET CHARLOTTE
Production Company: Released by 20th Century-Fox [Associates and Aldrich Production]
Producer-Director: **Robert Aldrich**
Screenplay: Henry Farrell and Lukas Heller, from original story by Henry Farrell

Cinematographer: Joseph Biroc
Editor: Michael Luciano
Art Direction: William Glasgow
Music: Frank DeVol
Cast: Bette Davis (Charlotte Hollis), Olivia de Havilland (Miriam Deering), Joseph Cotton (Drew Bayliss), Agnes Moorehead (Velma Cruther), Cecil Kellaway (Harry Willis), Victor Buono (Sam Hollis), Mary Astor (Jewel Mayhew), Wesley Addy (Sheriff Luke Standish), William Campbell (Paul Marchand), Bruce Dern (John Mayhew), George Kennedy (Foreman)
Length: 133 minutes

1966
THE FLIGHT OF THE PHOENIX
Production Company: Released by 20th Century-Fox [Associates and Aldrich Production]
Producer-Director: **Robert Aldrich**
Screenplay: Lukas Heller, based on novel *The Flight of the Phoenix* by Elleston Trevor
Cinematographer: Joseph Biroc
Editor: Michael Luciano
Art Direction: William Glasgow
Music: Frank DeVol
Cast: James Stewart (Frank Towns), Richard Attenborough (Lew Moran), Peter Finch (Captain Harris), Hardy Kruger (Heinrich Dorfmann), Ernest Borgnine (Trucker Cobb), Ian Bannen (Crow), Christian Marquand (Dr. Renaud), Ronald Fraser (Sergeant Watson), Dan Duryea (Standish), George Kennedy (Bellamy), Gabriele Tinti (Gabriele)
Length: 147 minutes

1967
THE DIRTY DOZEN
Production Company: Released by MGM [MKH Productions]
Producer: Kenneth Hyman
Director: **Robert Aldrich**
Screenplay: Nunnally Johnson and Lukas Heller, based on novel *The Dirty Dozen* by E. M. Nathanson
Cinematographer: Edward Scaife

Editor: Michael Luciano
Art Direction: W. E. Hutchinson
Music: Frank DeVol
Cast: Lee Marvin (Major Reisman), Ernest Borgnine (General Worden), Charles Bronson (Joseph Wladislaw), Jim Brown (Robert Jefferson), John Cassavetes (Victor Franko), Richard Jaeckel (Sgt. Bowren), George Kennedy (Major Armbruster), Trini Lopez (Pedro Jiminez), Ralph Meeker (Captain Kinder), Robert Ryan (Colonel Everett Dasher Breed), Telly Savalas (Archer Maggott), Clint Walker (Samson Posey), Donald Sutherland (Vernon Pinkley), Robert Webber (General Denton), Tom Busby (Vladek), Ben Carruthers (Gilpin), Stuart Cooper (Lever), Al Mancini (Bravos), Colin Maitland (Sawyer)
Length: 145 minutes

1968
THE LEGEND OF LYLAH CLARE
Production Company: Released by MGM [Associates and Aldrich Production]
Producer-Director: **Robert Aldrich**
Screenplay: Hugo Butler and Jean Rouverol, based on teleplay by Robert Thom and Edward de Blasio
Cinematographer: Joseph Biroc
Editor: Michael Luciano
Art Direction: George W. Davis and William Glasgow
Music: Frank DeVol
Cast: Kim Novak (Lylah Clare/Elsa Brinkman), Peter Finch (Lewis Zarkan), Ernest Borgnine (Barney Sheean), Milton Selzer (Bart Langner), Rossella Falk (Rossella), Gabriele Tinti (Paolo), Michael Murphy (Mark Peter Sheean), Coral Browne (Molly Luther), Valentina Cortese (Countess Bozo Bedoni), Nick Dennis (Nick), Dave Willock (Cameraman)
Length: 130 minutes

1968
THE KILLING OF SISTER GEORGE
Production Company: Released by ABC Palomar International [Associates and Aldrich Production]
Producer-Director: **Robert Aldrich**

Screenplay: Lukas Heller, based on play *The Killing of Sister George* by Frank Marcus
Cinematographer: Joseph Biroc
Editor: Michael Luciano
Art Direction: William Glasgow
Music: Gerald Fried
Cast: Beryl Reid (June Buckridge/"Sister George"), Susannah York ("Childie" McNaught), Coral Browne (Mercy Croft), Ronald Fraser (Leo Lockhart), Patricia Medina (Betty Thaxter)
Length: 138 minutes

1970
TOO LATE THE HERO
Production Company: Released by Cinerama Releasing Corporation [ABC-Palomar, Associates and Aldrich Production]
Producer-Director: **Robert Aldrich**
Screenplay: **Robert Aldrich** and Lukas Heller, based on original story by **Robert Aldrich** and Robert Sherman
Cinematographer: Joseph Biroc
Editor: Michael Luciano
Art Direction: James Vance
Music: Gerald Fried
Cast: Michael Caine (Pvt. Tosh Hearne), Cliff Robertson (Lt. jg. Sam Lawson), Henry Fonda (Capt. John G. Nolan), Ian Bannen (Pvt. Thornton), Harry Andrews (Lt. Col. Thompson), Denholm Elliot (Capt. Hornsby), Ronald Fraser (Pvt. Campbell), Ken Takakura (Major Yamaguchi)
Length: 144 minutes

1971
THE GRISSOM GANG
Production Company: Released by Cinerama Releasing Corporation [ABC Pictures, Associates and Aldrich Production]
Producer-Director: **Robert Aldrich**
Screenplay: Leon Griffiths, based on novel *No Orchids for Miss Blandish* by James Hadley Chase
Cinematographer: Joseph Biroc
Editor: Michael Luciano

Art Direction: James Vance
Music: Gerald Fried
Cast: Kim Darby (Barbara Blandish), Scott Wilson (Slim Grissom), Tony Musante (Eddie Hagen), Irene Daily (Ma Grissom), Robert Lansing (Dave Fenner), Connie Stevens (Anna Borg), Joey Faye (Woppy), Don Keefer (Doc), Ralph Waite (Mace), Wesley Addy (John Blandish), Dave Willock (Rocky), Matt Clark (Bailey)
Length: 128 minutes

1972
ULZANA'S RAID
Production Company: Released by Universal Pictures [Carter DeHaven, Associates and Aldrich Production]
Producer: Carter DeHaven
Director: **Robert Aldrich**
Screenplay: Alan Sharp
Cinematographer: Joseph Biroc
Editor: Michael Luciano
Art Direction: James Vance
Music: Frank DeVol
Cast: Burt Lancaster (McIntosh), Bruce Davison (Lt. Garnett DeBuin), Jorge Luke (Ke-ni-tay), Richard Jaeckel (the Sergeant), Joaquim Martinez (Ulzana), Lloyd Bochner (Captain Gates), Douglass Watson (Major Wainwright), Karl Swenson (Rukeyser), Dran Hamilton (Mrs. Rioran)
Length: 105 minutes

1973
EMPEROR OF THE NORTH
Production Company: Released by 20th Century-Fox [Inter-Hemisphere Productions]
Producer: Stanley Hough
Director: **Robert Aldrich**
Screenplay: Christopher Knopf
Cinematographer: Joseph Biroc
Editor: Michael Luciano
Art Direction: Jack Martin Smith
Music: Frank DeVol

Cast: Lee Marvin (A No. 1), Ernest Borgnine (Shack), Keith Carradine (Ciga-
ret), Charles Tyner (Cracker), Harry Ceasar (Coaly), Matt Clark (Yardlet),
Elisha Cook (Gray Cat), Dave Willock (Groundhog)
Length: 118 minutes

1974
THE LONGEST YARD
Production Company: Released by Paramount
Producer: Albert S. Ruddy
Director: **Robert Aldrich**
Screenplay: Tracy Keenan Wynn, from story by Albert S. Ruddy
Cinematographer: Joseph Biroc
Editor: Michael Luciano: Frank Capachione, Allan Jacobs, and George Hively
for football sequences
Music: Frank DeVol
Cast: Burt Reynolds (Paul Crewe), Eddie Albert (Warden Hazen), Ed Lauter
(Capt. Knauer), Michael Conrad (Nate Scarboro), James Hampton (Care-
taker), Harry Caesar (Granville), John Steadman (Pop), Charles Tyner
(Unger), Richard Kiel (Samson), Ray Nitschke (Bogdanski), Mike Henry (Rass-
meusen), Joe Kapp (a Guard), Bernadette Peters (Warden's secretary), Anitra
Ford (Melissa)
Length: 121 minutes

1975
HUSTLE
Production Company: Released by Paramount [Ro-Burt Productions]
Producer-Director: **Robert Aldrich**
Screenplay: Steve Shagan
Cinematographer: Joseph Biroc
Editor: Michael Luciano
Art Direction: Hilyard Brown
Music: Frank DeVol
Cast: Burt Reynolds (Lt. Phil Gaines), Catherine Deneuve (Nicole Britton),
Ben Johnson (Marty Hollinger), Paul Winfield (Sgt. Louis Belgrave), Eddie
Albert (Leo Sellers), Eileen Brennan (Paula Hollinger), Ernest Borgnine (Capt.
Santoro), Jack Carter (Herbie Dalitz), Catherine Bach (Peggy Summers),
David Spielberg (Bellamy), James Hampton (Bus Driver)
Length: 120 minutes

1977
TWILIGHT'S LAST GLEAMING
Production Company: Released by Allied Artists [Lorimar Presentation of a Geria Production]
Producer: Merv Adelson
Director: **Robert Aldrich**
Screenplay: Ronald M. Cohen and Edward Huesbsch, based on novel *Viper Three* by Walter Wager
Cinematographer: Robert Hauser
Editor: Michael Luciano
Art Direction: Werner Achmann
Music: Jerry Goldsmith
Cast: Burt Lancaster (Lawrence Dell), Richard Widmark (Gen. Martin Mac-Kenzie), Charles Durning (President David Stevens), Melvyn Douglas (Zachariah Guthrie), Paul Winfield (Powell), Burt Young (Gravas), Joseph Cotton (Arthur Renfrew), Gerald S. O'Loughlin (Gen. Michael O'Rourke), Richard Jaeckel (Capt. Towne), Roscoe Lee Brown (James Forrest), William Marshall (William Klinger), Leif Erickson (Ralph Whitaker), Charles McGraw (Gen. Crane), William Smith (Hoxey)
Length: 146 minutes

1977
THE CHOIRBOYS
Production Company: Released by Universal-M.C.A. [Lorimar-Airone Production]
Producers: Merv Adelson, Lee Rich
Director: **Robert Aldrich**
Screenplay: Christopher Knopf and [uncredited] Joseph Wambaugh, based on novel *The Choirboys* by Joseph Wambaugh
Cinematographer: Joseph Biroc
Editor: Maury Winetrobe, William Martin
Art Direction: Bill Kenney
Music: Frank DeVol
Cast: Charles Durning (Spermwhale Whalen), Louis Gossett Jr. (Calvin Motts), Perry King (Baxter Slate), Clyde Kasatsu (Francis Tanaguchi), Stephen Macht (Spencer Van Moot), Tim McIntyre (Roscoe Rules), Randy Quaid (Dean Proust), Don Stroud (Sam Lyles), James Woods (Harold Bloomguard),

Burt Young (Scuzzi), Robert Webber (Riggs), Blair Brown (Kimberly Lyles), Barbara Rhoades (Hadley), George Di Cenzo (Lt. Grimsley), Charles Haid (Nick Yanov), David Speilberg (Lt. Finque), Jim Davis (Capt. Drobeck), Phyllis Davis (Foxy/Gina)
Length: 119 minutes

1979
THE FRISCO KID
Production Company: Released by Warner Brothers
Producer: Mace Neufeld
Director: **Robert Aldrich**
Screenplay: Michael Ellis and Frank Shaw
Cinematographer: Robert B. Hauser
Editor: Maury Winetrobe, Irving Rosenblum, Jack Horger
Production Design: Terence Marsh
Music: Frank DeVol
Cast: Gene Wilder (Rabbi Avram Belinski), Harrison Ford (Tommy Lillard), Ramon Bieri (Jones), George Di Cenzo (Darryl Diggs), William Smith (Matt Diggs), Val Bisoglio (Chief Gray Cloud), Penny Peyser (Rosalie), Jack Somack (Samuel Bender)
Length: 122 minutes

1981
. . . ALL THE MARBLES
Production Company: Released by United Artists
Producer: William Aldrich
Director: **Robert Aldrich**
Screenplay: Mel Frohman
Cinematographer: Joseph Biroc
Editor: Irving C. Rosenblum and Richard Lane
Music: Frank DeVol
Cast: Peter Falk (Harry Sears), Vicki Frederick (Iris), Laurene Landon (Molly), Burt Young (Eddie Cisco), Richard Jaeckel (Referee)
Length: 113 minutes

ROBERT ALDRICH

INTERVIEWS

"No China Dolls," Says Director Aldrich

HOWARD McCLAY / 1953

THERE'S SURE TO BE A "new look" in MGM's *The Big Leaguer* if
Robert Aldrich has his way.

Aldrich, currently readying the production, his first directorial assignment, said:

"There'll be no traditional makeup for any of the players. The men will
wear none at all, except for character or action requirements such as scars
and bruises, and the women will be allowed only what they would normally
use for the street or for a dinner date, depending on the situation.

"They won't be look-alike beauties," he concedes. "They'll look human
and natural, instead of like china dolls."

This sounds like pretty startling talk, especially coming from a youngster
(he's thirty-three) for his first time out as a full-fledged feature director. But
Aldrich is a seasoned veteran in the industry. He's been learning the funda-
mentals of directing since 1942 as assistant to some of the top men in the
business. He's authored a half-dozen successful screenplays, and has been
production manager or associate producer on several major releases for
Columbia, 20th Century-Fox, and United Artists in the past five years.

In 1952 he directed twenty-two films for television, seventeen of which
were for NBC's "The Doctor" series. He believes that many of the new techniques developed to meet the economic and physical limitations of video
are applicable to the production of feature pictures.

His "no makeup" ruling, which will affect Edward G. Robinson, Vera

From *Los Angeles Daily News*, 5 February 1953.

Ellen, Richard Jaeckel and others in *The Big Leaguer* cast, is a result of his TV experience and has been given the green light by MGM executives after they viewed some of his NBC films and found nothing unattractive about the appearance of "bare faced" players.

Another Aldrich innovation at MGM is that every scene of his first feature, including interiors, will be shot on location at Melbourne, Florida, home of the N.Y. Giants' farm club. Instead of building special sets, Aldrich will use existing structures and will play his action against whatever backgrounds are available at the location site.

This is a common practice in the television field, where set construction costs get out of hand unless the same set is used over and over again, as in some of our more popular series shows.

"For the dramatic vignettes you see on television," Aldrich explained, "set construction is a forbidden luxury. So, if the scene takes place in a 9 × 12 room, then the director must find a room that size which is suitable, even though it has been used before.

"Sometimes, with such limitations of space and movement, you can come up with some very realistic results."

An Interview with Robert Aldrich

GEORGE N. FENIN / 1956

FENIN: *First let me congratulate you for the enthusiastic reception Europe gave to your two latest films,* Autumn Leaves, *winner in the Berlin Film Festival, and* Attack, *winner of the Pasinetti Prize at the Venice Film Festival. These recognitions, following upon the Silver Lion award to* The Big Knife *at last year's Venice festival, would seem to represent the esteem in which European critics hold your talent and integrity.*

ALDRICH: Thank you for your kind remarks. I am very sensitive to the reaction of European critics, and do believe that a director should always take into consideration the public and the critics—in the United States as well as overseas—in order to find assurance and courage in his work.

FENIN: *I noticed that* Autumn Leaves, *which I consider substantially important for its message, did not get critical recognition from the American press. To my mind, you tried in this film to throw some light on one important facet of the complex psychic problem confronting modern society. Neurosis and psychopathy are on the increase; such a phenomenon and its causes have necessarily to be treated within the proper context of our society.*

ALDRICH: You are quite right in stressing the importance of this condition. I believe that the lack of psychological maturity in too many Americans is what causes their instabilities. They will not accept failure, defeat, or poverty. They want to be "successful" at all costs, in business or in love, in politics or in any other sphere of their lives. Thus, economic pressure, among other

From *Film Culture* II (1956): 8–9. Reprinted by permission.

things, causes a chain reaction system which provokes, ultimately, a series of shocks. From there on, it is up to the individual who will run through the various stages of instability. This problem, being on a gradual increase as you stated, has to be dealt with more deeply and more completely on the screen in the future. I hope to contribute more to it.

FENIN: *About* Attack: *while Norman Brooks's play* The Fragile Fox *impressed many critics, it was not a "popular" success. Ever since seeing the play, I hoped it would be brought to the screen. Your adaptation follows the original text faithfully without the usual "castrations" which so often mar Hollywood's versions of literary and theatrical works. As with* The Big Knife, *it has resulted in a filmic presentation of a frank and honest drama. I doubt it could have been transferred with such integrity to the screen in certain other countries. Do you think that* Attack, *exposing, as it does, the brutality and uselessness of war, may properly be considered a humble addition to the anti-war cinema, started by such classics as Renoir's* La Grande Illusion *and Milestone's* All Quiet on the Western Front?

ALDRICH: I certainly hope so. I recently invited Lewis Milestone to see *Attack* and he liked it. For me, it is a sincere plea for peace, a document in its genre which I sincerely trust people will understand clearly.

FENIN: *Your efforts to present some vitally human themes as a reflection and as an analysis of our tormented times qualify you as a member of the "new school" of American cinema. In this capacity, how would you define a director's creative responsibility today—in aesthetic, social, and moral terms?*

ALDRICH: Such responsibility, which must be expressed by personal style and must be based on a high moral standard and a sincere and constructive concern for the progress of fellow beings, is very difficult to maintain. Here and in Europe, people often don't realize fully the difficulties of a director. You cannot always make good films. Economic strangleholds demand that you sometimes direct commercial films. With their revenues you may then make your own "good" films without any compromises. I am no exception to this rule, but I am most sincerely trying to maintain good standards in my films and to express myself in them. Others simply do not follow this rule. Take Alfred Hitchcock, for example. It surprises me that he enjoys such great success in some quarters in France. For me, the director of *Rear Window* and *To Catch a Thief,* to mention only two of his recent films, is an efficient master of tricks, but he never conveys human warmth in his films. I see in him craftsmanship only, no creation.

FENIN: *You were mentioning personal style . . .*
ALDRICH: Yes. I think my films have a style which expresses my personality, my behavior patterns. This style may not show during filming, but later, in the final editing stages. At that moment, when my work finally takes definite shape and harmony, I am glad to see that the style is there, that I have been faithful to the creative urge, to the patterns of its development and expression.

FENIN: *Aesthetically, then, do you have absolute freedom of expression? Or are you forced to accept a script even if you don't like it to avoid being "put on ice," as a director once told me?*
ALDRICH: I try to select my scripts, but let's be very frank. On your own films you are entirely free and responsible. On the others, simply not.

FENIN: *Budd Schulberg recently declared that the intellectual situation of screenwriters in Hollywood is worse than that of the negroes in the South before the Civil War. Is it a fact that today the screenwriter has no freedom of expression and is being coerced by commercialism and blacklisting practices?*
ALDRICH: I don't agree completely with Schulberg, although I realize why he must prefer to produce his films in the East rather than in Hollywood. In my opinion, the lack of writing talent on the West Coast results from the simple fact that there are so few good writers. A well known writer carries much more independence with producers than a rising or unknown one. As far as blacklisting is concerned, I agree that the situation in Hollywood is terrible and shocking. Many themes are still taboo and creative intelligence has a difficult time once the displeasure of some groups is incurred.

FENIN: *You have been fighting for a revision of the Production Code, I know.*
ALDRICH: And I believe the final goal ought to be no censorship at all. This would have to come in a gradual process of revision, but revision should be left to the creators of the films. The fight is still going on strongly, of course.

FENIN: *What are your preferences in films and directors, American and foreign?*
ALDRICH: *Shane, Wuthering Heights, Panic in the Streets, Jeux Interdits, Ger-*

vaise, Wages of Fear, Paisan, Open City, La Strada, Umberto D., Bicycle Thief. I like Wyler, Kazan, Stevens, Ford and Nick Ray—when they try—and Clément, Clouzot (the Clouzot of *Wages of Fear,* not *Diabolique*) Fellini, de Sica, the early Rossellini.

FENIN: *As you know, I followed several phases of the location shooting of your new film* Garment Center. *Can you tell us something about this production?*

ALDRICH: *Garment Center* is part of an agreement between Columbia Pictures and me. I agreed to direct it on condition that I later direct another film from an unproduced play *Until Proven Guilty,* which is of particular interest to me. *Garment Center* is, in my opinion, the first pro-labor picture; in it I am trying to emphasize another particular aspect of our times—the tragedy of the small businessman, caught between the ever-expanding large corporations and the pressures of organized labor. The small businessman has often, in order to stay alive, to compromise with graft and blackmail. He is usually made to realize that there is no place for him in our society. The struggle of this group for existence has impressed me deeply. The structure of our economy is based on the middle man, but there has been a definite change, a passing to mammoth trends and patterns. This sort of development cannot remain unobserved in our cinema. That is why *Garment Center* should be an unusually frank film. Much of its material has been gathered from actual events, for example, the murder of Mr. Lurye, a labor organizer who was killed by gangsters in New York some years ago.

FENIN: *Besides Lee J. Cobb and Joseph Wiseman, who are established actors, I noticed four newcomers in the cast: Kerwin Mathews, Robert Loggia, Gia Scala, and Valerie French. Do you approve of such a practice?*

ALDRICH: No indeed. In an expensive production such as *Garment Center,* the presence of four newcomers can seriously overburden the director. But such were the terms of the agreement with Columbia, and they had to be honored.

FENIN: *What comes next after* Garment Center?

ALDRICH: Starting in January of 1957, I will have to work on two projects. One is *Kinderspiel,* a story of the rebellion of the world's children against their parents in view of an impending nuclear war. I plan to film this in Germany with Anthony Quinn and a German actress. Also, my agenda calls for *Pom-*

meroy, a comedy to be made in Great Britain with Broderick Crawford and Diana Dors. In between, I hope to make *Until Proven Guilty* in Omaha in the spring. This will be a political film based on social conformity as expressed through the experiences of a teacher wrongly accused of molesting his adolescent pupils.

FENIN: *Have you ever considered making a film about New York's melting pot, this example of living democracy, as Walt Whitman said?*

ALDRICH: Yes, I have. But I would like to treat only one side of it, that is to say, the Puerto Rican situation, stressing the isolationist policy that confronts the immigrants and their own tragic problems of assimilation. I understand Elia Kazan is planning a film along these lines. However, if he doesn't make it, I shall be glad to do it myself. It will be of the utmost importance, I am sure. And only an independent producer would be able to make it with freedom of research, evaluation, and expression. Such problems, I believe, cannot be ignored any longer.

Robert Aldrich

GEORGE ADDISON / 1962

GEORGE ADDISON: *Mr. Aldrich, since, for once, we have plenty of time at our disposal, could we follow through on your films in chronological order?*
ROBERT ALDRICH: There's nothing I'd like better.

GA: *Perhaps you might first like to tell us what prompted you to become a film director?*
RA: I was always interested in show business. Back in my school days at the University of Virginia, I made quite a good deal of extra money booking jazz bands and dance bands. I did it both ways: I would book school bands around the countryside and I would bring in professional bands to entertain the school. But the bands that interested me most were those that ran through motion picture projectors. I developed a taste for show business but decided that films, not music, were what I wanted to do.

In 1941 I went to Hollywood and got a job, through a family friend, at RKO. I did everything from production clerk to clapper boy, and then I got some second assistant director jobs. However, try as I might, I could never break into the ranks of first assistant directors, so I quit RKO in 1944. Then I did get various first assistant jobs, with such directors as Lewis Milestone, Jean Renoir, Charles Chaplin, Joseph Losey, William Wellman, Robert Rossen, and Abraham Polosky. I also served a stretch with the ill-fated Enterprise Studios as a production executive. Then I felt I was ready to direct. But that is not easy, so first I made the *China Smith* television series and—

From *Film Index* 6 (1962): 1–4. Reprinted by permission.

GA: *Before we go on, would you like to say some words about the films you worked on as assistant director and your impressions of the directors involved?*

RA: I was an assistant to Lewis Milestone on four films—*A Walk in the Sun, Arch of Triumph, No Minor Vices,* and *The Red Pony.* Milly is and was a brilliant cutter. While directors pretended to cut in the camera, he really did. Sometimes it's a shortcoming, however, making for rigidity. Let's say it was *Arch of Triumph* with Ingrid Berman and Charles Boyer. Maybe Bergman didn't feel for Boyer at the door what she did by the time she got to the bed. But if you cut by the camera, too bad. Economy is the great value of cutting. I do it occasionally, but combined with a rehearsal period. That way you're not locked in.

I was an assistant to William Wellman on *The Story of G.I. Joe.* The thing about Wellman was his complete, physical, masculine dominance of the entire scene, his obvious control of the situation. He was the star. There were no minor disagreements, only major ones. No peripheral nonsense.

Jean Renoir is much more Stanislavski-inclined than he would ever tell. He's looking for truth in his own framework—but he wouldn't put it that way. On *The Southerner* he took the actors up to Stockton to get used to the country, he said. He was really trying to figure what the story was all about under the guise of having the actors get used to the farmers.

Joe Losey has the capacity to have love affairs with actors. I never could do that, but at least now I like them. Losey romances them to death, and as a result they're always better than they have a right to be. Take *The Prowler* for instance. Evelyn Keyes gave the best performance she ever gave. Even Van Heflin, a bore, a dullard on the screen, was great. I find that in the handling of the stars—

GA: *Did Losey rehearse the players much before actual shooting?*

RA: Not as much as I do. Losey used to do some pre-shooting rehearsal, but I've found that complete rehearsals going on for two weeks before actual shooting starts is essential for me—and fine for the actors. I start with two days of reading to work out scenes and to get the actors into developing a full, rounded conception of their characters. I then do actual dress rehearsals of all studio and location scenes. It allows me to visualize each scene and to be able to extract the needed drama, cohesion, and characterization. I am not one of these directors who can come on a set or location and immediately place his camera. I have to know the set or location and analyze it thoroughly beforehand. Then I know what I want. I feel this is also economical in the end, for when the actual shooting begins, both actors and myself have a firm idea about each scene. This does not rule out further changes, however. It also helps me for I have a weakness for high-blown dialogue which can be changed if it reads too flowery-like.

G A :   *Your first film as a full director was* The Big Leaguer?
R A :   Yes. I made that in 1953. It was made on location and was about the trials of a young ball-player in the minor leagues trying to get into the big time. Not to stretch a point, it was not a personal film of my status at the time. I feel the film was good, but not indicative of what I wanted to express in the motion picture medium. It was *World for Ransom* which first embodied what I wanted to say in films. It was mainly about two men with good and bad points. Both men believed in individual liberty, but the belief of one man was much weaker than the other because he had no respect for humanity. I believe that the enemy has to be known, and his good points even admired, before he can be fought intelligently and with dignity.

G A :   *I see you co-produced* World for Ransom *but your next film* Apache *you worked for producer Harold Hecht?*
R A :   As a matter of fact, I took the original novel to Hecht-Lancaster, but was not happy the way things ultimately turned out. They cut my ending and had the hero alive at the finish. I felt he could not possibly be re-accepted or survive, for progress had passed him by. I respected his audacity, courage, and dedication, but the world no longer had a place for his kind.

I then made *Vera Cruz,* again for Hecht-Lancaster, after which further disagreements had us parting forever. However, I liked this one, and it again had a hero and an anti-hero with the hero surviving only after choosing a rightful battle and destroying the anti-hero, whom he admired in spite of their disparate credos.

Then came *Kiss Me Deadly* and *The Big Knife. The Big Knife* was my first completely independent production, and it lost money. This, in spite of winning a prize at the Venice Film Festival in 1955 and taking in $1,250,000 with a negative cost of $400,000. The distributor made all the profit and I was left with less than the cost.

I had wanted to do *The Big Knife* for a long time. I admit to having a penchant for already set-up dramatic lines and conflicts, which is why most of my films have been adapted from either novels or plays. I did a script with James Poe from the Clifford Odets play, peddled it around the major studios in trying to get the actors and then finally made it as personal production, via deferred payment agreements. I do not feel it is exactly anti-Hollywood, for that would make it too sensational. To me it can apply to any sphere of business or the arts where man's natural liberty or freedom to express himself can be squelched by unworthy, incompetent, tyrannical leaders or bosses who don't deserve their powers.

But particularly, of course, the film was against the evils of a Hollywood whose enormous profits made it stoop to gangsterism and even murder, at times, to keep the empire intact.

Then again, Hollywood in 1955 was full of anachronistic executives who had not moved with the times, living in ivory towers of their own making. I wanted to puncture their false idealism. Even the hero of my film was a false realist, and I felt he had to be shown as a guilty tormented victim, for he had made half-concessions.

I feel I can think only in whole terms when it comes to the moral climate of my films. The characters have to be completely dedicated to their code of life, be it good or bad. That is why my unswerving heroes usually are killed by a system that is not ready for change, and the half-convinced may die by their own hand.

In my next film, *Attack,* the hero went all the way against incompetent authority in trying to kill a cowardly captain responsible for the deaths of his men. The captain was a neurotic weakling, made so by a harsh father. But this did not excuse his failure as an officer and a man. That is why I wanted to depict my utter contempt and loathing for this captain in making him do sadistic things that probably smacked of "grand guignol." The same goes for the cynical, fascistic private eye, Mike Hammer, in *Kiss Me Deadly.* Perhaps that is why it did not do as well at the box-office as the other Mickey Spillane films, which made a sort of anti-hero out of him. The public probably wants that.

Well, none of these films did well, so I signed a contract with Columbia for a film per year for three years, so I could make some money to put back into my own company, Associates and Aldrich. I made *Autumn Leaves* for Columbia from a novel I had purchased myself. I admired Joan Crawford, who is a "method" actress of her own concoction, but I could not get her to be a drab ageing woman, which threw off the balance of the picture.

GA: *You actually made* Autumn Leaves *before* Attack?
RA: Yes. *Attack* was moderately successful at the box-office, but not enough to ensure my complete, independent status.

GA: *Your next film at Columbia was* The Garment Jungle?
RA: Yes, I had only four days shooting left when Harry Cohn fired me. We did not agree on the way I had been making the film. On the surface it was about hoodlumism in the unions of the garment trade in New York. But I got interested in one of the lesser characters. He was an immigrant who had created a thriving business, but now, at forty-five, found himself being squeezed out by both big business and excessive labor demands and gangsterism. He was robust, dynamic and active, but also fettered by being Jewish, of which he was proud, but, perhaps, also sub-consciously angry, since it interfered with his complete freedom due to the survival of some brands of anti-Semitism. Well, the film was finished by Vincent Sherman. I have not seen it, or care to. It is not mine.

I sued Cohn to break my contract, but the case dragged on, and I could not direct a film for a year and a half.

In the interim I prepared various scripts, some of which I sold. The only one I really regretted selling was *Taras Bulba* on which I had worked for five years. This was the classic example of the hero who says, "Damn the odds! Destiny is not in control of me! I am in control of Destiny!"

I also produced a film, *The Ride Back,* with a young director, H. Allen Miner, whose documentary on tuna fishing I had admired. *The Ride Back* is a good western, with psychological overtones, dealing with a bitter deputy who has failed at everything in life, including his wife, and has to bring in a man accused of murder on a long trek from Mexico to Texas. The accused turns out to be the better human being on all accounts.

GA: *I believe that another of the scripts you prepared was* The Gamma People *directed by John Gilling in England in 1955 for Warwick?*
RA: Yes.

GA: *To go back in time for a moment, what other TV series were you employed on besides the* China Smith *series, which formed the basis for* World for Ransom?
RA: Well, I did do seventeen of *The Doctor* series for producer Marion Parsonnet.

GA: The Doctor *was live television, wasn't it?*

RA: Yes, it was. Live television was a strenuous proving ground for directors, and I've known more than one to crack up under the strain. On the one hand, the producer demanded high quality—which, of course, he never got—and on the other hand he wanted speed, speed and more speed! I wrote the scripts for three of seventeen that I directed.

GA: *Your next two features were made in Europe? Firstly* Ten Seconds to Hell?

RA: Charles Smadja of United Artists made a fabulous, bordering on brilliant deal with UFA for the use of their Berlin studios, staff, and equipment; and from a monetary point of view, the picture was beautifully produced at an amazingly low cost. Actually, the cost would have been much lower except for the German habit of constructing the walls of interior sets so sturdily they couldn't be moved—even when the art director's plans specifically designated that the walls were to be "wild." Also, I like to use a small camera crane on interiors but the one the UFA had was of an early vintage and far from small—and it had not seen service for quite some time. Both these factors caused aggravating and unnecessary delays.

GA: Ten Seconds to Hell *was not a critical or commercial success?*

RA: There were a number of reasons for that. When I finished my cut, it ran 131 minutes. It was released at eighty-nine minutes. Naturally, much of the cohesion and sense was lost. Admittedly, the scenario which I co-authored from Lawrence Bachmann's exciting novel *The Phoenix* was too long, too philosophical, and far too talky. But probably the chief factor for the film's failure was that after doing two fine films with Jack Palance *(The Big Knife and Attack)* we both ran out of the ability and/or the capacity to continue our professional rapport. Palance's was the pivotal part and when I lost control of him and he lost confidence in me, the resulting damage to the final film was catastrophic. Palance is a difficult person to get along with, but I blame myself entirely for this shortcoming. It is the director's responsibility to maintain harmonious working relationships on the set.

GA: *I believe you had exactly the same problems with Robert Mitchum on your next film* The Angry Hills?

RA: I couldn't get through to him at all. I was totally unable to find any personal or creative or even emotional routes to make Mitchum really function as an actor. I have seen Mr. Mitchum be too excellent too often to doubt for one minute that he is an extremely accomplished and gifted artist. And since the performance that I was able to extract from Mitchum was neither sensitive nor accomplished nor in any way gifted, my failure to connect with him is a liability that I alone must also assume.

But there were other problems with *The Angry Hills* that prevented its success. The picture was taken from a novel by Leon Uris and told about the resistance movement in Greece as it functioned during the first months of the German occupation. In this regard there was only one real problem— Uris had never been to Greece in his life! Consequently, the novel (and Uris's first draft screenplay) were far from being realistic or believable. When this was politely pointed out, the producer countered by sending Uris on a quick six-day, all-expenses-paid tour in a fervent, if foolish hope that such a jaunt might inspire some remarkable feat of literary endeavor. It was already the middle of May and the film was scheduled to start on July 1. This date couldn't be postponed because of contractual commitments. Thus we were forced to commence principal photography with a script that was only a third finished. Consequently, the rehearsal periods were sporadic, and even these never had any overall direction, since none of us knew where the film was really headed. So the film lost that most important quality of cohesion.

Both *Ten Seconds to Hell* and *The Angry Hills* are what I call marginal films—pictures that are not really good but could have been a lot better. The chief problem with filming in Europe is that few, if any, American directors are granted final contractual control over their European-based films. So when their work is finished and they have made their final cut, a collection of people whom the director has constantly battled throughout the production at long last have their belated innings. They seize upon his film and mutilate it almost beyond recognition. Often, as happened with *The Angry Hills,* the distribution company itself—in this case, MGM—lends its supposed "good" offices to this wanton butchery. In my version, *The Angry Hills* ran a little under two hours, but the release time was more like an hour and a half!

GA: *But doesn't much the same distributor-mutilation occur in Hollywood?*
RA: Not nearly to the same extent, and certainly never to me. In Hollywood film can usually be cut, scored, dubbed, previewed, and re-cut before submission to that divine final arbiter—the almighty distributor—for his studied,

thoughtful, and knowledgeable perusal. By that time the director will have the anticipatory advantage of seeing and responding to many audiences' varied reactions and is therefore fortified with certain built-in defenses that, if he is at all adroit, usually are impregnable. In such cases, the film usually goes out with only minor and unimportant alterations. But, regrettably, such is not the case with Americans who undertake directorial chores for European producers.

GA: *In 1960, on behalf of your Associates and Aldrich Company, you acquired the screen rights to John O'Hara's 1940 short story "Now We Know"?*
RA: I wanted to make a film with Katharine Hepburn, and I bought this properly with her specifically in mind. She accepted, subject to her approval of script and co-stars. I assigned Halstead Welles to do the screenplay. I collaborated on it myself. But we had a lot of trouble. There's very little action in the story. It's a simple love story involving a Manhattan bus driver and a younger woman with a higher social and educational background. We were unable to lick this problem and our screenplay had too much talk. So the project never got off the ground.

GA: *Your next picture was* The Last Sunset *with Kirk Douglas?*
RA: That was a toughie. I found it extremely difficult personally to do the picture. But in this business, you have to stay alive. You have to take assignments like this to make money to eat, to buy more properties and try and float another project and to get some more scripts written. And yet on assignments like this you must still do a professional, workmanlike job. But opportunities to take assignments like this are becoming more and more scarce in America because there are less and less pictures.

GA: *So you returned to Europe to do* Sodom and Gomorrah?
RA: But this time I specified in my contract that I was to make the final cut. Even so, I had trouble. My cut was two hours and fifty-one minutes. They cut it down to two hours and thirty-six minutes. I took them to court. They argued that as my contract was signed in America it was null and void in Italy. The court threw that argument out, so I was able to stop the film's release in the mutilated version the producers wanted. But it was a qualified victory. The producers agreed to let me do the recutting and thus they were able to save face. And when I was finished, the film came out at two hours

thirty-four minutes—two minutes shorter than the length they originally wanted.

GA: *Couldn't you have insisted on the full length version being released?*
RA: I could have. The law was on my side. But to do that I would have had to permanently impound the film, let them sue me for five or six and one-half million dollars and fight it through all the courts. That would have taken three or four years, so you have to find some operational rapport that you can live with and that doesn't allow total damage. About 70 percent of the film is the way I wanted it. There was a very funny aftermath to all this, though I didn't think it was funny at the time—I was furious. I wanted Dimitri Tiomkin to do the music score. Well, they didn't want to spend the money and who needs an American composer, etc. But I kept arguing that Tiomkin would be great and finally I wore them down. Tiomkin was signed up and he charged them a fortune! He came over to Rome to look at the picture and he sits down in the cutting room. We get down to the last reel and I could sense he wasn't totally happy and I came up to him near the end and he said, "I don't buy it." I asked him what he meant. He said, "I don't buy the concept." I said, "What do you mean you don't buy the concept? What don't you like?" He said, "I don't believe she turned to salt." I just sat there and dropped my head. Finally I got up, put on my coat, and started out of the room. He said, "Where are you going? What can I do? What can I say? I can't do anything I don't believe in." I asked him, "What the hell would you have me do? Re-shoot it, re-write, the Bible? You don't buy the concept! Now how in hell am I going to combat that?" We had a very unpleasant farewell in the cutting room. Finally I walked out with a few four-letter words. And the funny thing is—like the joke where the guy gives the headwaiter hell and then has to go back to get his briefcase—we both end up on the same plane to Paris! He sat at one end of the plane and I looked this way and he looked the other. Of course, I was furious, but later, you know, after two or three months, it was funny. I think it's a riot now, but it wasn't funny then.

GA: *You would say that the director is the most important man behind any film?*
RA: I'm not very fond of producers, but you must say, sir, that some producers create the film. Hal Wallis, for example, like or dislike his pictures, he creates the Hal Wallis films. Nobody can say that Frank Tashlin or Norman Taurog or these kind of guys created the pictures Wallis produces. It's not fair

to say that only directors create in this country. It's a bad example because it's a miserable film, but Frank Ross carried *The Robe* around for ten or fifteen years before it was made. I don't care what anyone says. Frank Ross created *The Robe.*

GA: *Let us now move onto* What Ever Happened to Baby Jane?
RA: I took it to ten companies before I could get the money to make that film. The tenth company, Seven Arts, wouldn't make the picture without enormous guarantees, without heavy economic contributions from me and my company, with enormous penalties from me and my company, with no reward for me and my company, except nominal, unless the picture was highly profitable, which fortunately for me, it was. But say it wasn't so profitable. Say it had just broke even, what would have happened? Bette Davis and Joan Crawford would have received a reasonably good recompense for four or five months' work, the distributor would have made a small fortune, the lending company Seven Arts would have received a handsome interest on their money, their overhead would be paid, their lawyers and my lawyers and Bette Davis's lawyer and Joan Crawford's lawyers and everyone else's lawyers would have been paid in full. For what? Why? How did it happen? It happened because one man wanted to make a picture. It happened because one man gave up eight or nine months of his life to make that picture, plus six or eight months of researching and writing the script. And what does he get out of it? Nothing!

Interview with Robert Aldrich

IAN CAMERON AND MARK SHIVAS/ 1963

THIS INTERVIEW WAS RECORDED when Robert Aldrich was in London for the opening of *Sodom and Gomorrah*. We had not at that time seen *Baby Jane*.

Q: *We see on one set of the credits of* Sodom and Gomorrah *that there's a "director, Italian version." How much, in fact, did he do?*
A: He didn't do anything really. The Italian subsidy system makes it necessary to have an Italian name. It's a technicality. And so you pick a name. I asked him to start to do the second unit. He unfortunately didn't want to do it quite the way I envisaged, so I think his life span was about four days. But to get the subsidies, it's necessary to have an Italian director and in your contract you recognise and allow for this as you do with the screenwriter, who is Hugo Butler. In the Italian version credits there are all kinds of other gentlemen who had nothing to do with the film.

Q: *What made you decide to make the film in the first place?*
A: A couple of things. One: I think every director wants to make one biblical spectacle. I think he's probably unwise if he wants to make more than one, but I think it's something that you should do, or would like to do to see if you can make a picture that is not repetitive or so cliché or imitative. Also, I don't say this irreverently, but I think you'd like to make—if you think it's a challenge to make a biblical picture—one that's not in the Christ period, or

From *Movie* 8 (April 1963: 8–10. Reprinted by permission.

that you don't have to really be stuck with that ending. You know that you can't very well have Him live, and everybody is a little tired of the Shadow and the Feet. But seriously, you want some other period in which you can have more imaginative and creative freedom. You don't want to be inhibited by what everybody expects so that you can really only tell one story. This was a story that was two thousand years before Christ, or 1,900. It seemed to have much more promise. And there is a political-social comparison, as obliquely and lightly as it's done in the film. The social-moral decay of Sodom then and the decline of integrity and maybe political morality today. We tried to do it without being too obvious. I made a picture about McCarthy once and I asked one of my—he was—friends if he really got the message, and his reply was "Between the fornication and the fighting I can't find the message." It might well be that that same friend would see *Sodom and Gomorrah* and say much the same thing, I don't know. It's hard to find where the balance in what must be a mass audience picture lies.

Q: *It seems to be as much about capitalism as about any particular varieties of sodomy . . .*
A: I would say that's possible. There are some liberties taken of course. The Hebrews were just as indulgent and just as debauched in their attitudes towards slavery as were the Sodomites, but you had to find some moral contrast, you know, or a '62 audience has a right to ask "Why did they stay down on the farm? Why didn't they move into Sodom the day they got there?" You may remember, in the Bible, Lot and his fellows were in there for nineteen years. You can't make this tenable in a modern context. How were they doing it for nineteen years to find salvation, you know. It's pretty late.

Q: *What about* Whatever Happened to Baby Jane?
A: Oh, I think it's a pretty good film! It couldn't be any more different than the last one. It's quite intense and very personal. Small in terms of what it has to do with. It has to do with two sisters who live in an active hate for each other. It's quite a picture, I think. It's been very well received in America, which doesn't always mean anything, but it's surprising because I thought it would be not so well received there and very well received here.

Q: *Were you intending to use these two decayed actresses as a symbol of the decline of Hollywood?*

A: Not really. It's a more personal story than that. It doesn't have—the French may think it does, I'm not sure, you never can tell—a social significance in terms of what happened to them has happened to the industrial film complex. It's a much more personal, involved story. I'm sure that people will read things into it that weren't intended, you know. Depending who they are, you won't deny it, but it doesn't have that as a plan.

Q: *There were such implications intended in* The Big Knife, *though?*
A: That was quite a different kind of picture, an attack on certain behaviour patterns among filmmakers. But that's not true of *Baby Jane.* It's not a story about films. It's a story about people. It's about the demise of a child prodigy who just didn't mature emotionally or intellectually. It's not against the industry, it's against her family.

Q: *I hear that you had trouble getting finance for the film. . . .*
A: Nobody would finance it. I'm too cynical, too old now, to be surprised, but I was amused that people couldn't see the chemical combustibility of these two ladies who were so different, you know. They act differently and they think differently. Their attitudes are so different, you'd put them in a room and you know that they've got to—in terms of theatre—explode. They just can't inhabit the same area together without having a friction situation.

Q: *When you work do you do a lot of improvisation and wait to see how things develop?*
A: No, well on these kinds of films, films like *The Big Knife, Kiss Me Deadly* or *Attack,* or *Baby Jane,* films that my own company makes, the really personal films, the budgets are limited, the schedules so short that you require two to three weeks rehearsal in order to make those schedules. So you just can't take the luxury of a shooting continuity or develop a pattern; you must have that pattern pretty well developed by the end of those two or three weeks. *Baby Jane* was shot in thirty-four days, which was really four days over schedule, two of them which were due to Davis being ill, and one we had no sun at the beach. So in fact we shot it in thirty-one days. You don't have that latitude in thirty-one days; you must rehearse and know where you're going.

Q: *Have you ever been able to work on films like, say,* Vera Cruz *with plenty of time and improvisation?*
A: *Vera Cruz* was total improvisation because the script was always finished about five minutes before we shot it, and we'd sit right down and work it out

and then shoot it as we went along. I'm not sure that that's the right way to work. It's easier, perhaps, on a western or a big, sprawling, physical picture. But not on a small and tense personal picture. I think you get much more range of character if you know the whole thing before you start and you sit down and examine it and build it layer by layer rather than discover three-quarters of the way through the picture that he's not that kind of a feller at all.

Q : *Was* Apache *made in an improvising way, too?*
A : Same thing. Basic difference between *Apache* and *Vera Cruz* was the time factor. *Vera Cruz* came after *Apache,* which was by then quite successful. So there wasn't the time pressure on *Vera Cruz* and *Apache* was done in thirty-four days. It was a very athletic picture, and we moved all over making it. You did improvise, but only as best you could in the time you had. On *Vera Cruz* you did it as well as you could, and then you got it and shot it, and then you'd move on.

Q : *You were saying that writing it beforehand gave you more intensity, but the Jean Peters character in* Apache *was one of the most successful things you've done.*
A : She's an extraordinarily gifted woman. It was a shame she disappeared from the film scene. She was going through a very difficult time in her life then and she had a personal animosity towards Burt Lancaster and she hated the corporate contract she had with Fox. Now you put those things all together and she was out to vindicate her own belief in herself and she was marvellous to work with. She was trying, I guess, harder than anybody I've ever worked with, but not for the usual professional reasons that "I'd like to be good."

Q : Apache *was the first of your films which you would "own," was it?*
A : Probably, yes. We made a little picture that nobody liked and very few people saw that I would have to take responsibility for, parts of which I like very much—called *World for Ransom.* Parts of it were pretty bad, but it was made in ten days.

Q : Apache *seems more like Losey than many of your other films. You did work with him once, didn't you?*
A : Yes, I did two or three films as Joe's assistant. Put it this way: it's a Losey-

like subject. He tried to buy *Bronco Apache* the novel, and he came quite close, but there was a problem of money. We had talked about it three or four years before it was made. It could be that there are Losey carry-overs; I'm not conscious of what they are, but they're quite likely to be there.

Q: *You didn't want the ending on* Apache *that was on it?*
A: And in all fairness to Lancaster nor did he. Hecht and United Artists wanted Lancaster to be able to live, but it made a joke out of the whole film. What was the film about, what was he running away from, what was his fight to preserve his own very strange but very personal integrity if he wasn't going to get killed? He lived a life one kind of way. Now the only way to make that life believable is to end it in death. If he goes back to the bawling baby, and everyone says "Isn't that nice," well then the whole front part of the film is not very honest.

Q: *There's a certain similarity between the relationship between McIntire hunting Lancaster in* Apache *and Lancaster and Cooper in* Vera Cruz.
A: McIntire's, of course, was one of understanding and possible admiration. The Cooper character, we tried to imply, had a deep and fond affection for the Lancaster character.

Q: *We all like* Kiss Me Deadly, *but hear that you don't!*
A: Oh no, that's not true. I like this one very much and I'm very proud of it. If you remember when it was made was the time all the New Wave directors were editors on *Cahiers*. And they read into it many more things than were intended. And I think it was Truffaut who asked me at Venice the following year if I wasn't proud and happy or something about the things that *Cahiers* had said about it. And I'm a lot older and wiser now, and I suppose I should have said "Yes" and let it go at that. But I said something to the effect that I was very glad they said it, but I couldn't really take credit for all those rather deep and significant thoughts because they weren't all intended. I'm glad that they were there; maybe some of them were subconscious, but I thought a lot of them were read in. And naturally, if you had been the author of this kind of thing, you would have felt a little bit cheated, and I think they did. I think they didn't resent it, but they felt a little hurt . . . No, I like the picture very much. I just don't think it was as important a film as some people thought it was.

Q : *It doesn't at all have the wish-fulfilment of Mickey Spillane does it?*
A : Oh, no. That was the film that my friend said that between the fornication and the fighting he couldn't find the message. It was done at a time that you tried to say that the ends do not justify the means. It was a time in America when the McCarthy thing was in full bloom and that was the principal anti-Spillane attitude of the picture, that it was an anti-Spillane picture about Spillane. It was anti-McCarthy and anti-Bomb in a minor way. Bezzerides was co-author of the idea.

Q : *Bezzerides wrote* The Angry Hills *too, didn't he?*
A : Yes. Leon Uris started it until we found out that he'd never been to Greece, which seemed silly because the novel that he wrote was about Greece. Since none of us had been to Greece, we thought we'd better get somebody who knew something about it and so we went and spent some time there. I guess from the result that we didn't spend enough time. We had to start because Mitchum was on salary, because they had a start date, because they had studio committments, and the script wasn't satisfactorily polished. It wasn't ready to begin. And I think the finished film shows that, a loose wandering quality that doesn't enhance it at all and needn't have been there if we'd had another couple of months. You get locked in to those situations and it's difficult to know what to do about them.

Q : *Still, it's the picture I like most of your more recent ones.*
A : I think *Baby Jane* may change your mind; it's back to the old days of *Attack* and *The Big Knife*. By the way, we're contemplating a tour with the two ladies from *Baby Jane* which would be a ball. I don't say it would be exactly pleasant, but when it was over it would be very memorable!

Q : Ten Seconds to Hell *was the most mutilated of your films?*
A : Yes. I made a big mistake, a number of mistakes. One: I wrote the script with Teddi Sherman. And second: I don't think anyone ever read the script before we started the picture. They really thought it was going to be an adventure picture with Martine Carol taking off her clothes once or twice. Well, it never was that, so their degree of disappointment . . . the picture could have been bad or mediocre or whatever you like, but that was the kind of a picture it always was. The area of disappointment between the distributor and myself was that they had expected one kind of film, a dramatisation

of the Bachmann novel. Well the script was never changed from the day it was submitted, budgeted and agreed and cast and started, until we finished. So when they came on the scene in Berlin and saw this picture, which was pretty melancholy, they were terribly shocked. It wasn't the kind of film they expected at all. So they overreacted to what they saw. They chopped it to pieces. I think everybody had a hand in the re-editing.

So I don't think it was the picture it should have been. But it was my script. Some directors have the capacity to edit their own work, but I don't think I'm one of those.

Q : *You had a long business association with Jack Palance, didn't you?*
A : Well, that picture ended it. It was a very violent ending. He didn't like the role and he didn't like the film and I guess he knew something earlier than the rest of us, because we thought it was pretty good at the time. He had more insight than we did, maybe. We speak, but that's just about all. It's a shame because I think he's a really fine actor, but perhaps it's unwise to try more than two pictures with that kind of a personality. It can be pretty abrasive. You can be pretty strong minded about what you want.

In *Attack* he was wonderful, and also in *The Big Knife*, although a lot of people felt that he should be more handsome. I for one regret the falling out. But . . . it happens.

Q : Attack *was extremely anti-heroic. What were your particular intentions in making it?*
A : Basically it's an anti-war film. You start from the cliché "War is Hell" and you try and refine that into a personal statement of the unnecessary heroics that induce people to get into a war-psychology. And reverse that war-psychology into saying that it's a pretty ugly business. The war department refused co-operation and it looked for a while as though it wasn't going to be made. But we devised methods to make it look reasonably acceptable and realistic and went ahead.

Q : *What are you going to do next?*
A : It's not being evasive, but I really don't know. *Baby Jane* has become so successful that it makes the next picture a little more troublesome than it would be normally. *Baby Jane* will take some nursing now. I have a big, kind of flamboyant fun-western I would like to do.

Q: *There was an Anglo-German movie you were going to make at one time. . . .*
A: That's tied up in the German courts. That's a film by Lukas Heller based
on a BBC Television play called *Cross of Iron*. And I would gather that it came
too close to the meat of the matter, because we were enjoined by a German
film that said that if these Nazis were still alive and could sue. . . . That
shocked us a little bit; we thought that would make better box-office, but I
don't think the Germans agreed.

Q: *You could make it out of Germany, couldn't you?*
A: You could if you could get the goddam property out of the court. You
either pay for the deal that they didn't make, or you could get the property
back. But you can't do both. Not not get paid and not get the property. If we
don't get the property back, then give us the money, you know. At the
moment it's impounded in the Charlottenburg, Berlin, and we wait.

Robert Aldrich

PETER BOGDANOVICH/1965

THE FRENCH WERE THE FIRST to point out the brilliance of
Robert Aldrich's freewheeling movie version of the Mickey Spillane/Mike
Hammer thriller *Kiss Me Deadly,* an annihilating crime melodrama that starts
with a woman dressed only in raincoat and high heels running in panic
down a dark road, and ends with a nuclear explosion in a Malibu beach
house. I remember my old friend writer/critic Eugene Archer laughing as he
said Aldrich's picture was so refreshingly perverse that even the title came on
backward, as indeed it does in the opening roll-up: *Deadly Kiss Me.* Similar
orneriness can be perceived in the name of Aldrich's first independent company, not Aldrich and Associates, but rather the Associates and Aldrich.

Having been trained as an assistant to picture makers of such Olympian
height as Jean Renoir and Charles Chaplin (among others), Aldrich was way
ahead in the fifties, a decade before the system finally crumbled; he was first
singled out by Europeans, winning the Silver Award in Venice for his version
of Clifford Odets' savage Hollywood drama *The Big Knife*—a play that he,
Renoir, and I all had in common: we each staged it—the Italian Critics Prize
for the Jack Palance war film *Attack,* the Berlin Festival Award for the Joan
Crawford weepie-creepie *Autumn Leaves.* His biggest commercial successes
were Burt Lancaster as an American Indian in *Apache;* Gary Cooper versus
Lancaster in the satirical *Vera Cruz;* the classic Bette Davis–Joan Crawford

From *Who the Devil Made It* by Peter Bogdanovich (New York: Alfred A. Knopf, 1997). Copyright © 1997 by Ivy Moon Company. Used by permission of Alfred A. Knopf, a division of
Random House, Inc.

duel of malice, *What Ever Happened to Baby Jane?;* the rousing World War II adventure *The Dirty Dozen;* and the football drama *The Longest Yard.* Which shows the range of his anger. All the Aldrich movies are in some way angry. He even made a picture called *The Angry Hills*—the archetypal Aldrich title, right before *Sodom and Gomorrah*—though both those films were recut much against his will.

My brief interview with Aldrich was recorded in 1965 for a little article (never printed because the magazine went out of business) on the picture he had just finished shooting, *The Flight of the Phoenix;* a few other films are discussed, too. I always meant to augment our talk, because I felt Aldrich had such a strong, definite voice, had made some fascinating pictures, and also because he was among the very first independent American filmmakers of the post–Korean War period; a survivor of the end of the studio system, he led the way of the independent in the midfifties, and again in the midsixties—before, in some ways, giving in to the ultimate pull of Hollywood. In his last years he became more often a director for hire. He worked up to the end and died, through hospital errors, much too young. Though our conversation remained fragmentary, I've included it not only because of its intrinsic interest or because a discussion around one picture reveals a certain attitude about all of them, but also because Aldrich serves as a perfect transitional figure between the "A" or "B" studio director and the struggling independent, who has become much more the norm today.

Our paths crossed only a few times: I saw him pacing outside the theatre for an opening of one of his films, wished him good luck and moved on as he turned to look at the posters displayed outside; window shopping near Central Park South; on the set of *Hush . . . Hush, Sweet Charlotte,* coping with Joan Crawford in red wig—a fairly terrifying sight—before she took ill and was replaced by Olivia de Havilland; at a meeting of the Directors Guild Board, where he led a vote to support a request of mine on a picture even though he didn't agree with my wish.

The sense of his being on the run and a bit out of breath is rather a normal place for independent producers and directors, pressed to set up their next film before the current one runs out. It was a state unknown in the old studio days for anyone as good as Bob Aldrich. He tried a number of times to find independent stability but it eluded him to the end. In the late sixties, he blew everything he had earned—from his biggest success, *The Dirty Dozen*—in buying a studio and trying to fill and use it; this failed and Bob never again recovered his footing. *Hustle* was the title of an interesting Aldrich picture, and hustling became a way of life for the independent director. Most of his failed pictures are more compelling than a lot of people's successes.

At heart a true maverick, Aldrich respected this trait in others. When John Cassavetes outraged the Hollywood Establishment by coming to blows with a producer (Stanley Kramer) for recutting his picture (*A Child Is Waiting*), Cassavetes told me the town silently blacklisted him: he was out of work for nearly two years. That John was among the most talented young actors *and* directors did not faze anyone—except Bob Aldrich, who broke the unspoken blacklist by hiring Cassavetes as one of his *Dirty Dozen*—a small role which Aldrich then encouraged Cassavetes to enlarge for himself into one of the leads. It became probably the best performance in the movie and John was nominated for a Best Supporting Actor Oscar; his career was back on track. In a world of bottom-line business, Aldrich always backed the artist, right or wrong. Being the black sheep and poor relations of a prominent banking family, Bob had been an insider/outsider from the beginning, preparing him well for the place he ended up—an insider/outsider in Hollywood's mainstream: a part of and apart from.

Our brief conversation happened on August 12, 1965, near sound stages at Fox, where Aldrich was preparing to shoot; I began by asking him what it was about the book *The Flight of the Phoenix* that most interested him in making his latest feature . . .

ROBERT ALDRICH: It's much more than an adventure story, but it has all the wonderful entertainment ingredients of an adventure story; superimposed on that is the survival dilemma of what men will and will not do to stay alive under pressurized conditions; third is the twist that I don't think has ever been done in film before, which makes the surprise ending not just a gimmick. It makes it a whole, almost reasonable, ending. There are no parallels. You can't say it's like some other kind of picture, and you hope it isn't.

PETER BOGDANOVICH: *You've dealt before with the theme of men under pressure:* Ten Seconds to Hell *[1959],* Attack *[1956], et cetera.*
RA: Yes, how men will combat those excessive pressures to stay alive, and how they will weaken, and how they won't crumble.

P B :   *Is the picture very violent?*

R A :   No, strangely, not very. There's only a brief episode of violence and it's neurotic, not physical. It's only physical in that they have to overcome [Ernest] Borgnine, who's tremendously disturbed by an incident. But as such there is no violence in the picture at all. There's an offscreen killing—you never see that.

P B :   *Did you improvise a lot, or at all?*

R A :   I'll tell you what really happens—and it happens often with big films: you end up with a film that is a little longer than you would normally want, and probably a little fuller than you originally expected. Because you *do* improvise. The screenwriter, Lukas Heller, takes liberties with the book that help the film, and you take liberties with the screenplay that you think help the film, and to that degree a great deal has been added since the original conception.

P B :   *Did you improvise with the actors on the set?*

R A :   Oh, yes—always. We had a three-week rehearsal period before the picture. We talked about different approaches that you would expect from the script.

P B :   *More than on, say, your last two pictures?*

R A :   I would think more, just because of the personalities of the people involved: there were seven or eight nationalities represented, and some things—no matter how well you write them in English—just don't sound that well when they come out in a thick French accent, or a thick Italian accent, and the actor would say: "I know the point of the scene—wouldn't it be a lot funnier if I said, 'Zaba-zaba-zaba' instead of the other way around?" And you say, "Of course it would." Obviously. If you were French or Italian, you would have thought of it first.

P B :   *You didn't do as much extemporaneous stuff as you did, say, on* Vera Cruz *[1954], on which I understand you improvised an awful lot.*

R A :   No, because the script for *Vera Cruz* had many sections that would say: "And the Arabs took the town," and we would shoot for seventeen days.

PB: *Were you glad to get back to a world of men after two of your last films [*Whatever Happened to Baby Jane? *(1962) and* Hush . . . Hush, Sweet Charlotte *(1965)] both had two female leads?*
RA: That implies that—

PB: *That you weren't happy on those—no, I didn't mean that.*
RA: But it was a big relief to work with an all-male cast. And we only had one bit of trouble on the whole picture—it was the day we had the one female in front of the camera. So it *is* different: there are certain latitudes you can take with men. It's just not possible to wake up and say, "I think the whole thing stinks—let's reverse the scene and go off to the other side." Not very many women are capable of that kind of inversion—they like to stick to what they've practiced and rehearsed.

PB: *Really?*
RA: Not every man welcomes that either—but you take less of a chance.

PB: *Borgnine and [Dan] Duryea are the only two in the cast with whom you've worked before.*
RA: Yes. My son [William Aldrich] has a part in the picture, but it's very small. Everybody else I'd never worked with.

PB: *After all your recent studio work, were you happy to be back on location?*
RA: Location was wonderful. We had wonderful weather; it didn't get as hot as it was supposed to—got to 120 degrees, but it *should* be 130 degrees down there that time of year. And you have much more latitude outdoors—you're not so confined; I get along wonderfully well with [cinematographer] Joe Biroc and it's not so confining—you feel much more at ease.

PB: *With this film, were you purposely trying to get away from the horror/shock kind of thing you've done lately?*
RA: Yes—I don't want to be a middle-aged Hitchcock. I think any director gets better by doing a variety of films. I don't think he should do any *one* kind. For my personal taste, *Charlotte* and *Jane* were a little too close together. If there had been two or three films in between, I'd have been a lot better off.

PB: *How did you come to do them one after the other?*
RA: I get along wonderfully well with Bette Davis and I really enjoyed work-

ing with her. She's a terribly exciting personality, and that reflects in *your* work as well as hers; I found the story for *her* and it seemed kind of pretentious to postpone on the grounds that you didn't want to do two pictures alike too close together, because the story was there and she was there and I was there. In retrospect, I probably should have had more in between—but there was really no reason to wait to do it.

PB: *I liked de Havilland.*
RA: Oh, she was wonderful.

PB: *She was better than Crawford would have been.*
RA: Oh, much better. I think probably the casting damaged the picture commercially, but it helped the picture enormously in believability. Crawford was Crawford and very good, but she'd never have given that kind of role the nuances de Havilland did.

PB: *Well, I felt that de Havilland seemed intrinsically more of a bitch somehow.*
RA: Also, if de Havilland steps out of the cab, we're not *sure* the butler did it. Anyone else steps out of the cab, you know the butler did it, and the story's over.

PB: *How did the cast of* The Flight of the Phoenix *[1966] get along?*
RA: Everybody says "no problems," and it's never, never true. As long as I've been around—almost twenty-five years—I've never been on a picture that there wasn't a beef. This picture, which is a tragic tale, is without one single, personal abrasion. Because these guys [all-star cast: James Stewart, Richard Attenborough, Ernest Borgnine, Hardy Krüger, Peter Finch, etcetera] are terribly individualistic and they couldn't be more un-alike. I was prepared, just by the nature of things, that there would be unpleasant days— maybe quite a few of them. And I don't know what happened. They just had an enormous regard and respect for each other around that table while we were rehearsing, and we went on location at just about the right time. We only rehearsed about a week and a half together and it was pleasant together; everybody got the same kind of treatment; nobody was favored.

PB: *How was Jimmy Stewart?*
RA: Marvelous. I thought there might be some kind of collision because

some of these are—not different kinds of actors, but they have a different set of standards concerning what are good films, what constitutes a good film, than probably Stewart does and I thought there could be a variety of collisions. Being more film-conscious than most major American actors, these guys all have known every single one of his pictures, and seen them, and just honestly flattered him as opposed to kissing his ass. He couldn't believe *that* many people knew that *much* about his own pictures and other pictures. And they just got along wonderfully well.

P B :   *While casting the picture, were you specifically looking for them to be very different from each other?*
R A :   No, the key to the casting of the whole picture was an idea that the young, intelligent engineer-type be German. And there was a great deal of resistance in my own little group whether this was wise or not, because you take on many things people will read in—more than anything the script may refer to—by this man being German; you take on many problems of political and social theory. Then, having thought about that for a long time, I didn't think the worries were valid. Having decided on the idea, we agreed only two guys could play the part, maybe three. I thought the ideal was Krüger and we were lucky enough to get him. Having gotten Krüger and having gotten Stewart—that already changed the complexion of the kind of picture it could be. Then I said—having been a fan of Attenborough's for a long time— wouldn't it be sensational if we got Attenborough for the other big, big part. And we were lucky enough to get Attenborough. Now, having gotten Stewart, Attenborough and Krüger, then, gee, why not have a much broader-based film? A picture with more international aspects.

P B :   *Originally, the cast was supposed to be all one nationality?*
R A :   Well, in the book they were all British, and we had changed that to predominantly American with a sprinkling of others. That kind of snow-ballad. Krüger was the key—once we decided to make the young engineer a German . . .

P B :   *Had you decided from the outset you wanted Stewart for the part?*
R A :   No, here's what happened: we found this book because we got a big break—I have a guy in England who reads galleys for me; he told me about it—and we got in the bidding very early. Then, about a month later, *Life*

came out with a rave review of the book: the price skyrocketed and every-body got terribly involved in trying to buy it. We managed to prevail and we got the book. No sooner had we signed the contract than I got a call from Stewart's agent: "Is it really true that you own *Flight of the Phoenix?*" I said, "Yes, why?" He said, "Well, I've been trying to buy it for the last two weeks for Jimmy Stewart." I said, "Well, I presume he wanted to buy it because he wanted to play it. He could play it; he'd be marvelous, he'd be just wonderful." But we hadn't started the screenplay and the arrangement we would make here is that he would agree to play it on the basis of the book. I didn't want to get into a long negotiation where now he'd have to see the screenplay and approve the other cast. And he was most cooperative, loved the part. And that's how we got Stewart.

PB: *Did you prepare the role for Stewart, change it in any way?*
RA: Once we knew he was doing it, we certainly wrote the part for what Stewart *seems* to be. We took his characteristics as an actor into account.

PB: *Watching* The Garment Jungle *[1957], I felt I could tell which parts you had directed and which you hadn't. Did you ever see the film put together?*
RA: No. It was a very sad experience.

PB: *Did you direct most of it?*
RA: I'm *told* that's what happened. The Directors Guild asked if I wanted arbitration, I said no.

PB: *It looked as if you directed a lot of it. I mentioned this to Lee J. Cobb the other day and he said, "How could you tell?" I think he was kidding though.*
RA: He wasn't kidding. Cobb was one of the sore points on that film. He had an old, long-standing relationship with [Columbia chief] Harry Cohn; Cobb and I didn't get along. He's a very strong-willed actor—a wonderful actor, but . . . That could have been a wonderful picture. It just ran out of guts in the middle. Strangely, I've always been sorry I didn't reconcile with Cohn because I do think he made an awful mistake, and a fair mistake, but he was quite a man. We never spoke again—after.

PB: *You said a lot was cut from* Ten Seconds to Hell.
RA: Yes. I was producer on that and took my name off because about a half

hour was cut, and it doesn't make any sense to me now. The reasons why these men behave the way they do were all deleted out of the beginning of the picture—that was the whole opening. Because this is pretty factually what happened when people came back to cities like Berlin. There was just no way to get enough to eat. And to keep their families from starving they took these dangerous jobs.

PB: *It's fascinating that so many bombs didn't detonate.*
RA: The British really shook up the Germans: they devised a detonating device for which there was no timetable—it could sit there a week, two weeks, or two days, or two hours. You never knew when the bomb was going to go off once it was there.

PB: *You used that in* Ten Seconds to Hell.
RA: We didn't say it was the British, but it was them—a Mercury bomb; it could sit there for two months.

PB: *Under what circumstances did you make your second feature,* World for Ranson *[1954]?*
RA: Working night and day on a six-day week, and then a five, and we made *World for Ransom* in eleven days. We made it for ninety-five thousand dollars or something—but nobody got paid.

PB: *And you made* Baby Jane *very inexpensively.*
RA: Yes.

PB: *Because you did it fast?*
RA: We did it fast and everybody took no money and got a piece. Davis got sixty thousand dollars and Crawford got twenty-five thousand. And *Charlotte*, by the time we throw in Crawford's illness and everything, I think Davis took $125,000; well, Jesus Christ, that's some difference.

PB: *As a result of* Baby Jane, *haven't you had more ease and freedom in getting financing?*
RA: It always goes back to the same problems: who's in the picture? how much is it going to cost?

PB: *Really? You don't find as a result of* Baby Jane *that you . . .*

RA: Well, I made a career mistake I'm just about recovering from. After *The Big Knife* [1955], *Kiss Me Deadly* [1955] and *Attack* on top of *Apache* [1954] and *Vera Cruz*—I really had more latitude with that unbroken string than now. Because, remember, after *Attack* I made my three dogs in a row.

PB: *Are you talking about* Autumn Leaves *[1956]?*

RA: Well, *Autumn Leaves* did nothing to embellish my reputation.

PB: *I quite liked it, thought it was funny.*

RA: I didn't mind it either—I liked a lot of things in it that were really corny—I'm not unproud of it. But, you know, *Garment Jungle* was a disaster, and *The Angry Hills* [1959] was a catastrophe. Then, you know, given a different leading man, I think we did a goddam respectable job with *Sodom and Gomorrah* [1961]. I don't think you could do any more with that. If you had a guy you believed was Lot, I think the picture would've worked. Also, a half hour was cut out. Everybody should do a biblical picture—once.

PB: *Is that why you did it?*

RA: Hell, yes.

PB: *I didn't realize that* Attack *and* The Big Knife *had been that successful.*

RA: They were economically successful: *Attack* was a very profitable picture, but it didn't cost too much money. The French liked *Kiss Me Deadly* so much, the Hollywood community liked *The Big Knife,* Europeans generally liked *Attack.* All this made a lot of things come easier: actresses, actors. It was a whole kind of wave—you know, snowballed—good opportunity. But that was all negated by the things that followed. Because the films I wanted to do, I just couldn't get to do, and I spent three years on a marvelous group of projects. That's a sad history.

PB: *Are any of these the pictures you are planning now?*

RA: Yes, we have great hopes for these particular projects—one called *The Legend of Lylah Clare*—which we hope to do with Jeanne Moreau—and Paul Bowles's novel *The Sheltering Sky. Lylah Clare* should be done in this country; *Sheltering Sky* should be done in Morocco.

P B : *Did you direct any of* The Ride Back *[1957], which lists your company as producer?*

R A : No—a lot of people ask me that—but Oscar Rudolph, who was a friend of mine, does all of those second units. That came the last two days. It was not that it wasn't directed well—it was directed wonderfully well—but he [director H. Allen Miner] just ran out of money and had to finish the picture in X amount of days. There was a lot left to do and we just had to bring Oscar in.

P B : *Have you planned to do that again—produce a film with another director?*

R A : Yes, but with a different kind of operation: you've got to be close to it—you can't be away from it—somebody's got to watch the store. They never should have gotten me in that position in the first place, then it wouldn't have happened; you can't be doing a picture while somebody else is, and expect to watch the other picture carefully.

P B : *I guess I'm one of the few in America who saw the foreign version of* The Angry Hills, *with that great dance scene, which was so much better in its original version. A lot of lines in the American version now make no sense.*

R A : They don't work now. And Mitchum, you know, has a wonderful capacity for drinking. It was hot as hell that summer. He wanted to drink some beer—it wasn't beer—I don't know what the hell it was, but he was drinking something. [Actor] Leslie Phillips drank along with him—and remember, we had to cover two different versions—by the time all this was finished, poor Leslie was loaded. Not Mitchum, but Phillips.

P B . *You wrote a magazine article about financing.*

R A : There's no way to finance films that deal with the American scene that are controversial that may not be built-in moneymakers, that alienate certain portions of the American public. The financier's in the business to make money. If he sees in this case that his capital is in jeopardy, he's not going to make the picture. We have yet to develop a way to finance those kind of pictures.

P B : *You had this problem on* Baby Jane.

R A : *Baby Jane* proved the point that it was entertaining, it wasn't even controversial. The problem really was whether you liked the subject matter or

not. What happens if you want to make a picture on Vietnam. I don't necessarily mean it's *my* position, but what happens if I don't like our government's position on Vietnam and I want to do a film about that? I *don't* like
it—the government's position on Vietnam—and there's not a *chance* to make
a film about that. Now, other countries have ways in which they make films
on unpopular subjects.

PB: *Do you think, as a result, that American filmmakers are falling behind foreign
filmmakers?*
RA: There isn't a doubt in the world. It's nonsense to think our culture, our
education, our exposure is such that we can't knowingly deal with these subjects—we can. Nobody's found a way to finance these kinds of pictures. The
market's there; I'm sure it is. It's like proving the world is round. Until you
do it, nobody's going to find out.

PB: *Is there some intrinsic difference between American filmmakers and European
filmmakers?*
RA: I think the problem is, they don't have much hope. Where can they
look to say, "If I really was clever and I did *that,* I could do a real picture"?
What chance do you have to get an unpopular picture made? You just
haven't. You go back, I'm sure, and you say, "I have to do a picture in two
and a half days for TV for so much; you finish by six o'clock . . ." Everybody's
entitled to dream, but that's kind of a hopeless dream; I don't see any chance
of fruition.

PB: *But how did people in the old days—like John Ford, Howard Hawks—make
great films? Didn't they have the same problems you have today?*
RA: No, not quite true because then the distributor said we can average out;
you can no longer average out. Every picture is a bookkeeping entry. Either
it loses its money or it *doesn't* lose its money. They used to make thirty pictures of which twenty-seven make money and three lose; they didn't care
because it averages out—you take the house's gamble. But the house can't
gamble anymore.

Interview with Robert Aldrich

JOEL GREENBERG/1968

THE THALBERG BUILDING, Culver City, California: follow its
long plain corridors, climb a couple of flights of prosaic stairs and turn several corners and you will eventually reach an office that sometimes serves as
the temporary headquarters of the Associates and Aldrich, Inc. company. An
inner room, rather murky and cluttered, its main furnishings a mountainous
desk and a number of big black leather chairs, discloses a burly, bespectacled
man who looks as if he might have been a formidable college footballer. This
is Robert Aldrich, and he was indeed a formidable college footballer. He is
now an even more formidable veteran of countless Hollywood in-battles,
and creator of a body of films which at their best reflect his own urban-
American energy and his preoccupation with the morality and ethics of violence in an amoral, violent world. Over Coca Cola, he talks briskly and often
pungently of the vicissitudes of a movie director's career, and after the interview—although it is well past office hours and the building is practically
deserted—he will confer long into the evening with a colleague on the preparation of their new film. Movie-making, for Robert Aldrich, is clearly a
twenty-four-hour a day activity.

JOEL GREENBERG: *How did you enter movies?*
ROBERT ALDRICH: I was about to leave the University of Virginia in 1941
when I approached an uncle who had some movie interests in California. He
gave me a production job for six weeks at $25 per week saying, "I never want

From *Sight and Sound*, 37.1 (Winter 1968–69): 8–13. Reprinted by permission.

to see you again." My job was that of production clerk, a position that has since been done away with. It was the lowest form of human life here, the guy below the book-keeper and below the tea boy. They were finally unionised about 1942 or 1943 and became third or fourth assistants.

I made the jump from fourth to first assistant director rather hurriedly thanks to World War II. I was thrown out of the Air Corps after a day and a half because of some old football injuries, and owing to the wartime shortage of young manpower I quickly rose from first assistant to production manager.

J G : *What were some of the pictures you worked on at this period?*
R A : I was very lucky in my assignments. I worked with Lewis Milestone on about four or five pictures when he was just about at the peak of his career—although *he* mightn't consider it the peak. I worked with Chaplin, with Joseph Losey and Bill Wellman, and also with some terribly bad directors whom there's no point in naming—although you learn just as much from the bad ones as you do from the good ones, strangely.

J G : *What were Enterprise Studios like to work for?*
R A : Enterprise embodied a really brilliant idea of a communal way to make films. It was a brand new departure, the first time I can remember that independent filmmakers had all the money they needed. But we wasted—that's presumptuous—the *company* wasted an awful lot of money, energy, and effort on bad material, on improperly developed material, because its story selection and picture execution were not what they should have been.

There's an ethnic saying here: "A fish stinks from the head." Well, there was no head of that studio. There were a lot of very talented, experienced, intelligent people among its various branches, but there was no knowledgeable guy to run the shop.

But for about two or three years before it went down the drain I would guess that it had a better esprit de corps, and more interest and excitement going for it among its employees, from the labourer to the star, than any place in Hollywood. Personal relationships between the employees and management were extraordinary, and they paid the top dollar to all technicians. Thus they got the best technicians from every major studio in town.

J G : *Did Enterprise have an ethic, an orientation towards stories with social significance?*

RA: I think that happened, but it would be unfair to say that was its 'aim.' As the Irish say, this was just before the 'troubles,' and the talented people in that period—there were exceptions, of course—tended to be more liberal than the untalented people, and because they were more liberal they got caught up in social processes that had political manifestations which later proved to be economically difficult to live with. In its search for talented and interesting people Enterprise hired a great many followers of that persuasion, and its pictures consequently began to acquire more and more social content.

JG: *Which of the outstanding pictures at Enterprise did you work on?*
RA: I don't think there were any "outstanding" pictures. The studio's main problem was that it had one hit and about nine disasters. The hit was *Body and Soul,* which cost a million dollars more than it should have cost because its director, Robert Rossen, was given his head. Abraham Polonsky, although he'd written a marvellous script, really interfered too much. Bob Roberts, who was a dear and good friend, never really pretended to be a producer, and as I said there was nobody at the head of the studio to pull us all up short.

JG: *What was your contribution to* Force of Evil?
RA: On that I was production manager *and* assistant director. Polonsky, who wrote and directed it, is a terribly talented and gifted man. Blacklisted during what we laughingly refer to as the "dark days"—during which his work was to be found on television under a considerable variety of different names—he is now back in town and has done work at Universal.
    You're led to believe that most of the formerly blacklisted people are back. It's not quite true. The rehabilitation process varies in direct proportion to their talent or their need. If they were marginal, or if they were sporadic in their output, you just find that they're not working.

JG: *How did you come to direct your first feature,* The Big Leaguer?
RA: At M-G-M they'd formed a unit jokingly called "the sons of the pioneers" in which sons of producers who had worked with Louis B. Mayer were producing tiny little features. Dore Schary, who didn't have a very outstanding record here, was nevertheless a pretty wise fellow, and he recognized—in his capacity as studio production head—that with fellows like that as producers you had to have directors who knew what they were doing. Herbie Baker,

who wrote the screenplay for *The Big Leaguer,* a baseball story, had been with Carl Foreman at Enterprise and suggested my name to Schary. That's now I got to do the film.

Before that I did some filmed television shows in New York, including a lot of the *China Smith* series starring the late Dan Duryea. The photographer was Joe Biroc, and the producer was Bernie Tabakin. It was a fun show—we were knocking these episodes out in two days each—and one day I conceived the idea of making a feature the next time we closed down.

So during ten spare days another fellow and I sat down and wrote a story which became *World for Ransom.* To get enough money to finish the film we took on a couple of commercials, a beer commercial and an Eversharp commercial, and interrupted the picture to shoot them. It was a strange and very enjoyable experience and—except for the end result—a marvelous collaboration. It really had no sets and thanks to Joe Biroc we had reflections in water where there was no water, and all kinds of silly things. I've always looked back on *World for Ransom* with a wistful kind of happy feeling.

J G : *How did you become associated with Hecht-Lancaster?*

R A : That went back earlier than *World for Ransom,* to the time when they were still kind of sprawling and struggling and had gone to Columbia on a two-picture deal. They needed someone to watch the store because Harold Hecht wasn't too well acquainted with the physical and financial side of picturemaking and wanted an experienced production manager. I went there as "assistant to the producer," which was really just a glorified way of paying me more money so that I could be their production manager.

J G : *And your first film for them as director was* Apache?

R A : Yes. They let me do it because they wanted a "bright young man" they didn't have to pay much money to. A great deal of what I wanted to say about the Red Indians in *Apache* was lost. The original script ended with the hero, Massai (played by Burt Lancaster), going back up to a shack to be shot needlessly in the back by Federal troops. That was the script I'd been given, that was the script I'd approved, and that was the script I'd shot. Two or three days before shooting on the picture was due to finish United Artists prevailed upon Hecht to shoot two endings. I don't know how it is in other countries, but in this country when you have somebody suggest two endings you know they're going to use the other one. So I refused to shoot the alternative ending and for about two days Burt agreed that the original ending was what this picture was all about.

Then for reasons best known to himself he changed his mind. Now once Burt had changed his mind it made little difference if I refused to direct the other ending because the next day they could have got someone who would. The point was lost because a $500-a-week director had no hope of prevailing against Hecht-Lancaster and United Artists. With the original ending I think the picture would have been more—"significant" is a pompous word—but I think it would have been more important. You make a picture about one thing, the inevitability of Massai's death. His courage is measured against the inevitable. The whole preceding two hours becomes redundant if at the end he can just walk way.

J G : *Did you have a more amicable relationship with Burt Lancaster on* Vera Cruz?

R A : Burt is not an easy man to get along with, but quite responsive. On *Apache* we had a much better relationship, I think, than either of us anticipated. On *Vera Cruz* it was less amicable. This was because Burt, until he directed *The Kentuckian,* thought he was going to be a director, and when you're directing your first great big picture you don't welcome somebody else thinking he is going to be its director. There were also a few differences of opinions about concepts and about action. Since Burt directed *The Kentuckian* I think he's probably a more valuable actor.

J G : Kiss Me Deadly *has become a kind of "cult" picture, particularly among some European critics. What are your views on it?*

R A : I was very proud of the film. I think it represented a whole breakthrough for me. In terms of style, in terms of the way we tried to make it, it provided a marvellous showcase to display my own ideas of movie-making. In that sense it was an enormous "first" for me. I've never denied that. I think what irritates some people—and I've been misquoted about this so many times—is that they think I have disowned the importance of the film. I haven't. What I have said is that it has an importance juxtaposed against a particular political background, an importance that's not justified if it's juxtaposed against another one that by accident happens to fit. It did have a basic significance in *our* political framework that we thought rather important in those McCarthy times: that the end did not justify the means. Once you got outside the United States the whole importance of that disappeared, and the French and others read into it all sorts of terribly profound observations. Now the moment you denied that alleged profundity they thought you were discrediting your own work and their opinion of it, which wasn't the case.

J G :   *To what extent did you use Mickey Spillane's original book?*
R A :   The book had nothing. We just took the title and threw the rest away. The scriptwriter, A. I. Bezzerides, did a marvellous job, contributing a great deal of inventiveness to the picture. That devilish box, for example—an obvious atom bomb symbol—was mostly his idea. To achieve the ticking and hissing sound that's heard every time the box is opened we used the sound of an airplane exhaust overdubbed with the sound made by human vocal chords when someone breathes out noisily.

J G :   *At what point did you form your own company, The Associates and Aldrich?*
R A :   I formed it at the close of *Kiss Me Deadly*, retaining many of the people— film editor Michael Luciano, cameraman Joe Biroc, prop-men, assistants— who had been with me before on most of the television stuff, certainly on *World for Ransom*.

J G :   Did The Big Knife *upset people here in Hollywood?*
R A :   It certainly did. It was a critical success but economically it was, to say the least, a disappointment. I'd love to be able to say that it failed commercially because it was too uncompromising: that would make me out to be a courageous guy. But there were other factors, the chief one being that lay audiences could not accept Jack Palance as a movie star. They didn't associate him with a guy who could or could not decide to take $5000 per week. We failed to communicate to the mass audience—not to the critics, not to selective audiences—that it was not primarily a monetary problem; it was a problem of internal integrity such as you or I or the guy at the gas station might have. I don't know that this dilemma could have been resolved anyhow. The original play had been done on Broadway with John Garfield, who was dead by the time we came to do the picture. If you'd had an electric, charming guy like Garfield in the lead you would have solved half the problem but I don't think you could ever have solved the other half.

JG: *Autumn Leaves* seems to have been a very uncharacteristic subject?

RA: I guess self-survival made me do that one. People were getting pretty collective in their criticism of the violence and anger and wrath in my pictures, although these things weren't intentional, and I thought it was about time I made a soap opera. I was also a great fan of the Butlers—Jean Rouverol and Hugo Butler—and this was her original story. I had always been a Joan Crawford fan too, but we had big problems with her on *Autumn Leaves*. About a week before work on the picture began, Miss Crawford wanted her own writer to come in and rewrite, which I refused to allow her to do. At two a.m. on the morning before we were due to start shooting I received a 'phone call saying she wouldn't be there later that day unless her writer could attend, to which I responded that if her writer showed up we would not shoot.

Looking back, I really think that's the only way you can properly deal with Miss Crawford. The writer didn't show up but she did, and we proceeded. But she didn't talk to me for about four or five days. She took direction, she did what she was supposed to do, but there was no personal communication. Then one day she was doing a scene terribly effectively: I forget which one. I was really touched, and when she looked up after finishing it I tried not to be obvious in wiping away a tear. That broke the ice, and from then on we were good friends for a long long time.

JG: *What was your main anti-war argument in* Attack?

RA: Well, not the usual "war is hell" thing but the corrupting influence that war can have on the most normal, average human beings, what terrible things it makes them capable of that they wouldn't be capable of otherwise. I'm very proud of the film. I never saw *The Fragile Fox,* the play on which it is based, but I read it and thought that it said through the characters many things that I would like to have said about anti-war attitudes. We had just been through a cycle of markedly unsuccessful preachment pictures in California, and I thought that if you could make this film really honestly and with a good cast, the characters saying what you'd like to say by just playing the parts, it would be a welcome change. It worked that way and, although many people prophesied that it wouldn't make money, it did; the trouble was that it was cross-collateralised against *The Big Knife* so nobody ever saw any of the money.

JG: *What were the circumstances of your quitting direction of* The Garment Jungle?

RA: That was a strange experience. I don't remember another occasion of a guy getting fired for wanting to shoot the picture that he'd been assigned. Usually, if you're fired, it's for wanting to change the script. The film's producer, Harry Kleiner, had written a terribly tough, controversial script and as we started getting into it—it was shaping up as a pretty good picture—they suddenly realised that they had no intention of making that kind of a document; they wanted to make "boy meets girl in a dress factory." I was pretty stubborn, and Harry Cohn, the head of Columbia, was pretty stubborn, and they wanted to change the focus, the force, the direction of the picture. I wouldn't do it and Cohn fired me. I've never seen the finished film, although I'm told that about half or two-thirds of it is mine.

I had a great fondness for Cohn. Naturally I think he was wrong in firing me but that's beside the point. I think he ran a marvellous studio. I think that system is better, I think he did it as well as anybody could do it. He wasn't in the money business, he was in the movie business. I had a chance to have a reconciliation with him later—a reconciliation in terms of doing other work—and I didn't go. I've always regretted it.

JG: *What went wrong with* The Angry Hills *and* Ten Seconds to Hell?

RA: *The Angry Hills* is disappointing not because it's not a good picture but because it *could* have been good. It had a potential that was never even remotely realised. *Ten Seconds to Hell,* on the other hand, is a bad picture. Why, I've never been quite sure. Some of it has to do with my writing, some of it has to do with the story, some of it with the fact that United Artists didn't know what kind of picture it was. If it's bad it's bad, but that's as good as you could make it. Thus you feel embarrassed maybe about *Ten Seconds to Hell,* but you feel sad about *The Angry Hills.* No matter if I did *Ten Seconds to Hell* tomorrow I wouldn't know how to make it any better. I'd know how to make *The Angry Hills* better in a thousand ways.

JG: The Last Sunset?

RA: A very unpleasant experience. The whole thing started badly, went on badly, ended up badly. Dalton Trumbo had done a screenplay. This was just towards the end of the McCarthy period and he had yet to be given a screen credit, though Preminger had promised him one for *Exodus.* He quit his concentration on *The Last Sunset* to concentrate on the Preminger picture and by the time he came back to our film it was too late to save it.

Now I think that all things considered, Trumbo was 2000 percent right. There was an enormous principle involved here. He was the first writer to break through the blacklist, he was going to force a change in the whole California concept of blacklisted writers. That was certainly much more important than making Kirk Douglas look well, but it didn't solve the problem of making *The Last Sunset* any better. Rock Hudson emerged more creditably from it than anyone. I found him to be terribly hard-working and dedicated and very serious: no nonsense, no "I've got to look good." Or "Is this the right side?" If everybody in that picture, from producer to writer to other actors, had approached it with the same dedication it would have been a lot better. That's not my way of saying that Mr. Hudson is Laurence Olivier, but he was certainly much more honestly involved in that venture than anybody else I can think of.

J G :   *Were Davis and Crawford your initial choices for the two principal parts in* What Ever Happened to Baby Jane?
R A :   Yes, right from the beginning. I'd never met Davis. I did write her a letter saying that she might not want to do the picture but she would have to admit it was the best role she'd ever had, and if she didn't feel that way she shouldn't see me. After two weeks she wrote back declaring that it was rather presumptuous of me to say that, but it was certainly a good enough role to warrant discussion.

J G :   *Was there any ill feeling between the two stars on the set of* Baby Jane?
R A :   None. I think it's proper to say that they really detested each other, but they behaved absolutely perfectly: no upstaging, not an abrasive word in public. Nor did Miss Davis allow any enmity with Miss Crawford to colour her playing of the scenes in which she was supposed to torment her. People who loved the violence of it read that into it and thought it was inherent, but it wasn't. They both behaved in a wonderfully professional manner.

J G :   *How did you find Victor Buono?*
R A :   I'd seen him in an *Untouchables* episode on television playing a large cameo character called Mr. Moon. He was fabulous. Davis didn't like him at first: she thought he was too grotesque. Victor obviously sensed her attitude,

but he never commented and it was never openly displayed. Halfway through the film—we don't really get along, but this is a small instance of the kind of lady she can be when she wants to—she smiled at him and said: "I want you to know that at the beginning of this picture I did everything I could to persuade Bob not to use you and I'd like to apologise because you're just marvelous." And he was.

J G : *Is it true that Davis didn't like herself in the part when she first saw it run?*
R A : She'd never seen the complete picture before seeing it with me at Cannes, and I don't think she was prepared for the experience of seeing it among lots of people. She, more than I, decided on her Baby Jane make-up, that ugly chalky mask. I'd say it was 80 percent Davis and 20 percent Aldrich, whereas on *Hush, Hush, Sweet Charlotte* it was very close to 50–50, maybe 55 percent Aldrich and 45 percent Davis. She did not realise, I think, what the cumulative effect of seeing herself like that would be. About five minutes into the picture I heard this quiet but kind of desperate sobbing beside me and turned to her wondering what the hell was the matter. "I just look awful," she wept. "Do I really look that awful."

Miss Davis is a strange lady. She has been misled so many times, and placed her confidence so many times in situations and/or people that didn't pay off, that she's naturally terribly hesitant to trust anybody. Once she trusts you, however, she's marvelous.

J G : *Were you pleased with her performance in* Baby Jane?
R A : I thought she was wonderful. But I also thought—the public won't agree, and certainly the critics won't agree—that the job she did in *Hush, Hush, Sweet Charlotte,* because it was a much more difficult, narrow-edge part, and took much more talent and time and thought and care, was a better performance than *Baby Jane,* which was such a bravura, all-out Gothic eye-catcher that everybody thought it superior.

J G : *What was the origin of* Hush, Hush, Sweet Charlotte?
R A : It came from a three- or four-page original idea by Henry Farrell, author of the *Baby Jane* novel, that I found very exciting. I also wanted to re-team Davis and Crawford. Then Miss Crawford fell ill and was replaced by Olivia de Havilland. And Crawford was sick, seriously sick. If she'd been faking, as some reports then suggested, either the insurance company would never

have paid the claim or she would never had been insurable again. Insurance companies here are terribly tough, there's no such thing as a made-up ailment that they pay you off on.

Eventually the insurance company offered us the alternatives of finding a replacement for Miss Crawford or scrapping the picture. As you can well imagine, there were great arguments about whom we should get. A number of ladies were considered, all of whom for a variety of reasons were not acceptable to all parties. There was also a contractual problem in that Davis had star approval. Until then it had been academic because she had approved Crawford, but it now became vitally important.

Obviously the ideal candidates would have been Vivien Leigh and Katharine Hepburn. Now it's not necessary that it should become a matter of public record why Davis didn't want either of those ladies. It is fair to say however that it had nothing to do with their talent. But there are deep-seated personal and historical reasons why she didn't want them. I won't say that Olivia was third choice, but Olivia was the first choice that was acceptable.

J G : *What script problems did you have on* The Dirty Dozen?
R A : Metro-Goldwyn-Mayer and the producer Kenneth Hyman had bought the property, a novel by E. M. Nathanson, after I had tried to acquire it when it wasn't even in galleys, just a step outside. Then they had about four or five scripts, the last one written by Nunnally Johnson. This would have made a very good, very acceptable 1945 war picture. But I don't think that a 1945 war picture is necessarily a good 1967 war picture. So I brought in Lukas Heller. Metro must have had about $300,000 tied up in aborted *Dirty Dozen* scripts by then, and I wanted a whole new concept. Well, despite considerable resistance, we got a whole new concept, and with the exception of Bosley Crowther I think you will discover that most people adored—that's a pretty rich word—were fascinated by the anarchy of the picture's first two-thirds and were excited and/or stimulated and/or entertained by the last third. The first two-thirds were Mr. Heller's contribution toward making it a 1967 picture and not a 1947 picture and the last third was a pretty high-class, well-done war adventure.

J G : *How do you go about preparing your films?*
R A : I give my art director, William Glasgow, a concept and he comes back with the drawings. It's very subtle. Sometimes it gets terribly complicated

when we used a model, but very rarely; we did use one on *Charlotte* and *The Legend of Lylah Clare.* As I approve or disapprove of his suggestions his ideas snowball and gradually become better and better. Glasgow did a marvellous job on *4 for Texas,* and an even better one on *Charlotte* which doesn't show because it's in black and white. I believe I gave him his first credit as an art director, and we have been associated ever since. He's a very dedicated, quiet kind of fellow, and also very stubborn.

JG: *Do you pre-plan your films in detail?*

RA: It might seem a silly thing to say, but one pre-plans one's pictures if there's time. What you find is that you run out of time. You can't let other things intrude on rehearsals even though you'll pay for it later. You concentrate on rehearsals at the expense of other things so you often have to do a certain amount of improvising while shooting. Ideally, I'd like to pre-plan my pictures in their entirety, and on some there's time to do that. Hitchcock is said to do it. Milestone did it. I think it's too rigid. We used to have terrible problems with Milestone. He's a marvelous cutter and director, but he would pre-plan and pre-sketch a scene so much that if an actor wanted to depart from it by even one little bit the whole preparation went for nothing.

JG: *How do you view the contemporary filmmaking scenes here and in Europe?*

RA: Among contemporary European directors, I love Godard and Chabrol; I think Chabrol is terribly underrated. As for Hollywood—I could be wrong, this is not a nationalistic point of view—but it's my opinion that we have just as many talented directors and actors here as anywhere else in the world. What has happened is that this industry has gone into the money business and not into the film business, and since they are in the money business they tend to look for guarantees and protections and things like that before everything else. Because of the inundation of the more honest, more frank European pictures we were breaking away from that tendency for quite a while, but now that's been offset owing to the enormous revenues that American films can make through being sold to television. All of a sudden there's a fresh upsurge of this conservative, play-it-safe, let's-sell-it-by-the-foot, very average mundane material.

And I don't know the answer to that. We have such staggering labour costs here. I don't say they are unfair but they are high. You can't make a good film without taking time over it. *Morgan* cost no money, but Karel Reisz took sixty-six days to make *Morgan.* Well, you can't shoot sixty-six days in this country for under two million dollars.

I don't know how you are going to break through at the idea level. A guy comes to you and says he wants to make a daring, controversial piece of material. Now to make that well, to make it as well as the Europeans make it, he's got to take the same amount of time. But he can't do that because the Americans in charge of handing out the money aren't going to give him the required amount. They might give him—if he's an extremely talented, well-known guy and the ideas aren't too explosive—one-tenth of the money he needs. But one-tenth of the money he needs is not going to buy him one-third of the time he needs, so he can't come over with a good picture. And I don't know the solution.

Interview with Robert Aldrich

ALAIN SILVER / 1970

T HE FOLLOWING INTERVIEW conducted by Alain Silver was com-
missioned by *Film Comment* Magazine in November 1970 and recorded on
the afternoon of December 21, 1970 in Robert Aldrich's office at the then
Aldrich Studios, 201 North Occidental Boulevard, Los Angeles, California.
Aldrich was then in the process of supervising editing of *The Grissom Gang*.
Also present during the interview was Jerry Pam, Aldrich's press agent. This
text was edited from a transcription of approximately one hour and forty-
five minutes of recorded time and includes a substantial amount of material
which was omitted from the version published in *Film Comment* (Spring 1972)
for reasons of length. Also incorporated here are some remarks and observations made by Aldrich during an informal half-hour conversation after the
tape recorder was turned off.

SILVER: *I want to ask about your tie, which you drape around your neck the
same way Barney Sheean does in* The Legend of Lylah Clare.
ALDRICH: That's a dull joke actually. When I first came out here I used to
be reasonably athletic, enough to stay in shape. Then came a time in the '50s
that I put on forty pounds, and I just didn't have the time or the money to
get a brand new wardrobe. So it became expeditious not to button my shirt,
simply because I couldn't. By the time I had enough money to buy new

From Alain Silver and James Ursini, *What Ever Happened to Robert Aldrich?: His Life and His
Films* (New York: Limelight Editions, 1995), 343–60. Reprinted by permission of Limelight
Editions.

shirts, it had become a habit. I don't know but you hang on to those idiosyncrasies. So I gave it to Ernie Borgnine—Barney Sheean was a poor man's Harry
Cohn.

SILVER: *No tape decks arrayed behind the desk?*
ALDRICH: We thought about it, but it doesn't work. It only worked with
Cohn.

SILVER: *I was originally planning to start with the standard line about your early
career as production clerk and assistant director or "How to build a small studio
empire in thirty years . . ."*
ALDRICH: Well, thanks for the small empire. But if I were starting out
today, I'd marry some producer's daughter or illegitimate cousin—the only
way to start in this business is at the top.

SILVER: *Well, then how did you get that first job directing a feature?*
ALDRICH: Mayer before his decline, before he was overthrown by Dore
Schary, had wanted to put the sons of the guys who helped him form Metro
into production work; and they had this thing called the "Sons of the Pioneers." That was really the name of it. Matt Rapf was one of them. Arthur
Loew was one. Three or four guys whose fathers had been helpful in first
forming Metro. Under Schary they made seven or eight pictures. I had been
at Enterprise [Studios], and Herbert Baker, who had written one of the pictures for [Stanley] Kramer [*So This is New York*] was doing a baseball picture
with Matt Rapf. And Herbie told him, "There's a very bright guy in town
who's done a lot of productions; he's doing television now in New York. You
should get this guy. He's a very good athlete. He knows athletes." Well, there
was nobody there [in this unit at MGM] who really had any production experience. So they were looking for "bright young guys" who'd been on the
firing line for a while, someone they thought they could give an opportunity
to and who knew what he was doing, because they didn't. So we made that
picture with Eddie Robinson in what is now Cape Kennedy in sixteen, seventeen days, out of nowhere. The world wasn't waiting for that picture. It was
a picture about the New York Giants and Metro had the foresight to open it
in Brooklyn; so you can't have expected it to do very well.

So nothing much came out of it; and I did some more television and *World
for Ransom*. Hecht and Lancaster saw *World for Ransom* and liked it; and out

of that, not out of *The Big Leaguer* came *Apache.* On the strength of *World of Ransom,* I got *Apache.* I had worked for Hecht-Lancaster before, under a different relationship. They made two pictures, *Ten Tall Men* and a Frank Tashlin picture [*The First Time*] on which I was associate producer or assistant to the producer or something. We had an argument over the credit on those films; but we had a pretty good relationship.

SILVER: *When did the problem with the ending come up?*
ALDRICH: The problem started with the [Paul I.] Wellman novel. [Joe] Losey had wanted to buy it and couldn't. I had wanted to buy it myself but couldn't afford it. In the novel, Massai hears his son being born, suspects that it may be a trap, but goes in anyway; and they kill him. That's the inevitable conclusion of the story, that he be killed. The internal relationships between [Jean] Peters as Nalinle and Lancaster as Massai, between Massai and the Army, Massai and the other Apaches, they're all built on the inevitability of his death. Of course, United Artists and Hecht became apprehensive of that so-called downbeat ending. I made noise but they didn't hear me. Burt held out for a week or so; but they finally convinced him. Well, United Artists is the money and Burt is the talent, so then you go through the steps, but you know they're going to use the happy ending.

SILVER: *The last shot, from the helicopter, moving back, which anticipates the ending of* The Big Knife, *was that planned for Massai's death? Didn't you shoot both versions?*
ALDRICH: He was shot coming out of the corn field, but we merely went through the motions on that. I'm not sure that the other ending would have cut together. We never assembled it, because we knew from the day we shot the two endings, we'd be stuck with the happy one. It was an economic decision.

SILVER: *I think it was Truffaut who suggested that* The Big Knife*'s economic failure was because it was too moral at a time when psychology was in vogue. Your pictures seem to be as much about survival as about morality.*
ALDRICH: Well, you usually have a set of principles that you try to identify with the "good guys"; and a set of values of which you disapprove that identify the "bad guys." I seldom did but in that Truffaut piece, I think I referred to my father, who saw only one of my pictures before he died, and that was

The Big Knife. So the explanation of its failure is simple. My father was a man of considerable means and reasonably intelligent but very old school. When he saw the picture, he asked, "Tell me one thing. Am I to understand that his [Castle's] choice was to take or not take $5,000 a week?" I said, "Yes." "Well then, you'll never have a successful picture." I asked, "Why not?" "Because there is no choice." That may seem to demean my father's sophistication; but it doesn't really. He saw something that [Clifford] Odets and me and Jim Poe and Charlie Castle, we never saw.

SILVER: *Did any of your family or school background in economics relate in any way to those early jobs, to breaking in?*
ALDRICH: It had some bearing. I broke in when they were making filmed television in New York. They really didn't know how to make filmed television there; they just didn't have a clue. All they were paying directors was scale. Who the hell wanted to go live in New York and work for scale? Only guys who had never directed or couldn't get a shot. Walter Blake, who is now associate producer on most of my pictures, convinced these people who were doing the Camay soap shows that I was a genius waiting behind a rock out here. I had been assistant director on a Chaplin picture [*Limelight*], so he told them that I had directed Chaplin. Nobody directs Chaplin except Chaplin, but these guys didn't know the difference. So I went back to New York and did, I don't know, thirty or forty shows.

SILVER: *It was kind of a fluke then?*
ALDRICH: Luck, luck . . .

SILVER: *And those few months in New York established you more than all the assistantships and other production work?*
ALDRICH: They couldn't care less. That opened the door enough for the first step inside. But otherwise it's no different than if any sergeant in the world tells a captain, "I can do the lieutenant's job." Nobody's going to believe you. All those years they don't mean as much as you might think they mean. They mean that much in terms of personal gratification, but if you're in a very tough league with a lot of rookie players, it doesn't make that much difference that you can run or punt or pass as well as the next guy. The guy calling the signals, they'll give him a tryout. But your experience or knowledge don't really have much to do with that "trial period."

And waiting out that period is always tough. Someone once said that lasting power is the most important power. Especially in this business. Staying at the plate or staying at the table, staying in the game, is the essential. You can't allow yourself to get passed over or pushed aside. Very, very talented people got pushed aside and remained unused. That's the problem: staying at the table.

SILVER: *You seem to have a fair share of luck "at the table"?*
ALDRICH: An old joke. Because there are so many of those talented people, if you must make a choice between luck and talent, you have to opt for luck. It's nice to have some of both, or a lot of both; but if you can't, luck is the answer. Nowhere else more so than in this business. The right place, the right time, the right script, all the right auspices—they made the difference to directors, writers, actors.

SILVER: *Is it really necessary nowadays to act as your own producer in order to remain a director?*
ALDRICH: Well, yes, you lessen the enemy. Then you only have the distributor to fight. There's always a problem whether it's a producer or a financing company, when someone wants to intrude into your sphere; but it is considerably lessened if you don't have a separate producer. One discovers that during any kind of "growth" in this industry. Growth is a pompous word; but we do shut our eyes to thievery—at what level do we participate? Do we endorse it? Probably we're all guilty of that at some time.

SILVER: *But has money or unwillingness to "shut your eyes" ever really hampered you?*
ALDRICH: I think I made three very good movies, *The Big Knife, Attack,* and *Kiss Me Deadly.* I worked almost for nothing, economically, on those movies. They got caught up in the system and were not profitable pictures. Things that you hoped would explode out of good movies didn't quite happen. And I came back to this country, after having made some dogs in Europe, to cash in on what I thought would see me through another period of trials, namely my considerable ownership in these former projects. They cost so little that I thought they had to have a large equity! TV sales, at least. I found that I had almost no equity, or at best nominal. I think my fifty percent in those three pictures was $35,000; not each but altogether, of which I had to pay a

large part to my producer representative who watched the store. So you end up with $20,000 for half of three pictures; and you begin to understand, you have a graphic lesson in what the ground rules are. And they are: you don't get yours, they get theirs. You have to divide up. [When it's] between you and them or [between] you and you, you become cynical in terms of what preference to give survival and what preference to give material that might make a fine film which nobody or very few would go to see. That was the break. When I came back from working in Europe in '58, I really started to work on the theory of how to stay at the table. I realized that, just by the law of averages, if you're careful in choosing projects and settling costs, your tastes and knowledge will, out of every six or seven pictures, produce one that makes a good deal of profitable return for everybody. I also realized that, for all the critical acclaim, *The Big Knife* and *Attack* and *Kiss Me Deadly* could not keep me in the ball game. I added a few disasters of my own after that.

SILVER: Kiss Me Deadly, *wasn't always one of your favorites.*
ALDRICH: People have always said that. What I thought, it happened quite often with French critics, particularly when Truffaut and Chabrol and all those guys were at *Cahiers,* was that they read many, many things into *Kiss Me Deadly.* I appreciated their enthusiasm, but I just couldn't take a bow for it. Because *Kiss Me Deadly,* at its depth, had to do with the McCarthy Era, the end justifying the means, and the kind of materialistic society that paid off in choice rewards, sometimes money, sometimes girls, sometimes other things. But it wasn't as profound as many of the French thought it was. I did like it; it did everything I hoped it would do and more. I think I did a good job on it, that everybody connected with it did a good job; but it isn't that deep a piece of piercing philosophy as the French thought it was.

SILVER: *You've called* Kiss Me Deadly *an anti-McCarthy picture. Although Stanley Hoff is a composite of Mayer and Cohn, whom we're already mentioned, the McCarthy figure seems more physically present in* The Big Knife. *When Danziger raises his arm in a kind of neo-Fascist salute, "Hail, Columbia," both meanings are there.*
ALDRICH: Well, of course, he [Hoff] is McCarthy. But I'm terribly ambivalent about the Hoff character. When we made *The Big Knife,* Harry Cohn and Jack Warner were still in full flower, and Mayer was only recently fallen. Nobody had seen the abyss. We'd had twenty years of petty dictators run-

ning the industry during which time everybody worked and everybody got paid, maybe not enough, but they weren't on relief. Seventeen years later you wonder if the industry is really more healthy in terms of creativity. Are we making more or better pictures without that central control? But when everybody worked under those guys, they hated them. So we took the drum roll from Nuremberg and put it under the Hoff character's entrances and exits. But, you know, you can have a certain fondness for the way Cohn and Mayer got things done. Cohn took a while to realize that I did *The Big Knife*. Halfway through the "honeymoon" period when I was signed with Columbia, he asked me "Did you do *The Big Knife?*" I said, "Yes." "You son of a bitch. If I'd known that you never would have been here." The Hoff crying came from Mayer, who is reported to have been able to cry at the drop of an option. But the big rebuff that Odets suffered was at the hands of Columbia, so there was more of Cohn in the original play than there was of Mayer.

SILVER: *What made you use those long takes in* The Big Knife *and also in* World for Ransom *and* Kiss Me Deadly?

ALDRICH: It has a direct relation to economy and personnel. Ernie Laszlo is a very good cameraman, but his trademark isn't speed. That was a problem. *The Big Knife* was made in sixteen days, and *Kiss Me Deadly* was made in twenty-two days. If you elect to go with a cameraman that's not very, very fast, you have to, up front, make the decision that you are not going to get the kind of cutting coverage you'd normally like to have. You have to sacrifice setups and hope the performances are good enough, because they're cast in concrete. On *Attack,* made in the same period, I wanted Joe Biroc, who is almost twice as fast. That gives you an opportunity to work with a one-camera system, which I used until the time I came back from Italy, and still get twice as much coverage. So the selection of the cameraman sets a good deal of the style of the picture. You have a five or six page sequence which needs to be lighted once, and it'll take three to five times longer to light it for six or seven close-ups or cutaways. So you did it in a master.

SILVER: *You have some recurring framing concepts. For example, you may place characters in close shot foreground, frame left, and frame right will be another figure visible in depth of focus, with perhaps a lamp or some other object further restricting the space. You started doing that in television and you do it, for instance, in both* The Big Knife *and* The Angry Hills. *Those are several years apart, with different cameramen in different countries, and yet strikingly similar in visual conception. How much time and detail do you put into planning your shots, how precisely do you know what you want in advance of shooting?*

ALDRICH: You have—I think "style" is a pompous word—but you have a certain way of doing things. Ordinarily, when you block out the scenes you have in mind the kind of composition that would lend itself to what you want to say in that sequence. With quick lenses, you can stage in depth, you can pose something in the foreground and build up enough to hold something else in the background. I never use Panavision lenses because the staging will fall off to such a degree that you'll have to let somebody go [out of focus], either keep the guy in front sharp and forget the guy in back or dial back and forth which is always disconcerting. When we block the scenes, we have those four ugly faces in South Dakota: the modified "Rushmore" the medium "Rushmore," and the big "Rushmore." A big Rushmore puts a guy right up in the foreground with somebody back there. They're just "trade names" that I use with Biroc mostly, because we've been together so long.

Some scenes lend themselves to that kind of framing; but you'll find with a certain kind of dialogue scene, it's just not possible to do that. You look for ways, but it's not always there. And you can't bend a scene to fit the camera; it just doesn't work that way.

SILVER: *Why do you use all that foreground clutter?*

ALDRICH: Well, [Lewis] Milestone used to tell young hopefuls that there wasn't enough real interest in any frame to justify attention any longer than necessary. If you could find something to block off the concentration of the audience towards the point in the frame that interests you, if you could throw garbage in front of the camera to block off the rest of the apartment or the rest of the desert, [you might] possibly enhance the shot. You'll see Losey do it, and [Jules] Dassin do it, in terms of trying to limit the area of concentration. You can only do so much, so that the audience doesn't become aware. A lot of framing is done for that reason. That isn't always the motivating [factor], but it really is better than over-the-shoulder when you want to get rid of the rest of the room and just concentrate on what somebody is answering.

SILVER: *Are those the kind of shots that you block out in your mind ahead of time or put on your "worksheet"?*

ALDRICH: When you're through blocking a scene, at the end of a rehearsal, you know pretty much where the master angle's going to be, what kind of coverage you're going to have, and in most cases, where the camera's going to be. Now, what you don't know and what the bane of your existence is are the little things that you're going to add. When you're through with rehearsal, in theory, the script clerk should be able to give you a pretty close timing; yet it's always off by an hour. An hour because, when you actually do the scene, you add a second here or a second there, an extra bit of business here, two extra lines there. By the end of the picture you've put on sixty minutes. Now perhaps those sixty minutes will prove better or more important than sixty minutes that were in the picture originally. Probably not, but let's say twenty of those will stay and another forty will go. So, yes, you know pretty well where the camera's going to be when the time comes, but you may frequently alter or append to your original conception.

SILVER: *Do you actually change lines or add lines, before or during shooting, to any great extent?*
ALDRICH: Well, I don't think the script is holy. We change lines all the time to make it work. I like to work very closely with the writer in the first place. I wrote the original on the Sinatra picture [*4 for Texas*]; you could change that over and over and it was still a disaster. I did the original on *Too Late the Hero,* and Lukas Heller made it a much better script. There is no frozen reverence towards what's written. That's not to say that the writer didn't conceive of a proper line in the first place. He just wasn't privy to the pressures of the moment that might bring out a better line. I'm a great friend of [John] Cassavetes—some actors are critical of the "rigidity" of my concept, others are uncomfortable with the way John does his pictures. Everybody does it differently. I say to the actors, "Look, if you're uncomfortable with the line, come up with one that you are comfortable with that says the same thing." We try it once or twice. If it works, we keep it. If it doesn't, we throw it out. It's as simple as that.

SILVER: *You said once that you had a weakness for "flowery dialogue."*
ALDRICH: Well, look at *The Big Knife.* At the time, I thought that kind of theatrical flavoring was extraordinary. I'm afraid neither Jim Poe nor I were tough enough in editing some of Odets's phrases as we should have been. Both Poe and I—I did the first pass on *The Big Knife*—were more in awe of

Odets than we should have been; but he was giant then. He was not only a giant but his style was a fad. But when Poe did *Attack* right after that, we tried to keep the exaggerated or larger-than-life kind of attitude, in terms of speech pattern, out of it. I did two or three pictures with Hugo Butler, and he'd just go wild. I consider him a fine writer. Lukas Heller, with whom I've made four or five pictures, is more refined than Odets, a little larger-than-life, theatrical maybe, but flowery isn't the word. There's a lot less of that kind of dialogue in *The Grissom Gang*.

SILVER: *"Take a chance, Mr. Callahan. Love is a white bird, yet you cannot buy her."*
ALDRICH: *World for Ransom*. That's Butler. He wrote that script. Funny thing. There are optimists in this society, not many left, who thought that some day those guys would get postmortem credit for their work. So he wrote *World for Ransom,* and I put my name on it to try and get him the credit. And it went into arbitration with the Writer's Guild, and another guy [Lindsay Hardy] got total screen credit on it. It was a joke. He [Hardy] no more wrote that script than walk on water. Butler made that total screenplay.

SILVER: *Did you have any trouble with the Marian Carr character, the overtones of lesbianism?*
ALDRICH: We had more trouble with Madi Comfort handling the mike in *Kiss Me Deadly* than we did with that. We thought we would get in trouble with half the things in *World for Ransom*. Nobody ever questioned them; nobody seemed aware of it. We made that picture in ten days, ten and a half days. We ran out of money and went back to do some Eversharp [razorblade] commercials to get enough to finish it.

SILVER: *Was it envisioned as a kind of spinoff, to capitalize on the popularity of* China Smith?
ALDRICH: We had a break in the *China Smiths*—I did quite a few of them. We had about four weeks off, and we told [Bernard] Tabakin, who was producing the series, that if he could come up with a script, we would all donate our services. I guess that's literally what we did.

SILVER: *And you called Butler an optimist. How was it that you could be associated with him, Joe Losey, Chaplin, Jules Dassin, Abraham Polonsky—a significant number of blacklistees—and come out unscathed?*

ALDRICH: Well, you know, that's not a new question. I always answer that I was either too dumb or too young to be a Communist. If I had worked with Ring Lardner or Losey or [Robert] Rossen or Polonsky or Butler or [Dalton] Trumbo or any of those guys, who were five or ten years older than I was, earlier than I did, a kind of hero worship might have made it necessary for me to be a member of the party. But by the time I got into close contact with them, the heat was already on. They were already in trouble or about to be—the handwriting was on the wall. They weren't looking for recruits. It wasn't as much a matter of converting anybody anymore as a matter of personal survival, of who was going to Mexico, who was going to Paris, who was going to England. When I was assistant for a lot of them, they were on the verge of trouble. They were [like Dassin], making Music Master shorts for Piatagorsky and Rubenstein and Heifitz, just to get enough money to skip the country. I got served but nobody ever picked up the subpoena, and I was never called to testify. Just fortunate.

SILVER: *Other young directors who broke in around the same time and didn't get blacklisted, like Nicholas Ray or Sam Fuller, they haven't worked as steadily as you have either.*

ALDRICH: They are both very talented guys; and Nick had some major success. I think Nick got caught up in political problems, and that hurt his employability. If a guy is in a gray area, politically or socially, all he needs is one disaster to move him into a black area. Then people will say he's unemployable. Fuller is something else. He has great energy and a great eye, and a good batting average, too, which people forget if you get one or two dogs in a row. I think Sam is a gifted guy, but he has a tendency to tell people to shove it up their ass, which is the proper and correct thing to do at times, but it doesn't make getting the next assignment any easier.

SILVER: *What was the cause of your difficulties with Columbia on* The Garment Jungle?

ALDRICH: Very simple. Harry Kleiner had written a very, very good script, tough as nails. I had an across-the-room relationship with Cohn: he wanted me to come there; I didn't want to come there. He had certain projects; I didn't like them. But he offered me this script, and I said fine and went to New York to start shooting. A strange thing happened at the start. A girl I had known in New York, just a friend of a friend, called my wife to go out to lunch; and she told her, "I don't think Bob should make *Garment Jungle* until he gets it cleared." "What do you mean cleared?" She said, "Bob'll know what I mean. I can set up dinner with 'a guy.'" My wife told me this story; and I couldn't believe it, because this "guy" was Frank Costello's right hand man. So I called Cohn and he said, "That's bullshit. We've got this cleared and there's no problem." But when I went to dinner the next night with this "guy" who was very proper, very polite, terribly solicitous, he told me again, "Bob, don't make this picture. It hasn't been cleared. We'd like you to make it, no reason you shouldn't, but Mr. Cohn knows this has to be cleared." So I left for California the morning after, and I reported this to Cohn. Finally, after some hectic calls to Las Vegas, they discovered [that] a copy of the script had never been sent to be cleared. They ironed it out. But Cohn's little oversight could have caused trouble. As time went on, Cohn became more and more apprehensive about the project. And Lee Cobb was impossible. He had just come off a big triumph in "[Death of a] Salesman," he didn't want to be a rough father. He didn't want to have people dislike him. And it was necessary for him to be a tough, miserable son of a bitch, not a good guy. So every day someone or other would want me to soften the script. Then I got very sick on a Thursday night; I had the flu. Five o'clock Friday afternoon, [my agent] Ingo Preminger came up to see me and announced, "I don't know how to tell you this, but you're fired." I said, "You've got to be kidding." But I called up [Samuel] Briskin, and he wouldn't talk to me. I called up Cohn, and he wouldn't talk to me, so I figured I was fired.

SILVER: *What was your contractual arrangement with them that caused you to be out of work for some time?*
ALDRICH: Nothing. I didn't breech the contract, so they had to pay it out. They paid me and I sat home and I couldn't get a job. Now that year was over, and I could not get a job. It goes back to staying at the table. William Faulkner's the only guy I know who could go away to the back marshes of Mississippi and they'd never know the difference; he was so quiet and concealed. Anybody that stays away for a while, voluntarily or involuntarily, risks never coming back. Then somebody brought me *The Phoenix [Ten Seconds to Hell]*. I figured I might as well get out of town, so I rewrote it much to its detriment and went to Germany. I stayed [in Europe] to make *The Angry Hills* for Raymond Stross. He understood that Metro was buying film by the yard then, and Mitchum was reasonably hot. So they thought that as long as

it was an hour and a half with Mitchum and some Greek scenery, it would work. Obviously it didn't.

SILVER: *It was cut to that length after your cut, wasn't it?*
ALDRICH: Yeah. That's when they really do the old-fashioned thing. You asked me about producers. Well, the Strosses of this world just hang back there and let you work your ass off, till you're all through, and then say, "Fine. Good-bye. Thank you very much." Your director's cut or two previews don't mean a thing. Despite whatever promises about length or final cut they made to you, they take it back then and do what they were going to do in the first place.

SILVER: *It makes that end title rather ironic, "Finis. A Raymond Stross Production."*
ALDRICH: [laughs] It certainly does.

SILVER: *That whole question of final cut brings to mind that scene from* Lylah Clare, *the Sheean/Zarkan negotiation at the Brown Derby. I suppose part of the irony of that scene is that for all the past problems with producers, you have often filled both roles, Sheean's and Zarkan's, producer and director.*
ALDRICH: The irony, it seems to me, is that the system, at best, just doesn't work. Sure a producer has to be judicious about handing one or three or five million dollars to someone; but once it's done he should have enough confidence in himself, in his own choice, to back that guy. You don't have to make him a full partner, but at least support his decisions or don't go into it. In any case, are they qualified by being close enough to that material to make a judgment about cutting, six months, a year, or a year and a half later? Let's say a rough cut runs four hours, and the director has taken that four hours down to two. Now along comes a producer who says, "Take another twenty minutes out of it." How the hell does he know what's going on, that there isn't something more valuable than the next twenty minutes in the two hours you've already taken out. John Cassavetes had me look at his new picture [*Minnie and Moskowitz*] when it was three hours long. I liked it, but my comment was "they'll cut it." To whom are you as a director going to turn the picture over to cut? Why shouldn't Cassavetes have final word over that picture?

It's not a new moan and groan. I can rattle off twenty pictures, mine included, that would be helped enormously if they were cut. But to whom are you going to entrust that task? We are in that position now with the picture that we're making for ABC. Marty Baum, who up until a year ago was an agent, runs ABC. Has he, in that year, learned all there is to know about cutting? And yet I know that, when I turn the picture in, the distributor [ABC] will make changes. That doesn't make my life happy or worry-free. Because it's like having a professional who's designed a car discover that somebody's gardener is going to come along and change the position of the front wheels.

SILVER: *Some years after the fact, are you still dissatisfied with* The Legend of Lylah Clare?
ALDRICH: I think it has a number of flaws. I was about to bum rap Kim Novak, when we were talking about this the other day, and I realized that would be pretty unfair. Because people forget that Novak can act. I really didn't do her justice. But there are some stars whose motion picture image is so large, so firmly and deeply rooted in the public mind, that an audience comes to a movie with a preconception about that person. And that preconception makes "reality," or any kind of myth that's contrary to that preconceived reality, impossible. To make this picture work, to make Lylah work, you had to be carried along into that myth. And we didn't accomplish that. Now, you know, you can blame it on a lot of things, but I'm the producer and I'm the director. I'm responsible for not communicating to that audience. I just didn't do it.

SILVER: *Perhaps the reason I'm asking about* Lylah Clare *is that I've always had the feeling it was particularly close to you as a project. You are sitting there now with a prop painting of Lylah from the movie hanging on the wall behind you.*
ALDRICH: Yes, I always thought that picture would work. With the exception of a change of leading ladies, I'd make the same picture, tomorrow, again. Of course, it still wouldn't make money.

SILVER: *Is your disappointment in it mainly financial then?*
ALDRICH: No. My disappointment with it is believability. I think Kim did a very good job, but she's very angry with me. I used a German voice for her during the German period, because nobody can speak with that kind of accent, they really can't. So I brought over a German actress of some repute

and worked for a long time to get it done well. Of course, she was furious because, quite properly, her ego tells her that she does a good German accent. It may be good; but it's not good enough. Things like that make the difference. So audiences never believed that picture, and that's why it didn't work. You find people who like bits of it—Peter Finch or the Italian women or Borgnine—and then you'll find some who took the whole concept as an affront.

SILVER: *You can't help but see in it, I think, a reflection of that vulgarization which Hollywood has subjected people to. That freeze-frame at the end—the bared fangs—is genuinely savage, more savage than the whole of* The Big Knife *and perhaps more "antisocial" or "antiestablishment" in its implications than anything in* The Dirty Dozen *for all its controversy.*

ALDRICH: That ending was pretty good. But you can't get too many people to agree with that, I'd agree with you. With *The Dozen* two things happened. One, Heller and I stumbled onto the dissatisfaction, particularly on the part of the younger public, with the establishment. I'd like to say we anticipated that kind of success; but we didn't really. If you read the book, however, that kind of antiauthoritarian attitudes, that point of view, isn't there; and Heller did an excellent screenplay. So we got on a wave that we never knew was coming; not a wave, a tidal wave. But we didn't see it forming.

SILVER: *And you made a lot of money.*

ALDRICH: Oh, Christ! One of the sad rewards of this business is that when money comes in that fast, some of it has to stick. Somebody has to pay you.

SILVER: *What about the problems with* The Killing of Sister George? *Did you see them coming? Would that even be a problem, an "X" rating, if you made it today?*

ALDRICH: Well, I'd have to suggest that you rephrase your question. "Is that an 'X' today?" depends on who you make it for. If you made it for Metro, Mr. Valenti and his hatchet men would go and say that it was a family picture, you'd probably get a "G" for it. If you made it as an independent, it would probably still be an "X." They might consider it for an "R" or "GP," for a minute.

SILVER: *Is it just that you had the bad fortune of being one of the first to arrive at the ratings board—after all that pre-publicity—before they realized that if all the pictures like* Sister George *were "X's" that they would end up with too many on their hands?*

ALDRICH: A number of things happened. It's tiresome to think about them; not because this question isn't welcome, but because I didn't know who to fight. You know that we tried to get ABC to join us in a suit against the [Los Angeles] *Times*, in a suit against KMPC [a Los Angeles radio station], but they wouldn't. So we went ahead and sued the *Times* anyway, by ourselves; and we asked the Federal Communications Commission to revoke the license of KMPC, which they didn't do. Two years have gone by, and you find Valenti battling the press up in San Francisco and paraphrasing word for word our indictment about censorship of movies, which is a little ludicrous. But the big problem was that the majors never believed they could make profitable "X" pictures. They jumped to the conclusion that "X" was a dirty letter. Once *Midnight Cowboy* came out and was very profitable and won awards, they wanted to take the "dirty" label off. So they drew up a whole new bill of particulars. Everything that was made by a major studio for a cost of at least X amount of dollars suddenly had some redeeming, "artful" feature and became an "R." I guess we're the only business in the world that has retroactive legislation of that sort. But we had finished production on *Sister George* before those abc's of the "X's" were out. People think that Preminger changed the Code. That's bullshit. The Code was changed on narcotics when Fox bought *Hatful of Rain*. It was changed on profanity when Warners made *Virginia Woolf* and didn't care. It was changed on sex when Metro won that re-rating on *Ryan's Daughter*. The majors, the fellows in the club, they pay the dues and they prescribe the rules. Eventually, ABC behaved a lot better over *Sister George*'s rating than they did about economic issues.

SILVER: *In that economic context, how about an old project such as* Too Late the Hero, *which you've said had been lying around in a drawer for a decade and which quite a few people had probably pegged—correctly as it turned out—as a loser, how does it still come to be made?*

ALDRICH: When you've had a big, big success, people who should know better lose their perspective about your infallibility. Right away it's "Let's make another one!" Let's go back and buy the first novel of some guy who, ten novels later, wrote a hit. That's ludicrous. You may have better projects, but you can't sell better projects, you really can't. ABC wanted another *Dirty Dozen*. The only other "*Dirty Dozen*" I had in the drawer was one I wrote in

1959 with Bob Sherman. So we pulled out *Too Late the Hero,* and they thought it was sensational. So did Metro. But at Metro they wanted a budget of nine million seven [hundred thousand] to make it, which was too high. Well, we'd had *Lylah Clare* in the store for a couple of years, and Metro was in a buying mood, so I said, "What about something like *The Big Knife?*" And we made *Lylah Clare.* Now I think we have some extraordinarily good, fresh projects. But *Hero* was less than successful, so now all our properties are scrutinized at a whole other level. It can get terribly sad, but it's true that your opinion is only as good as your last picture.

SILVER: *You've got* The Grissom Gang *roughly assembled now. Are you satisfied with it at this stage?*
ALDRICH: I think it's a good picture. It's a personal story, but yet it has quite a bit of violence. Still, I think it's quite sentimental.

SILVER: *How did you come to pick Scott Wilson for the picture?*
ALDRICH: It was like a play-off in the National League. The system is that we had a nomination, then ABC had one, then we had one, then they had one, until we had exhausted a series of three each. We had a notion of who they wanted and who they didn't. I'd seen Scott Wilson in several pictures and liked him; and of all those that ABC would be likely to nominate, he was the least objectionable. So we played the cards; we nominated someone that we knew they did not like to knock off someone that they really wanted. And again it was really luck. He is much better than the actor we originally wanted for the picture. But if ABC had put him out of sequence, nominated him in another position, we'd have ended up with somebody else. He would have been knocked off. *The Grissom Gang* may or may not make money. It's not a commercially oriented picture. It won't make money for us because it's crosscollateralized back against our lawsuit with ABC.

We had a big western called *Rebellion.* It was at the very heart of our lawsuit with them. It was *Vera Cruz* with balls, energy, and real sex. They approved the project. They had a major commitment; and we came up with a budget of seven million dollars. Now, I don't blame them for not wanting to make the picture for seven million. I do blame them for not honoring their contracts, for not trying to find a way out, a compromise solution. We spent a lot of time preparing that picture. Seven million was too big a risk for them to take on that material, from their position. And yet I think just as many people will go broke trying to make *Easy Rider* sequels, for a little money, as went broke trying to follow up *Sound of Music*. That's studio management. As with *Greatest Mother* or *Too Late the Hero*, you have to be terribly careful about not making a picture that will be affected by a change in the audience's framework of acceptance between the time you start and the time you finish. That's an enormous problem. Whatever you say today risks strongly going out of date in the fifteen month time-lag between the start of shooting and release.

SILVER: *So you make* The Grissom Gang, *a '30s picture.*
ALDRICH: That has something to do with it. Yes.

SILVER: *How does this affect future projects. Does this mean it's time for* Genghis Khan's Bicycle?
ALDRICH: [laughs] We lost the rights to that. I think it's being made into a musical.

SILVER: Vengeance Is Mine, *the gangster script with Bezzerides?*
ALDRICH: He and I were paid by a couple of Italians who have been suing us ever since, so I guess that's out, too. That was the story of a mythical [Lucky] Luciano set in Sicily during World War II. The projects we have on the fire at the moment, in order of likelihood, are *Rage of Honor; What Ever Happened to Dear Daisy?; Coffee, Tea, or Me; Billy Two Hats; The Crowded Bed;* something tentatively called *The Plaza.*

SILVER: *You've hung on to some projects for a long time and gotten quite passionate about them. You said in an old interview, "Taras Bulba is me." How did you feel when it ended up sold to Yul Brynner, the one actor you didn't want?*
ALDRICH: You know I sold it to another guy. That's when I came back from England with no money at all, when the tax guys put a sign on my house to sell it. That's when I cashed in those three pictures I mentioned earlier to United Artists for twenty grand. We had no money. I had breakfast most mornings about 6:30 at a restaurant nobody knew was open in the morning; but this guy, Joe Kaufman, came in there two or three mornings in a row. I should have been smart enough to know that this bum would never get up at 6:30 in the morning for nothing. The third morning, he asked me, "What did you ever do with that script, *Taras Bulba?*" I said, "I still have it." Then

he asked, "You want to sell it?"; and I said, "Sure." "How much do you want for it?" I said, "I'll tell you what I've got into it: $61,491." It was some odd number like that, which I happened to know exactly. "How do you know that?" Well, the tax guy had been adding up all my assets to see what they were worth, and that's what he was counting for this picture. "Would you sell it for that?" I needed money, so "Sure!" The next day, he was there saying, "I've got the money. I'll give you an advance check for $15,000." This was fascinating. We had a buyer and a seller, four lawyers, *and* a tax guy. We drew up a contract in which he had to pay me $15,000 then pay the government the balance in installments, so I sold *Taras Bulba* to him. It was quarterly payments, and three months later a second check came to me to endorse over to the government; and it was signed by Harold Hecht. Joe bought it for him or sold it to him.

SILVER: *Maybe he read that interview. [laughter] Whatever happened to* The Greatest Mother of 'Em All?
ALDRICH: We made that mini-movie with Peter Finch, Alexandra Hay, and Ann Sothern just at the time that everybody was getting very sanctimonious about sex pictures. It's a half-hour movie, like a long trailer, and I think it's pretty good. But nobody wanted this thing about a broken-down Hollywood director who found a sixteen-year-old girl and shacked up with her and had a heart attack, etc. We spent $90,000 getting it mounted to show people what it was all about, which I thought was an ingenious piece of showmanship; but nobody else agreed with me. I also think that it was very stupid timing. If I had been bright enough, I would have realized that the cycle had passed. Whereas a year before that picture would have sold like hot cakes. So no more war pictures and no more "Hollywood" pictures for a while. I'm a sucker for them. I can't find any and I'm trying not to look. *Greatest Mother* was in the original ABC package. The turnaround on it, because of the ABC advance, would cost us a fortune. Without numbers that make sense, we'll probably let it drown.

SILVER: *What is* Rage of Honor *about?*
ALDRICH: It's another period picture, about an aging cowboy set in Northern California in 1929. It's collision between two eras, between his attitude and mores and the industrial progress of a small town. I think it's the best script we have.

SILVER: *Any cast in mind?*

ALDRICH: Well, anybody that reads it says John Wayne; and I've got to admit that Wayne could be marvelous. But I think the guy should be Joel McCrea. I don't know if McCrea is bankable or if he'd come out of retirement. Right now nothing is bankable, so you don't have to ask that question.

We'll probably change the title on *Aunt Alice*. As a matter of fact, I went to New York last week to give it to Helen Hayes, and we did change the title. I know she's not about to play in *that* kind of melodrama. They're fun, and they've always been profitable, but it's tough getting that kind of picture made today.

Coffee, Tea, or Me is from the pocket book about "stewardi." Not a single person likes our screenplay except me. Everybody says the book is great, the idea is great, but the script stinks. I don't agree. What we've done is taken the Doris Day formula and flipped it. We've got a virgin who's doing everything she can to get laid, because all the other stewardesses are swingers and having a great time; but she can't. No matter what happens, something always stops her. I respect these other opinions and start thinking, "Jesus Christ, I must be wrong." Then I take it home and read it again and I laugh myself to death, I think it's hysterical. So nobody likes it except me.

Bill Two Hats is a Western, a kind of small, personal, simple statement Western. A lot smaller in concept and budget than *Rebellion* was.

SILVER: *Your production budgets have never seemed inflated, yet you got criticized for making* The Dirty Dozen *and not contributing to Bobby Seale's defense fund.*

ALDRICH: And I noticed in the trade papers yesterday that something like eighty-one directors, forty-five writers, and seventy-eight composers condemn the industry for not freeing Angela Davis. These people don't think there's any gray area about the justice involved. I know that sounds conservative, but I don't mean to be. If I weren't wearing both hats, I'd like to make a picture that would free Angela Davis. But I don't want the producer part of me to lose so much money that he can't make the next one.

Up to Date with Robert Aldrich

HARRY RINGEL/1974

''THE LAND THAT MAJOR STUDIOS are on will become so expensive that they will no longer be able to function where they are,'' Robert Aldrich forecast in 1968, the year *The Dirty Dozen* allowed him to buy his way out of the Hollywood system. "The business will scatter into a number of satellite studios such as mine."

Five financially disastrous—and ineffably personal—films later, Aldrich once again finds himself in need of a blockbuster. He hopes that it will be *The Longest Yard*: a *Dirty Dozen* variation he is filming for Albert Ruddy and Paramount, in which an imprisoned professional football player (Burt Reynolds) leads a team of misfits against warden Eddie Albert's semi-pro guards' team. He is filming at Reidsville (Georgia) State Prison, on a football field which Paramount has constructed there. His cast includes just as many real prisoners and football players as it does actors playing them—with "absolutely no women allowed on the set," I am told, until the climactic football game is completed.

Silver-haired and burly at fifty-five, Aldrich moves resolutely through this quiet hurricane of personalities. When he is not studying his storyboards (no drawings; only scribbled entries, ordered sequentially, like "Sonny gets hurt" and "Guardsmen fumble"), he is conferring with favourite cameraman Joe Biroc. Ironically, Paramount has given Aldrich as much freedom as he could wish. "He is a proven director," explains boom man Jaime Contrerez, who first worked with Aldrich on *Vera Cruz* (1954). "And a wizard with technique.

From *Sight and Sound* 43.3 (Summer 1974): 166–69. Reprinted by permission.

Like John Huston, only better. He *prepares* like John Huston." "He moves along like a TV director, when he has control of a film," adds the unit publicist, Dave Davies. Both must be right. By lunchtime, when I interview Aldrich, close to a dozen shots are completed. Filmmaking is still a serious business for Robert Aldrich.

HARRY RINGEL: *This film,* The Longest Yard, *has nothing whatsoever to do with the Aldrich Studios?*
ROBERT ALDRICH: There are no more Aldrich Studios.

HR: *So* Variety *is accurate in quoting you as terming the whole venture "a disaster"?*
RA: Right.

HR: *If you had a chance, would you try again?*
RA: Well, we built a better mousetrap but the mice went out of business. The equipment here is ours. We rented it back from the people to whom we sold the studio. And if I do anything again, I'd build three new units: a sound unit, a camera unit, an electrical unit. I wouldn't buy a studio again; but I would build those three units.

HR: *What was the working arrangement between you and ABC, as far as the Aldrich Studios films were concerned? Did you have free choice of projects?*
RA: We had a six picture deal with ABC. That was terminated after four pictures, with much mutual acrimony. Now in those pictures they had three approvals: budget, story, and cast. They could have had final editing, if it hadn't been satisfactory. But during those four pictures they never exercised any cutting control or any story control. The only time they did interfere was with the casting of Cliff Robertson in *Too Late the Hero,* and some of the casting in *The Grissom Gang,* which was the end of our relationship. But other than that, we had no casting problems, no budget problems.

HR: *Who wanted Cliff Robertson?*
RA: *They* wanted Cliff Robertson.

HR: *Who did you want?*
RA: Anybody but Cliff Robertson. You, me, anybody.

HR: *Is it coincidence or design that, in contrast to your early career, your more recent pictures haven't had any political focus?*
RA: That's presupposing that they haven't.

HR: *I'm thinking of* The Dirty Dozen *(1967), which grinds* Attack's *anti-authoritarian axe for the first reel, then focuses instead on the rehabilitation of the criminals.*
RA: The commercial success of *The Dirty Dozen* is reputed to be that it caught the wave of anti-authoritarian attitudes which were dormant, but became full-flown in 1967–68. I'd love to say we sat back there and knew that was going to happen during the release period of the picture. We knew that attitudes were there. But nobody knew people were going to identify with *The Dirty Dozen* so much as they did as a manifestation of their disagreement with the system. Probably, they did it out of proportion. But that's obviously in large part responsible for the success of that picture, over and above its intrinsic entertainment value. Younger people by the bushel thought it was an anti-establishment picture.

HR: *You've worked with repeated success in several genres: the Western, the war picture, the gangster film, the horror film. Do you ever try to pick up a theme you left undeveloped in some earlier film and work on it?*
RA: You try very, very hard—and unsuccessfully for a while—not to do any of the things you did in *The Big Knife.* You try hard not to do any of the things in *The Dirty Dozen* that you did in *Attack.* It's pretty unimaginative to be repetitious and just steal from yourself. There are some situations where similar attitudes are inescapable. *Too Late the Hero* and *Flight of the Phoenix,* with all their differences, are still just patrol pictures. It's *x* number of men trying to get from here to there and back, or from here to there and survive. So there are a number of built-in, inescapable similarities which you try to camouflage, but they're set. They're standard. You can camouflage them, but you can't escape them.

HR: *The Legend of Lylah Clare (1968), your last studio [MGM] film before moving to the Aldrich Studios, seems loaded with personal touches. Is the film in any sense autobiographical?*
RA: Oh no. I teased Borgnine into taking a couple of personal idiosyncrasies and putting them over the Cohn-Mayer character, but no, I think it's auto-

biographical only in that we may have exaggerated Peter Finch's impatience at suffering fools, and that he has to be more patient than he's willing to be.

HR: *What about the highbrow French critics, the producer's* Big Knife *philistinism, the* Dirty Dozen *marquee?*
RA: Oh sure, there were a couple of obvious zingers, but nothing autobiographical in the story context. Only a couple of jokes within jokes.

HR: *Was Kim Novak's character based on one particular sex symbol, or was she an amalgamation of myths?*
RA: Amalgamation of myths. The teleplay which Tuesday Weld did, and did marvelously, was much more strikingly fashioned to fit the Monroe mould, and we tried hard not to do that.

HR: Lylah Clare *has been compared to* 8 1/2, Vertigo, *and* The Big Knife. *Do you think any of those analogies hold up?*
RA: It's hard to tell, you know. A picture fails, and by "fail" you mean it doesn't make enough money to break even. It has nothing to do with how critically well received it is or isn't. Now, a great many buffs have an inordinate fondness for *Lylah*. But *Lylah Clare* was a failure, and if it's a failure, then you have to say that either the subject matter or the way you handled the subject matter didn't communicate itself to the people. And if it did, they didn't care about it. There are twenty-five cop-outs: who cared about Peter Finch, and is Kim Novak a joke in her own time? But there's *also* the fact that since you're the producer-director, since you bought the material, since you developed it, there is something apparent in the story or in the way you told it that people just aren't interested in. I've gotten extraordinarily high praise on this picture; I think inordinate, and unjustifiable. If the director-producer—and, for all intents and purposes in that picture, the writer—can't, with no limitation on money, communicate to an audience what he wants them to be interested in, fascinated in and/or amused by, then he has failed. Then he shouldn't have made that picture.

HR: *You blamed the failure of* Too Late the Hero (1969) *on the concomitance of Kent State; hardly enough reason for a film as good as that one not to succeed as well as it might have done.*
RA: There are different kinds of failures. There are failures you never think

are right or justifiable or understandable. For example, I put *Too Late the Hero*, *Flight of the Phoenix*, and *The Grissom Gang* in a category that says these are all fine movies, very well made films. People understood what they were about, what they aimed to say. They were entertaining and exciting and should have been a success. That they weren't means that something else was wrong besides the way the picture was made. Now, I don't put *Lylah Clare*, *Ten Seconds to Hell*, *Samson and Delilah* or whatever it was (*Sodom and Gomorrah*) in that category. Those I think were not well made, the story-telling functions were not done properly, inventively, interestingly enough. So those are the failures I understand. I'll *never* understand the failure of *The Grissom Gang*, *Too Late the Hero*, or *Flight of the Phoenix*, because they were marvelous movies.

H R :   Flight of the Phoenix *lost money?*

R A :   Oh yeah. Maybe in another five years *Phoenix* will break even. I don't know how to make those movies any better. You know, you usually go back and have second thoughts: if I'd only done this, if I'd only tried that. That's bullshit. Those were very well made movies. I don't mind taking the blame for the dogs, because everybody makes them. But I don't think those were dogs. I think they deserved to do infinitely better than they did.

H R :   *Thematically,* Too Late the Hero *seems to complete a statement on heroism which you began in* Attack *and continued in* The Dirty Dozen. Attack *being cynical,* Dirty Dozen *redemptive, and* Too Late the Hero *utterly random. Did you intend this sort of development?*

R A :   Reading your questions, you get as much out of the question as you do out of the answer. I would have thought, for example, that there is a *growth* in cynicism, rather than what you interpret as redemption. You see, there's one set of standards on a picture that you have any real control over, that you look for. You look for *that man*. It's really summed up in *The Big Knife*, when Wes Addy turns to Jack Palance and says, "Struggle, Charlie, you may still win a blessing." It's really not winning. Winning is terribly, terribly important; but you can be a winner if you lose better than the guy that won. It's a Hemingway extension with different kinds of nuances, because I would think that Hemingway couldn't accept not winning. I would think that Jack Palance wins when he commits suicide. I would think that much as I hate it, Cliff Robertson's character in *Too Late the Hero,* had it been played as I wanted it, would have won, even though he is killed and Michael Caine lives.

HR: *So your appreciation of Borgnine's villainy in* Emperor of the North *(1973) doesn't mean that you are mellowing?*
RA: When that contest is joined, there is a framework of mutual respect; and it has, or should have, the same influence as gladiators. Shack (Borgnine's character) had a total, singular, measurable authority corruption that only had to do with that train he guards. He might be a good father, he might be a nice guy, he might be a great fellow around the beer hall, but he had total integrity towards his corruption. Therefore, Lee Marvin's hobo character could have extraordinary respect for him in the arena. They would never have any conflicts outside the arena, and that's why Marvin doesn't kill him when he has the chance. And why Borgnine doesn't kill *him,* when he has the opportunity. Because they had extremely high mutual regard. It's the manner in which their dedication to doing their particular thing pays off.

Now, I know that to be true in terms of audience reaction. I don't know that to be true in terms which hurt the commercial acceptance of the picture. For example, we previewed *Emperor of the North* six or seven times, I guess. There is almost no applause, in any of the previews we took it to, when Borgnine gets thrown off the train.

HR: *You structured it that way.*
RA: Right. The applause is saved for the opportunistic guy (Keith Carradine), who is going along for the free ride. They're delighted when he gets thrown off. But Borgnine's character has his own integrity. He's not going to welsh on what he is. He stands for one particular thing. He doesn't vacillate. If there's a mellowing on my part, it's probably in the fact that in the process of growing older you sadly realise that there might be two sides to a question, instead of only one.

HR: *In* Ulzana's Raid *(1972), the arena is western civilisation.*
RA: You were very deft to have caught that. Not many people did. Your problem there is a marvelous story plotted around a big major star. The focus of that picture should have been between the Indian scout (Jorge Luke) and

the young lieutenant (Bruce Davison). Then you would have a very clear picture.

HR: *The Indian scout was submerged.*

RA: The guy who told you the power theory about how the more slowly you kill, the more power you draw from your victim. He was a marvelous actor, and that should have been the principal conflict. Now. You couldn't do that because (a) you couldn't get the picture financed, and (b) you couldn't get the picture made without a Burt Lancaster. Burt was playing an 1870 guy who had seen *Apache.* That was his frame of reference: he respected the Indians, because he knew more about them than the soldiers did. Yet you didn't feel hatred for Davison's character, because you were shown over and over again that he didn't know anything. He didn't know any better than to make those painful and irrational mistakes at the Indians' expense. So the film was saying at various levels that through ignorance of other peoples' cultures, behaviours, deities, customs, you do more damage to them than by intention.

HR: Ulzana's Raid*'s politics don't seem to matter so much as the codes of mascu-linity coming up against each other: a private conflict, out of which the most public conflicts could be drawn.*

RA: I wouldn't have thought it was purely masculine. Maybe "masculine" in the sense that it was done by a majority of masculine players. In theory, it was supposed to be metaphorical. In practice, it wasn't that important.

HR: *Let's go back to a film we have left out,* The Grissom Gang *(1971). The book, James Hadley Chase's* No Orchids for Miss Blandish, *had caused a minor uproar in World War II England, typified by George Orwell's remark that it "took for granted the most complete corruption and self-seeking as the norm of human behaviour." Were you aware of the book's reputation when you decided to film it?*

RA: I'd read the Orwell article a long time ago. I think his comments are well-taken and true. But *The Grissom Gang* should have been at the head of the nostalgia cycle, and should have taken off. Just think of the number of pictures between now and then that have been made about the 1930s, and how successful they have been. I think we read the scale absolutely perfectly. Never mind *The Godfather,* the Texas town picture (*The Last Picture Show*), the whole series of pictures which followed *The Grissom Gang.* I think the timing was perfect, the style of the picture was perfect. If you're asking me why that picture wasn't a success, I haven't a clue.

H R : *Basically, the script adds all the attic scenes and amplifies the love/hate rela-tionship between Slim (Scott Wilson) and Barbara Blandish (Kim Darby).*
R A : It's in the book. He's more retarded, but he's equally infatuated, taken by her. And what we finally did, I feel very sad about losing. In the book, Barbara Blandish jumps out of the window. In *The Grissom Gang*, she jumped in the river. We showed that version a number of times. The people in the audience came to respect her—not like her, respect her; and they were sad that the only person they had any "normal" identification with took her life. We finally figured that her life was lost and useless anyway, so why go through the dramatic ten minutes it took for her to escape from a cop and jump in the river with the intention of drowning? So we ended it as she drove away from her father, but we shot the other ending up in the Sacra-mento River. It was very effective, very well done, but it was like putting two periods. The picture was over when she drove out of the barnyard, alienated from her father. Nothing was ever going to happen to her again, her life was ruined, spent. So the drowning was just a redundancy which we didn't put in the picture.

H R : *You have commented on the relationship between pain and ecstasy in your films—which is never clearer than in* The Grissom Gang, *when Barbara Blandish climaxes while watching Slim knife his brother (Tony Musante). Does this reaction lock her into loving Slim, or liberate her to do so?*
R A : Kim and I talked about it. The only thing we hadn't thought of—and perhaps that shows a shallowness on my part—was that the orgasm would *free* her of the inhibition not to have an affair with Slim. I felt that by then she had an extraordinary fondness for him. He would do anything, which in his framework meant go against his mother, if she would only be sympa-thetic. Of course, the supreme gift was her giving him his manhood, which was questionable at best, the night before he died. So I didn't intend for that orgasm to foretell her eventually giving herself to Slim. I wanted *that* to come out of the fact that she knew he was going to die, and how often in any-body's life does even a dog love you that well, let alone a human being? The smallest reward in the world would be to give him his manhood, if that was possible. So had I thought about it, I probably wouldn't have let her do it, if

I had thought that the issue was going to be clouded by the moment of Tony Musante's death.

HR: *Healthy sexual relationships seem close to impossible in your films—and never more unlikely than here.*
RA: Possibly. We had a much sexier scene in the barn between Kim and Slim, the kind that gets the grain of the Beau Geste, the Beau Geste being the gift of his manhood. But we elected to go with the more gentle, tender one. I think it was right. Christ, we'd had ten yards of slobbering and saliva in that picture already, so we did it the gentle, tender way and it seemed to be much more effective.

HR: *You've never made a movie about children—though enough of your characters act like them. Accident or design?*
RA: It's mostly accident. We had some kids playing Crawford and Davis as children . . . Perhaps it's subconscious. I had terrible experiences when I was assistant to directors where there were kids in pictures. Like Milestone in *The Red Pony.* But I don't make any conscious effort not to make kid pictures.

HR: *Whatever happened to* Kinderspiel *[an unfilmed Aldrich property of the fifties]?*
RA: That script was owned by an actor, John Something-or-other. I had options on the property, and we optioned it and we optioned it and I could never get that picture planned. We even found a spot in Germany to make the picture, a sensational locale in the Hartz Mountains. We could have made a very favourable deal with the German studios to make the picture, but we could never get anybody to finance it. Today it's very political, very anti-war, but there's still nobody to finance it. The story is the Pied Piper, except that the Pied Piper is other children. And it's strangely violent, because a dwarf is set among the children to corrupt them. They find out that he's not a child, and they kill him. Then the children leave the adults, because the town is going to war. A brilliant script. Some day it'll be made by people interested in seeing the film, and not necessarily with stars.

HR: *I also lost track of* Taras Bulba *after your last interview with Truffaut. How did you finally lose it to Yul Brynner and Harold Hecht?*
RA: We had four or five *Taras Bulba* scripts, the last of which I thought was sensational. I took it all around the world and finally got it put together in

Yugoslavia with the English, and with Anthony Quinn to play the lead. Then United Artists pulled out of the scheme at the last moment, which caused me to come close to bankruptcy another time. When I came back to the United States, after having been in Europe for two years, I again thought I could put the damn thing together. So I met a guy in a restaurant one morning. He said, "How much have you got for *Taras Bulba?*" Well, the taxman had already put the "for sale" sign on my house. And I said, "About $65,000 in cash in a year and a half." He said, "Will you take $75,000 cash for it?" and I said I think so. He came back the next day and said, "I'll give you $25,000 cash, $25,000 in six months, and $25,000 in a year." He was a guy of some means. Not that kind of money but some means. So I went back to the taxman and said, "If I can get a letter to that effect, will you lift the lien on my house?" He agreed, so I sold it.

Now there's a before and after to that story. The before is that when I finished the second draft, not the final draft, I took it to Burt Lancaster. I said, "I think you should play Taras," and he said, "So do I, but I can't do it this year." I said, "I don't want to wait until next year, you know, you get hit by a taxi and what have I done with a year. I think it's a great script." He said, "I can't do it." Well, he didn't do it, and I didn't wait.

The after is that, through that exposure, Hecht-Lancaster knew about that script, and watched what happened to it. United Artists, who were their partners then, agreed to finance the script, and this man that I had met at the restaurant was an agent acting on their behalf. Obviously, had I known that Hecht-Lancaster wanted it, I wouldn't have sold it to them. Or I would have sold it to them on a different set of terms, with me directing and all kinds of things. So that's what happened to *Taras Bulba.*

H R :   *What about* Coffee, Tea, or Me?
R A :   We owned the book. We put a fortune into the book. Ted Flicker did a very funny, dirty script. We had our girl as the only hostess who was a virgin, who was trying not to be a virgin. In other words, we took the Doris Day formula of all those successful *Pillow Talk* movies and inverted it. Instead of the only girl in the office who was retaining her virginity, her friends were trying to get her laid, and something always happened to interfere. It was a very good script. ABC wouldn't make it, and when our option expired, CBS bought it and they went back to the straight title and the more mundane situation about stewardesses' lives.

H R : *Have you followed the TV-movies market at all?*

R A : No. You know, that's a life in itself. I've seen some things I've really admired on there. And I think we'll all be doing that kind of picture, not for TV but for some kind of distribution system, eventually. But I try very hard not to get involved.

H R : *I'd like to offer you the last part of the interview as a platform, to respond to criticisms people have levelled against you and your work over the past few years. For example, I don't believe that you ever replied, in print, to Bosley Crowther's accusation that* The Dirty Dozen *"encourages a spirit of brazen hooliganism" in its audience. Would you care to reply now?*

R A : You have to feel like a politician. If Crowther knocks you, you're in very good company. And I certainly would much rather have a spirit of "brazen hooliganism" than what passes for patriotism nowadays.

H R : *The* Christian Science Monitor's *criticism of an "uncomfortable woman-maligning streak" in* Emperor of the North?

R A : I've heard that people have said this. In fact, I got a letter from Vincent Canby telling me that I am anti-woman and anti-feminist. And I wrote him, though I very seldom write critics. It may be—but if it is, I'm wasting an awful lot of my non-working hours. I think women are a pain in the ass most of the time, but I'm sure women think men are a pain in the ass most of the time. I don't think it's anti-lib to say that women's goals collide with men's goals. It's all very well to say that the two can live harmoniously, but I don't think that's quite true.

H R : *In his review of* Emperor, *Canby calls you the best director of "this kind" of film working today.*

R A : I think I'm the best director in the world working in this kind of film. I don't think there's any doubt about it. The problem is, I'd like to work with some other kind of film.

H R : *Do we still have to make such distinctions?*

R A : He's talking about big, broad-actioned, multi-charactered, large-canvased, larger-than-life pictures. This comes out of a comparison with Peckinpah. Unfortunately, that *is* a kind of film. And also, unfortunately, if you do them well, people keep giving them to you. I'd love to do a musical. I don't see anybody offering me one. I'd love to do a comedy. But I don't get a chance.

H R :   *What do you think of Peckinpah's work?*

R A :   I think Peckinpah is a fine director. I don't think he's as good as I am, but I think he's a sensational director. I'm not sure I like the picture he made in Texas (*The Getaway*). I don't think that's as good as he can be. But some of his other pictures, like the Mexican picture with the Borgnine/Holden stock company (*The Wild Bunch*), I liked. But I think we did it before, with *Vera Cruz.*

H R :   *Joan Crawford's statement (quoted in* Films in Review, *June–July 1973) that you love "evil, horrendous, vile things"?*

R A :   Well, I'm very fond of Joan. If the shoe fits, put it on.

H R :   *Whenever one of your films is released, someone always gets worried about the violence. What is your position on the "monkey see, monkey do" theory of explicit violence in film?*

R A :   I'm at odds with Pastore as to what violence does to people. I don't think violence in movies creates other violence. On the contrary, I think it helps to expend violence. I think if you *see* it done, instead of going home and kicking the dog, maybe you just go home and kick the cat. It reduces the target area. You vicariously expend some of your antagonism against the people you don't like in the film.

H R :   *You once stated, concerning censorship, that "the final goal should be no censorship at all." Do you view the recent Supreme Court decision absolutely as a step in the wrong direction?*

R A :   As you may not know, I'm vice-president of the Screen Directors' Guild. We have taken a stand that is singularly the same as my own. There's no such thing as their dirty picture and our dirty picture. There are pictures which should be controlled for adult viewing that may be improper, and may exert undue influence on young people. But that's all.

H R :   *So even if they don't think* The Longest Yard *should be shown here in Glenville, Georgia, it should?*

R A :   Yes, sir.

Robert Aldrich: Making Good Movies with Instinct and Opportunism

DAVID STERRITT/1976

ROBERT ALDRICH IS ONE OF America's fiercest filmmakers. Critics have studied and debated the intricacies of his themes and techniques, while audiences have been caught up in—and sometimes put off by—the determination and sheer power of his style.

His work has always been controversial, but his hits speak for themselves—among many others *The Dirty Dozen, The Killing of Sister George, Attack,* and *What Ever Happened to Baby Jane?* And, most recently, *Hustle,* starring Burt Reynolds, Catherine Deneuvre, Eddie Albert, Ernest Borgnine, and Paul Winfield.

Aldrich's new project will be *Twilight's Last Gleaming,* an all-star action drama about the seizure of a U.S. missile base, to be filmed on location in Munich. Burt Lancaster, Roscoe Lee Brown, Joseph Cotton, and Melvyn Douglas will head the cast.

As you might be able to guess from looking at his films, Aldrich follows his own instincts and ideas as he gropes his way through the murky movie world. "There's no winning the critical game," he says. "If you're half smart, you abandon that elusive hope. You make the picture that you find attractive or interesting, and you make it as well as you can. If the critics like it, great. If they don't, forget them. There's no way to placate them, or to know what next year's in-vogue, trendy critical acceptance level is going to be . . ."

The Aldrich philosophy is predictably tough. "You make the picture that you want to make. . . . Sometimes you make it well, sometimes you make it badly. Nobody does a picture to make it unsuccessful, because X number of flops will eventually put you out of the game. And nobody looks forward to that."

Are there conscious, consistent themes—special Aldrich themes—running through the body of Aldrich's work, despite those "popular Hollywood surfaces"? Not surprisingly, it turns out that there are.

"The struggle for self-determination," says the filmmaker, "the struggle for what a character wants his life to be, ending up with the willingness to accept that life . . . I always look for that type of material . . . I look for characters who feel strongly about something to not be too concerned with the prevailing odds, but to struggle against those odds. . . .

"That is the stuff that heroes and heroines are made of. There's a line in *The Big Knife* where the friend of John Garfield says, 'Struggle, Charlie, you may still win a blessing.' I think it's the manner in which you struggle that entitles you to that blessing, if there is a blessing. That's the theme, whether the movie be *Taras Bulba* or *The Dirty Dozen* or *The Longest Yard*."

For all his seriousness as a film philosopher, Aldrich takes a grimly realistic view of the movie business. He theorizes sadly that "whether they like it or not, the major companies have embarked on a course that is going to end up with soft-core pornography movies for a mass audience. . . . That's the unavoidable conclusion to be drawn from *Last Tango in Paris* and other pictures. How many disaster pictures are tolerable, where is the next opportunity to make a breakthrough that is not TV fare?"

Aldrich predicts this "classy, star-populated, gentle, unabrasive pornography" largely on the basis of his experience with film financing, which he sees as a blind force whose main goal is to be in the right place at the right time to make the most money.

Aldrich's own thoughts are far from pornography when he says that he, personally, thinks the time is ripe for "a truly idealistic, revolutionary political picture. But I don't think you could get the financing for that right now, because it's an idea that hasn't penetrated the consciousness of the commercial people who lend you money . . . It's very hard to break barriers in getting financing through traditional channels . . ."

As for violence on screen, Aldrich feels that the MPAA (Motion Picture Association of America)—dispenser of movie ratings from G to X—"is more

lenient to violence than to sex . . . but that grows out of a historical substitu-
tion of violence for sex in the movies. . . . The sublimation of sex into violence was permissible in the old Hollywood code, and the current situation
is an outgrowth of that. . . .

"It has become very popular . . . to make anguished outcries about violence in films," continues the director. "And I think there's a certain amount
of merit to that. . . . But we live in a very violent world. I don't think violence
on film breeds violence in life. Violence in life breeds violence in films."

Aldrich became a filmmaker "the long, traditional, pretty dull" way. He
"got to like show business" while at the University of Virginia, and decided
it was "certainly much more interesting than any other line of endeavor."
He traveled to Hollywood and inched his way up from production worker to
director-writer-producer.

"It's a career marked mostly by good luck and opportunism," as he himself describes it, "and having been at the right place at the right time. And
when I did get the opportunity to direct, I could call on the experience of
having worked with some very talented directors and some terribly untalented directors. . . . Perhaps I didn't know what to do at some point, but I
hope I knew what *not* to do. . . ."

The Aldrich career has gone on for more than thirty-five years now—"you
would doubt its success from time to time, but it has been a *long* career," says
the director with a smile. Guessing at the reasons for his staying power, he
muses, "You have to realize what's wrong with the system, and the limits
within which you can change the system. You have to be tough within that
framework . . .

"I don't always know; I sometimes overstep how far you can push,
change, or resist. But if you roll over and play dead, you're a hack. Maybe
you're a hack anyway, but you're still there. . . . You must have a 'get lost'
attitude toward everyone else, up to the point where you'll be excommuni-
cated. If you can stay on that razor's edge, you've got a chance. That's all you
have—a chance. If you don't go too long between moderately successful pictures, you become known as a responsible and reliable commodity. . . ."

The biggest change in Hollywood, Aldrich believes, is that "the independent operators are in an noticeably improved situation, but only because the
studio guys—who always operated out of fear—are less courageous now. The
old studio moguls would take chances, even though they were driven by fear.
Their replacements, the committees of one or two or three, are less coura-

geous, with the same motivations of fear and greed. . . . They rely more on others, because they're not so sure what they think themselves.

"The demise of the star system is tragic," he adds. "The industry is getting more and more hooked on having to make bigger and bigger pictures with fewer and fewer people who are growing older and older. As for replacements, there's nobody on the bench. Nobody knows who will be the Steve McQueen of ten years from now, and the sad thing is, they don't care. . . ."

Are the movies "better than ever" as a whole? "Some are," says the filmmaker, "but probably for different reasons than the Motion Picture Association would have you think. They're better than ever because the competitive influence of the marketplace makes them be better to survive. The European pictures are often better—though that's a tide that goes in and out—so American pictures have to be better. TV is drab and dull, but it comes along with very rewarding works once in a while, even spectacular ones—so, to compete against a free industry, movies have to be better."

Aldrich recognizes the important position of television in today's world, but feels little temptation to work there. "With all the problems and ups and downs in movies," he says, "the basic reward is how well you can do your job. . . . The economics of TV are such that you aren't allowed to do your job as well as you can. So the enticement is money. I don't think the money is that good; and I also think the problems are greater, not lesser, and the interference is monumental. . . . Movies are more rewarding and less troublesome."

As for the stage, "I love theater, but not as a participant. I don't know theater; I've never done it. TV I did for years and years—it's a factor. . . . The money limitations affect the time limitations. The time limitations affect how well you can do your job. So you have to settle for less than you can do."

Aldrich gives the top TV creators some credit, however, saying that he couldn't do as well in twenty-four days as did the makers of *The Autobiography of Miss Jane Pittman* and *In this House of Brede,* even though he used to make feature films in nine days. "Maybe I've slowed down like everybody else," he smiles.

Slowed down or not, Aldrich continues to take great pleasure in his movie work, and to stand by his films. I mention a brief moment in *The Emperor of the North,* when a group of men standing over a game suddenly straighten up, and their motion is captured on film like the unfolding of a flower. Aldrich tells me that I am the first person to mention that scene to him, including people who were "very close to the picture." Then he explains:

"I'm a pro, and disciplined, and responsible. But every once in a while you have to be able to do something for yourself. . . . When you see the movie later, you take a moment of disproportionate pride in that moment. But it's very rarely communicable. It's for yourself—believe me, nobody's going to see it but you. . . ."

Aldrich Interview

PIERRE SAUVAGE/1976

THE LAST INTERVIEW WITH Robert Aldrich which we published was in *Movie 8*, at the time of *Sodom and Gomorrah*. This interview, recorded when *Hustle* was being released, deals with Aldrich's recent films and with his early days in the film industry.

Q: *Was* Hustle *already in script form when you first saw it?*
A: Yes, the script was submitted to Burt Reynolds when we were in Georgia making *The Longest Yard*. He liked the script very much and gave it to me. I liked it, but had some major reservations about the boy-girl relationship. Burt agreed, and so we collectively bought the property. It was twenty-five thousand against a hundred and fifty thousand; we put up twelve thousand five hundred each.

Q: *What appealed to you in the script?*
A: Well, I thought that if you had that obligatory love scene in the picture—the scene in the bar when Catherine says, "Just love me and I'll quit doing what I do" and he says "I'm unable to"—and if it were written properly, it would complete a unique love relationship. I never thought the picture was much of an action/adventure picture because the cop story's too thin; nothing really happens. But I did think there was a marvelous love story if the woman were foreign. In the screenplay she was American. But I thought that many Americans would find that unacceptable, that a man would seriously

From *Movie* 23 (Winter 1976–77): 50–64. Reprinted by permission.

consider a permanent love relationship with a prostitute. I thought a lot of that would dissipate if the prostitute were foreign.

Q : *You had decided that before you cast Deneuve?*
A : Oh, yeah. The only person we approached was Deneuve. Burt and I went to Paris, and sat and paid tribute—all the stuff you do—and explained to her what scene was missing and what we wanted that scene to say. I even did a rough draft of the scene. And on that basis she agreed to do the picture.

Q : *Did you work with Steve Shagan on the re-write?*
A : Shagan's a fine writer, but he's what I label "difficult." I don't mean to diminish his contribution, but he's not very malleable. Quite properly, he has pride of authorship. I guess it took three or four times to get that scene right. Also, I rely a great deal—more than many directors, I think—on an actor's response to the dialogue in terms of the character. But I like to get all that done in rehearsal, so I try very hard never to have any writer at rehearsals. Since I rehearse a couple of weeks, after two or three days the actors lose their inhibitions and say, "I understand why I have to say that, but isn't it better if I can say so and so?" And most of the time it is. Or if it isn't, it puts up a red flag, a signpost of why that is difficult to them. They may not have the right answer but they usually have the right instinct. Then you examine it and collectively find the right words. Many of the subtle changes that make a script work, or not, in my pictures are done in rehearsal. Not necessarily at the expense of the writer or script but to make it more comfortable for everybody. The only major rewrite in *Hustle* had to do with the tag [ending], which wasn't in the original, and the confrontation scene that really spelled out that she would be willing to forego her way of life if he would just accept her, but that he couldn't. And I thought that made it a very worthwhile, personal love story. Whether that's true or not will depend on the public.

Q : *Prior to rehearsal, do you participate activity in the writing process?*
A : Oh yeah. If you see a piece of material that you like—a play, a book, a screenplay—you buy an option on that, and then you either rework it yourself or rework it with the collaboration of the writer or with another writer. To buy this, we had certain built-in restrictions. We agreed that any major rewrites would be done by Shagan. That's a position I hate to be in and very

rarely am in. But in that case you have to work with the writer, which isn't always very healthy.

Q: *Except for some intermittent staccato effects—physical or psychological violence—the film is unusually low-keyed, certainly for you.*

A: I think that this picture'll never make it as an action picture. I think it has a great chance to make it as a personal relationship picture. Now once you say that to yourself, then you don't set up all the machinery, particularly in the beginning, to generate that immediate hook, so that people can't change to another channel. You're not involved in that; you're involved with the slow revelation of two people and their psychologically unconsummated romance. Either it works as a love story or it doesn't, because there's no gigantic action melodrama to sustain it. Without the love story it's second rate *Kojak*.

Q: *But at the same time you're going against an audience tendency to assume that the police story is going to be the main element in such a film.*

A: That's always true. I don't know how to overcome that. And I'm sure that it'll be sold that way and that people will go expecting to see that. If the audience expects to see *White Lightning* and they see something else, regardless of how good that something else is, they're going to be disappointed.

Q: *Yet there is, after all, a police story plot-line, and the Deneuve character and the love story are peripheral to that plot-line.*

A: Right. Except that I certainly wouldn't have made that picture and I'm reasonably sure that Burt wouldn't have made it without that man-woman relationship, because then it's pretty mundane.

Q: *And the main hook in the love story was that this was a physical relationship that was still, as you put it, psychologically unconsummated.*

A: Yeah, and the inability to come to grips with all the hang-ups that middle-class American Protestant working people may have about a love relationship with a woman who accepts money for sexual favours. To be able to overcome those and then not be rewarded after having lived through the agony of trying to overcome them—that is the basis for what is truly a very tender, moving personal relationship. Now whether that gets blurred and out of focus in the movie, I don't know.

Q: *At the same time you skirt really showing her at work in her profession.*

A: You see her after the fact. I think you come terribly close to having the audience, particularly ladies, accept a whore as a love object, and that if you were more explicit than phone calls or after-the-fact sexual encounters you'd never be able to make her the heroine. You see it done in foreign pictures and done very well. But I don't think we can handle it.

Q: *The idea used to be that a director should not waste close-ups, so as not to lessen their effect when he does use them. Yet* Hustle *is full of close-ups, which is not characteristic of your films. Did you simply feel this was a way of stressing the primacy of the personal, intimate relationship over the police story?*

A: That, and there is also the fact that if you have a story that is inherently slow, a dialogue picture rather than an action picture, the audience becomes less aware of the slowness and of the lack of action if they're presented with a variety of shots. They're fooled somewhat; they're deluded into thinking that there is less quiet or more action than there is.

Q: *In many of the intimate scenes, you did not in fact use a wide variety of angles but instead often stayed rather insistently on the faces.*

A: If it works as a story about the roles played by Deneuve and Reynolds, it works because of their chemistry and who they are in the picture, and so you want to get as close to them as possible. If it doesn't work, it doesn't work anyway. It doesn't make any difference where the camera is.

Q: *The political mockery you intended in* The Longest Yard *went virtually unnoticed. In* Hustle *there are rather insistent references to the Ben Johnson character being a "nobody," whose doubts about his daughter's death can thus be easily ignored in this society. Were you deliberately trying to make your political points inescapable this time?*

A: Part of that came from the original, and I happen to subscribe not to everything that Shagan says—we changed a lot of it—but to that, yes. Certainly the aftermath of Watergate is that we're living in a two-tier system of justice and a two-tier system of influence. It's more than the have and have-nots, it's a whole combination of inequality, and inequality has nothing to do with black anymore or brown or yellow. It has to do with who gets favoured treatment and who doesn't. I guess that the way Ben Johnson is treated is an exaggeration. But those people in America today don't have any muscle. If they steal a car, they go to jail for ten years, and the other guy steals ten million dollars and gets thirty days' suspended sentence. There is no equal justice. And I think that script came out of a time when everybody was painfully aware of that. We finished the picture December 1974 and it's being released in December 1975. I don't think it's quite as pressing today but it's still a painful subject.

Q : *The message also seems to be that the law is so inadequate, that one is justified in taking the law into one's own hands, as Reynolds does at the end of the picture, when he transforms the murder into self-defence. Do you really consider that a viable, positive proposition?*
A : Well, you could take the reverse and say that's a fascist position because it disregards the due process. But nothing was hurt. Eddie Albert was already killed; regardless of anything the policeman did, he's not going to change that set of affairs. Ben Johnson's marriage is full of holes that happened long before the suicide of his step-daughter, whom he thinks is his daughter. There is absolutely nothing factual to be changed—except the severity with which the law will deal with Ben Johnson. Now, you can take a purist position and say, no, Burt Reynolds should not do anything to change the course of justice or, you could take the humane position of why shouldn't Burt Reynolds protect a true innocent such as Ben Johnson and do what he does. I think that's forgivable, if not viable. You could take the position that if an officer of the law operates outside the law, what does the law mean, and be equally correct. I chose to argue it on the humanitarian basis. I don't pretend that makes it right.

Q : *I realise the idea was that Eddie Albert, for all his urbanity, was a true villain and ultimately even a symbol of corruption in this society, but that doesn't really change the fact that Ben Johnson seems to be almost randomly venting his frustration.*
A : There are two key lines. I don't think a picture can ever hang on two lines—if a viewer doesn't get the general concept, a line will never help or hurt a picture—but there are two key lines. One of them terribly natural and used by all of us in different walks of life: "I can't kill everybody." It's the final cry of frustration. "What are you going to do? There's no way to win. Maybe I am wrong but I've got to take my vengeance out on somebody. I can't fight City Hall. I can't fight an unnamed government, that usurps power." That, I

think, is a universal complaint. Burt's response to that is, "No, he didn't kill your daughter. He may have killed lots of other people but he didn't kill your daughter." Now, you put those two things together and they add up: what difference does it make whether Ben Johnson killed him? He should have been killed. And when Burt's friend, the black officer says, "You set him up like a hit man," Burt's response is true. No, he didn't. He didn't want to keep going in this case. It's the other guy who wanted to keep going. Burt in that instance *is* innocent. He did not set up A, B, C, D, to get Eddie Albert killed, although he's not unhappy at the twist of fate that made him to be the man who was killed.

Q : *But it did seem to be that Reynold's violence was presented as understandable and justifiable. When we see him kicking the shins of Jack Carter's crony we feel not simply that this is the way cops work, whether we like it or not, but that this is a fine, manly way to operate. And in the scene with the psychopathic murderer, the guy is shot, then Reynolds unnecessarily pumps more lead into him, ensuring that he is dead. Isn't that murder?*

A : It's a twenty-answer question. You know the guy is a psychopath, a guy that went to jail for life for killing four other people, who now is out and who's killed since then. You see two of the victims and you see a third person in imminent danger of being killed. So that takes away any question of whether it's right or not to kill that man because not to kill him means that an innocent woman is going to get killed. Then he's shot once, through the lady's shoulder, to get him killed: in fact shot twice. Burt shoots twice. Then Burt goes and shoots him three more times. And you're asking if the picture approves of that gratuitous shooting. Burt's answer is, "Those sons of bitches never die." His point of view obviously must be the picture's point of view: if you are a first-person witness to multiple homicide, why should you rely on a system that is less than perfect to let it happen again?

Q : *Do you really want the police to make those decisions?*

A : That's not a decision. If you see two people dead that this guy has killed, and he's holding a third one, and he's going to kill the third one, that's not the same decision as that of a cop who sees a guy reaching into his pocket for a package of cigarettes and uses that as an excuse to kill him.

Q : *The issue has to do with what happens after the first two shots, when the psychopath is down. . . .*

A: I could cop-out and say he's dead. But he isn't.

Q: *There's no reason to assume he is, but I wondered if you left that intentionally unclear?*
A: The hue and cry would be extraordinary if you labeled that he was alive and then Burt killed him. So it's left that you can draw your own conclusions. He was shot twice. Did he live or did he die? Would he have lived or would he have died?

Q: *I saw no reason to assume he was dead, and certainly no reason to assume that Reynolds knew he was already dead, and that being the case it would seem pretty clear that Burt just proceeds to make sure that he does die.*
A: I think that's a reasonable assumption. I'd go back to other pictures where people could technically raise the same question. When Eddie Albert is shot in *Attack,* is he killed with the first bullet or is he killed when the other nice guys shoot him? And does it make any difference? It's important that they have a collective guilt, and it's important that he be dead. And it's important that this guy is dead. That Burt kills him with the first shot or the fourth or fifth shot I think is unimportant. It's important that the woman be alive and that he be dead.

Q: *You say you changed the ending of the picture.*
A: He didn't die in the script, and she wasn't waiting for him at the airport. In other words, that relationship wasn't resolved.

Q: *It's an interesting choice for you to have made: the hero is unexpectedly killed in a trivial incident, a second-rate hold-up.*
A: Well, if it's trivial, I guess the director failed. Abe Polonsky, whom I have maybe more respect for than anybody in town, made that same point. And I gave him the same answer. If the viewer doesn't understand that when Burt's in that liquor store and the guy tells him to get his hands up, and he looks at the gun, he is thinking of what his own self-esteem means and of what's on the line, and that he has an opportunity just to play melody and avoid the unpleasant, then the director has failed. There are three cuts: Burt in medium shot, an insert of the gun, and a big, big head of Burt. The audience should realise that he's making up his mind whether to get involved or not get involved, knowing what getting involved would mean. And that he

thinks: "Fuck it, I've lived a particular way, and it's my job not to let people really get hurt. I can look the other way and nobody's going to be critical. But if I do, I will have lost my self-esteem and without my self-esteem what difference does it make that she's at the airport?" And he elects to act out what he is. But I've got to say that, since a lot of people I really admire did not understand that it's a *basic* choice, it has to be the director's fault. It has nothing to do with the actor or the writer. The director didn't draw that conclusion sufficiently strongly for the audience to understand it. And without that, the ending is soapy instead of sentimental. Whereas with that, you say, "Jesus, they finally fought their way through this. Are they going to happy live ever after, nobody knows. But they got a chance." And that's what should be sad. Not that he's dead but that they had a chance and they never had an opportunity to find out.

Q : *In many of your films the main character is confronted with a corrupt and corrupting system and ultimately decides not to go along with it.*
A : I guess you have a weakness for a certain kind of character. It's the same character in a number of pictures that keeps reappearing, characters that are bigger than life, that find their own integrity in doing what they do the way they do it, even if it causes their own deaths. They're more interesting, and more sincere. Considering what the odds are, what's involved, it becomes very expensive to have opinions that strong. So consequently they're more interesting people, more interesting characters. I would think that in all the movies that I particularly identified with, going back to *Attack* and *The Big Knife,* any of those kind of pictures, the guy says, "Fuck it, I'm going to do it my way." These guys thought they had a chance to win outside the system or against the system. And didn't. Or only did temporarily. And Polonsky in *Force of Evil* and *Body and Soul* says, "I probably will lose, but if winning means going along with that kind of system I'm not going to go along. And I think I have an outside chance of winning doing it my way." On *Body and Soul,* much against Abe's wishes, we shot an alternative ending, where Garfield leaves the ring, goes down an alley, and is shot, as he obviously would be. And when he falls his hand pulls off a one-sheet, and it says "Charlie Davis—Champion of the World." And I thought that was the proper ending for that picture. Abe didn't agree and neither did Rossen. I think that's the kind of guy that you find most admirable: a heroic figure, who understands that the probabilities are that he'll lose.

Q : *And you seem to admire characters who, although they may waver and hesi-tate, consider that integrity, a form of inner consistency, is a primary virtue.*
A : Yes, particularly if you add that integrity is really not worthwhile without self-esteem.

Q : *You were born 9 August 1918 in Cranston, Rhode Island. You attended the University of Virginia where you majored in . . .*
A : Football. No, Economics

Q : *Your father was a banker, was he not? At that time did you intend to go into banking?*
A : No, in Virginia I became head of what's called a dance society. I booked a lot of big bands—it was the big band era—I had the Dorsey brothers *et al.*, and one became fascinated with that particular aspect of show business. I said to myself, this is more fun than working in a bank or working in a news-paper. I was a film nut like everybody was at that time, and when we decided to go into show business, the most fascinating part of it then was film. Ergo, my decision to go to California in '41. I had completed four years of college, but I didn't get my degree because I wasn't very bright! Four glorious years. . . . I went to work for RKO as a production clerk, a position that doesn't exist anymore. It is the lowest form of human life. You are a gofer, you get coffee and you keep the time cards of the actors and the production report, and make out the call sheet, and if you're lucky and keep your nose clean, you eventually get to be a third assistant. And then you're on the assembly lines. Once you get to be a third then hopefully you get to be a second, and eventu-ally if you're again lucky, you get to be a first, and so on. I was a production clerk for about four or five months, at the end of which I got to be a second, and my first show as a second was with Michèle Morgan on her first Ameri-can picture, *Joan of Paris*. I did about two dozen pictures as a second. A lot of westerns.

Q : *You worked as an assistant to Zinnemann and Dassin.*
A : Yes, that was as a first. They made a series of musicals out here, with the great masters—Rubinstein, Piatigorsky, Heifetz—and that's where I assisted Dassin. With Zinnemann, I was going to go to Rome with them on *Teresa*. I prepared it, and then he had to postpone and I went to work for Metro, so I never actually assisted him. I was a first on a number of Edgar Kennedy and

Leon Errol shorts at RKO before I went with Renoir on *The Southerner* in '44.
From '44 to the end of '49—my last job as assistant was with Chaplin on
Limelight—was working all the time for a variety of directors: Milestone three
or four times, Losey, two or three times, Rossen, Polonsky, Wellman, Dassin,
Reis, lots of marvellous directors.

Q : *What do you think was the most important thing you learned working as an
assistant director, and from whom did you learn it?*
A : I think what you probably learn is what not to do as well as what to do.
I also worked for a lot of terrible directors who shall go nameless and you
told yourself you'd never make those same mistakes. It's a matter of assimilation and whose brains you can pick, trying to keep it for yourself later, and
what not to do. For example, Losey has absolutely extraordinary rapport
with actors. I don't think any other director I ever worked with ever had that
kind of personal communication. Now, he has other limitations. Milestone
is a great pre-cutter. He can think in his mind where he's going to use the
close-up, the medium shot; he really does pre-edit in his mind. Of course,
you would never be as good as that particular guy is in that particular field,
but you try to make yourself a composite of what you like and stay away
from the things you didn't like.

Q : *Were you already thinking then of becoming director?*
A : Oh, sure. The director is the creative hub of what makes a picture work,
and if you have any ambition, and you don't want to be a producer or a
writer, then you want to be a director.

Q : *You didn't have any say over which director you worked with at the time?*
A : No, as an independent, you weren't assigned; you went out and tried to
get a job. I was under contract only at Enterprise for a couple of years when
it was a small studio very close to this office.

Q : *You first became a director in television?*
A : Yeah, most of the good television coming out of New York was live—it
was the time of Playhouse 90 and Philco Playhouse—and not many film
directors would go to New York and do filmed television because it meant a
big economic disadvantage for them. But I was offered a half-hour doctor
series, *The Doctor*, for Proctor and Gamble, and I jumped at it. I was then very

successful with *China Smith,* and reasonably successful with Four-Star Playhouse. After that I did mostly pilots, which a) pay more money and b) require a little longer time and a little longer schedule and you get a chance to show off a little. I did pilots for the Michener series *Adventures in Paradise,* and *The Sundance Kid.* All the pilots sold and so that was an interesting way to make a living.

Q: *How did* Big Leaguer *come about?*
A: Metro was looking for some so-called bright young men to make a series of low-budget features. And somebody'd seen some of my work and I was invited to do *Big Leaguer* which was a picture about the New York Giants' baseball farm system. Edward G. Robinson had been out of films for two or three years and they thought it would be a wonderful way to get him back. We went to Melbourne, Florida, which is now Cape Kennedy, and made the picture there. I think it took all of sixteen days. It was a story about the New York Giants and they opened it in Brooklyn, so you can imagine that it didn't do very well. It wasn't a bad picture, but those pictures then were just thrown out on the market. They weren't expected to be sold. *World for Ransom* was much more fun and much more challenging. It was a blown up *China Smith,* which we did in ten days, and it looked like it was done in thirty or forty. It was an interesting picture, bits and pieces stolen from different directors, with a variety of styles and techniques. It was thievery in the night, but for ten days it was pretty good. I think the whole picture cost ninety thousand dollars: the economics were such that you had to have bizarre, outlandish kinds of situations to even be noticeable. So you make a potboiler and you try to make it as outrageous as possible so it has some marketable value. We sold it, made a little money, and it did rather well.

Q: *Your cut opened on a lesbian kiss, that was deleted from the picture?*
A: There's something borrowed from the Marlene Dietrich character in *Morocco,* and it's not dissimilar, and the inference and the thrust are still there but the kiss itself, I think, was lost to the code in those days.

Apache was moderately well received critically, and did very well. Everybody had bigger hopes for it but in those days that wasn't a very expensive picture, and Hecht-Lancaster (Hill was there but not yet a partner) did quite well on it. That was at that time a very progressively oriented company. It did a lot of marvellous things, and out of that association I got the chance to do *Vera Cruz.* It made a lot of money and gave us all a whole new thrust in our career. And you know that twenty years later we did another version of *Apache* [*Ulzana's Raid*] except that Burt this time played the John McIntire part: he played the scout and another guy played the Indian. Different picture, but same subject matter.

Q : *Your previous films were fairly classical in structure. Right from the beginning,* Kiss Me Deadly *strikes out in a new direction, with jarring angles, lighting, even credits. . . .*

A : We tried to have a very obvious stylized impact of energy. With the exception of possibly *World for Ransom,* you were trapped in a kind of traditional concept of what the material leant itself to. But on *Kiss Me Deadly* you had a chance to establish a very graphic, hard-hitting, short-cut, staccato kind of style for that movie. That wasn't brand new but it was new for that kind of film. Also I rehearse a great deal. Usually two weeks. And when you walk a picture—granted you walk it in an office or on an empty stage—you start to get visual impressions of how a scene would be most effective. It doesn't always work. You always have to make adjustments, so you can't have the built-in rigidity of saying, "This is how I'm going to do it," because sometimes you can't. But that was terribly helpful to me. I know that other people don't consider rehearsals always helpful but to me it's the difference between what the script says and what the picture says. There is a transition period before you freeze a concept when you still have the latitude to mentally experiment—it doesn't cost anything. You're thinking while the actors are working, and I think that's very valuable. Every picture from *Vera Cruz* on had a great deal of rehearsal.

Q : *You don't storyboard your films, do you?*
A : No. Milestone used to. And, with all due respect, occasionally he'd get stuck because he'd really done his homework and he was locked into a concept. It's very tough then to be fluid. On action pictures, for example *Longest Yard,* I feel you do have to have a continuity of action cuts, so you either stay up very late or get up very early and do great big worksheets that your assistant carries, so you know where you are. Because nobody else can know where you are, what goes here, why you're there, what you have to get, because no script is ever written like that. In that regard it's a half storyboard. Otherwise you'd find no way to put it all together.

Q: *You've enjoyed both critical and box-office success. When you're working, do you find there is any conflict between the two goals?*

A: No, I don't. I think this is an unusual medium. I admire a great deal directors who wait five, six, seven, eight years between pictures. But I don't agree with it. The more you do, the better you get, and I think to sit and wait five years for the right script, or a project that's important enough is foolish. Unless you have some certificate from your own personal God or you're going to live to 180, you miss more opportunities to get better at what you do. Writers get better by writing, actors get better by acting, and directors get better by directing. They can't get better by sitting in the living room and saying, "That script isn't good enough." It's certainly leisurely enough to do a picture a year. You should be able to do three pictures every two years, and do them well. It's not only economic, but it's philosophical. What are you going to sit home for? If that's not the best script, you do the best one you can find.

Q: *You've made several pictures dealing with Hollywood. Was your interest in the subject due to the fact that you happened to be working in the film industry, or did you see great symbolic value in its use?*

A: I think that both are true. You can't work here and not be fascinated by it, but there is also a saying that what happens in California this year will happen in the rest of the country in two years. And if that's true, what happens in Hollywood is going to happen in California in two years. What you have here is over-dramatic, over-theatrical, over-specialised, and it offers no dramatic, theatrical insight. You can see social and political issues in the white heat of the cauldron of what makes Hollywood work much sooner than you will see them in the rest of the country. In *Big Knife,* Odets saw them early on.

The play was six years old by the time we did the movie. The things Odets had to say about this community and the manner in which pictures were made or not made was very important, and it had to do again with political freedom. You could have made that picture in the middle of Nixon's administration and it would have been just as worthwhile. In fact, I think things have changed for the worse. Everything that was bad about the Mayer, Warner, Cohn regimes, is worse today, with none of the advantages. The advantages were that for all their evil and corruptness, which was rampant, you could get a decision. There was a sense of necessity to produce, to get on with the picturemaking process. And they weren't afraid. Today, the people who run the store are all afraid and the industry is run by committees or agents or committees of agents. Indecisiveness is the name of the game, not decisiveness. So I think you could make a better picture about the ills of Hollywood today, but it wouldn't be as exciting because these are not exciting people, they're dull people. Those were exciting people. Granted, evil and corrupt, but decisive. Today, they're bankers, they're not filmmakers. Where does it say that an agent knows a good script from a bad script? What entitles him to know a good director from a bad director? The fact that he sells him? Do you think the butcher knows the difference between a good cow and bad cow? They're merchants, but they're not in a mercantile undertaking. They're in an art hyphen craft undertaking, and that's not one that lends itself to be merchandised.

Q : Attack *was the first of several war films. You never served in the Army, did you?*
A : No, I was in the Motion Picture Unit of the Air Force for three days. I had two things wrong: a football knee and a perforated eardrum. *Attack* was a marvelous play by a playwright named Norman Brooks—he never did anything after that—called "Fragile Fox." Jim Poe did the script, a very good script. Again, ahead of its time, in terms of being anti-war, anti-military. I think the three pictures of mine that have suffered the most from bad timing are *Big Knife, Attack,* and *Sister George.* If each one of those pictures had been moved back five years, I think they would have been economically very successful. But they were premature, I think, in terms of the audience's receptivity.

Q : *Do you feel that your attitude towards war comes across exactly as you intended it to? I imagine that* The Dirty Dozen *was at least partly intended to suggest the ambiguity of heroism, and yet its violence was so dramatic that it probably distracted audiences from that point.*
A : I think that's a fair criticism. I think it stems from a dichotomy in my own opinion. I do think that war brings out both the best and the worst in men. But take the sequence at the end of *Dirty Dozen* where Jimmy Brown runs across the forecourt of the castle, and drops hand grenades in the ventilation systems that you know have already been saturated with gasoline. Now, what I was trying to do was say that under the circumstances it's not

only the Germans who do unkind and hideous, horrible things in the name of war, but that the Americans do it and anybody does it. The whole nature of war is dehumanising. There's no such thing as a nice war. Now American critics completely missed that, so they attacked the picture because of its violence, and for indulgence in violent heroics. Now, fascinatingly, European critics all picked up on the parallel between burning people alive and the use of napalm, whether they liked the picture or not. They all got the significance of what was being said. So you learn not to over-react to criticism whether it's favourable or unfavourable. There are some directors, some very good directors, who make a business, a *business,* of courting the critics. But then if the critic likes your picture, you'll never know whether or not it's just because you romanced him. I don't mean to single him out, but what would Altman do if the *New Yorker* didn't like his picture? He'd have a heart attack.

Q: *How would you characterize your runaway production phase?*
A: Oh, disaster. It cost me four bad films and the dissolution of a marriage—it can't be much more disastrous than that. But I couldn't find work after getting fired at Columbia on *Garment Jungle* after having shot two-thirds. They had showed me a script; I had wanted to do that script and I shot that script. That was a very, very tough picture, and halfway through it Cohn became frightened of how tough it was. It had some very strong things to say about the unions and about the mobs, and he wanted to soften the picture. He was aided and abetted in that by Lee Cobb, who wanted to be more heroic and not as tough. And I said, "Bullshit, I'm not going to change it." We had a number of sessions and I wouldn't sweeten up the picture. I then got the flu on a Friday and was very sick and had to take the day off. Well, they fired me that night. No, I never saw the picture—never will. But it could have been a good picture. So I was looking for a job, and I went to Europe and did *Ten Seconds to Hell.* Then I did *Angry Hills* and *Sodom and Gomorrah.* Sergio Leone was second-unit director on *Sodom and Gomorrah* and he was loafing and was terrible. He was up in Marrakesh and I was shooting in the south and had to take Saturday off because we had only Hebraic tribes working and they wouldn't work on Saturday. (The Italians wouldn't work on Sunday.) So I made the four-hour drive up to Marrakesh. Nobody knew I had come. And he had five or six thousand people working—and they were taking a three-hour Italian lunch. I was up on the buffs and I waited for about three hours while nothing happened and then four hours and still nothing

happened. I called him and I said, "Get your ticket and go back to Rome; you're through." He went back to Rome, and they had no director for the first Clint Eastwood picture and that's why he's a zillionaire and I'm broke.

Q : *Your adventure running your own studio from 1968 to 1973 must have had a considerable effect on your financial situation.*

A : We lost an awful lot of money. If we could have made two pictures a year, shooting at least forty days on each, it could have worked out. In other words, we needed eighty production days a year to make the studio break even. And it was the time when I hadn't made any successful pictures for a while, and we were in litigation with ABC. You can't rent a studio that's so well equipped for anything but great big pictures because the guys steal so much that if you're going to rent it for a twenty day picture they'll steal more than twenty days' worth of lights and cameras and lenses. So it required my either producing or directing two pictures a year, and because of the lack of success of *Too Late the Hero* and *Sister George* and *Grissom Gang,* we just weren't getting two pictures a year done. And the rent goes on, and the salaries go on, and the taxes go on whether or not you're shooting. So it was a miscalculation. But it was a marvelous studio. We did things very cheaply and very well but not often enough. For example, we were originally going to make *Too Late the Hero* for Metro, and their budget for the picture was ten million one. We made the same picture, I think probably better, with the same cast and everything for four million dollars cheaper. We could have kept doing that, but to do that you have to have a hit. We'd find properties, spend our own money to develop the properties, spend our own time to get actors interested, and then go to a distributor with the script, the actors, the budget, the schedule, and say "We want to start on Wednesday." That's the easiest way to do it. Because of all the money we lost in the studio, for a while we've had to go to the studios to get preproduction monies to buy and develop the properties. As a consequence of which you don't get the property you really want, and the script isn't really what you want and you've given away an awful lot to get the money. We're just coming out of that now, so we're really getting back in the business of financing our own preproduction. The only safeguard an independent has is to control the property, not have it controlled by the guy who's going to be his partner, because then the partner controls everything.

Q: *Do you have final cut on your pictures?*
A: No, I never asked for it. I could have gotten it a couple of times. I have uninterrupted supervision till after the second public preview. On the theory that if after two previews you can't convince anybody, even a moron, that that's the way the picture should be then those people are going to cut the picture anyway, regardless of whether you have a contract. And your job really is to be so expert at what you do that there can be no quarrel, and that everyone says, "Yeah, that's right." With the exception of about eighty feet in *Longest Yard* because of ego problems—not my ego, somebody else's—and fifteen feet on *Baby Jane* to satisfy the guy who put up the money, nobody's ever changed any picture of mine in the last ten or fifteen years. Burt Lancaster changed the foreign version of *Ulzana's Raid,* for what reason I don't know, but not the American version.

Q: *You obviously prefer to work as your own producer. What are the main advantage?*
A: Well you don't have anybody to answer to. Total independence. I've had some marvelous producers, but they're entitled to an explanation. You're a producer, you found the property, and you're entitled to have a guy tell you what he's doing or why he's doing it. And just the time it takes to tell somebody why you're doing something takes an amount of energy. You should be doing something else with that energy, not explaining things.

Q: *You've also developed a professional family, composed of people like cinematographer Joseph Biroc, film editor Michael Luciano, composer Frank DeVol . . .*
A: Well, you develop a professional shorthand. You say five words and they know what you mean, and they know how you work, and they trust you and you trust them, and they don't have to worry about being cautious around you.

Q: *Do you work closely with your cinematographers?*
A: Well, the last fifteen years have been with Biroc. We discuss the pictorial effect I want in terms of lighting, what the stop should be and what the focus depth should be. But not where the camera should be or what the lens should be, because I know where the camera goes I think better than they do. So that takes a little accommodation. In the last ten years I've also used a two-camera system. I find that you lose maybe five or ten percent on absolute right composition but you gain fifty percent on the fluidity of cutting

and the chance to change the pace of the picture. So I use two cameras even if I'm doing an insert of a doorknob. You can change the whole tempo of the scene in the cutting room over and over and over again. Instead of getting one close-up you get two close-ups, instead of one over the shoulder you get two over the shoulder, instead of one medium shot you get two medium shots, and you can generate enormous amount of energy. Let me explain something. Bette Davis knows more about the technical end of the business than any actor I know of. And on *Baby Jane* I couldn't get her to slow down enough, to make a point. She said that was an invasion of her creative capacity, that she couldn't wait. So I said, "Pick out a sequence, trust me and do it that way." She did and we cut the picture, and it worked. For example, when somebody comes in and lays the dead bird down in front of her, I wanted her to delay her reaction, so there's time for the cut to Crawford and then back to her reaction. Film is a time arrester. In fact, both reactions would be happening at the same time. But if you make them happen at the same time, it doesn't necessarily work, because you want one reaction to be off the other, even though both people see the bird at the same time. I think the highest compliment I've ever been paid as a director was to have Davis say, "I know what you mean." Now, Bette—never mind the picture—is much better in *Hush . . . Hush* than she is in *Baby Jane,* but only for that reason, that every reaction—and that's what film is really—every reaction is recorded. It's not lost in transition because you have to be on somebody else. That's very, very tough to do. But with two cameras you can do it and still not lose it. And you're not often going to be that lucky to work with people as intelligent and as knowledgeable as Davis, so from *Baby Jane* on I said, "Oh, fuck it, I'll use two cameras all the time." You spend more money for film, but you spend much less money on time. A picture that you would do maybe in fifty-five days you do in thirty-five days; it costs you five percent more on those thirty-five than it normally would but you've saved twenty days. We did *Longest Yard* in sixty-one days. Now the game took thirty-six days. But we had up to six cameras—there's no way of staging a football game with one camera. I had a marvelous time. But the end is a real steal from *Body and Soul.* There the Garfield character had thrown everything away and had to redeem his self-esteem more than anything else. Without the switch, without the main character having to regain his self-esteem after having sold everybody out, there's no pull, you don't care. So I just stole from Polonsky, stuck it on, wrote in the story of Jimmy's burning to death, and the funeral. None of that was in the script. And that kind of movie lent itself better to audience identification than *Body and Soul* Because it's longer and more complicated and you have a chance to bring the audience with you.

Q : *There seemed to be far more deliberate political overtones to the film than American critics saw in it.*
A : Eddie Albert is Nixon! When I put him in those clothes, and put the flag in there, and had the football talk, and the guy turning on and off the tape recorder—on the set, everybody said, "You can't do that Bob; you're going too far." I must say I thought I did go too far but obviously I didn't go half far enough, because nobody, nobody understood. Jesus, except for having a wife named Pat, we had everything in the picture. But nobody picked up on it.

Q : *The soundtracks of your films are unusually detailed and meticulous. On* The Longest Yard *you had a field day with bone-crunching sound effects and so on, partly with humorous intent.*
A : Some of it is, and some of it is to accentuate the realism. I hate films that have that synthetic quietness, and you can hear everybody talk. I don't agree with Mr. Altman about intelligibility, but I do think that in life you don't hear things as if in an isolation booth. So I spend a lot of time and extra effort to try and make sound busy and real and include noises from out in the street or across the hall, so that it has some believability and reality to it. Christ, you go to most California pictures, and when two people talk you don't hear a fucking thing, there's nothing on the track at all. I do think there are moments that you have to understand what the people are saying; it's a prerequisite to understanding what the story's about. So I do give the dialogue track precedence in most cases, but I also try and have four or five other things going on the sound track. I admit on *McCabe and Mrs. Miller,* I didn't know what the hell was going on for the first three reels. But I do think that's better than to have nothing on the track except one guy talking in the middle of downtown Los Angeles, and you don't hear anything else. For example, the opening scene in *Longest Yard* takes place on a Sunday up in the Hollywood hills. We had all the things going. It's near a freeway and you hear the thing, you hear the birds, the record player, the radio next door. And somebody went up there on a Sunday and got a track, and there were

church bells. Why didn't we think of that? It's not only in Rome that you hear the church bells, you hear them here too. So finally we got the church bells and put them in. We're always looking for things that would be at that scene at that time of day.

Q : *There is humor, and much irony, in many of your films, but* The Longest Yard *has more of it by far than any other. Have you ever thought of making a comedy?*
A : I'd really love to. But the problem in this town is that whether you like it or not people think of you in their framework, not in yours. So if they think of you as an action adventure director, you can break your balls, and nobody's going to give you a comedy. You say, "That's pretty funny, isn't it?" and they say, "yeah, but. . . ." The "yeah, but" is what kills you. I bought a play that Peter Sellers did in London a number of years ago called "Brou-haha." I had a marvelous script done. Nobody would let me do that movie.

Q : *In the forties, you worked with a lot of then future blacklistees, and you were briefly under contract at Enterprise Studios. What were your personal political attitudes at that time?*
A : If I'd come to California in '36 instead of '41 I'd have joined the party. Being a Communist then had nothing to do with wanting to mount the barricades. It had to do with a frame of mind, an attitude about politics and the picture business and the government and the Roosevelt administration. And it wasn't insidious and it wasn't cold war time. I think anybody with any brains in 1936 to '40 would have been a Communist. They were the brightest, they were the quickest, they were the best, and you found working with people of that persuasion more stimulating, more exciting. I never joined the party, nobody ever asked me to, and probably that's the reason, but you shared many, many attitudes about the political condition or you wouldn't have worked with them that much. History has proven that their liberal leanings were not trying to corrupt the government but were trying to make a better country. Nobody was stealing atomic secrets, you know, that's nonsense.

Q : *Would you characterise yourself today as a liberal still?*
A : Yeah. I can't imagine how people, certainly working people, can be Republicans, for example. It amazes me. And I can't imagine that people who work for a living are going to be Democrats much longer if something

doesn't happen. My guess is that my attitudes would be described as moderately left of the Democratic position. Not radical, but certainly more extreme than whatever the Democratic platform is, which is non-existent.

Q : *The fact that Nelson Rockefeller is your second cousin obviously hasn't coloured your views.*
A : He went out the door the day of Attica.

"I Can't Get Jimmy Carter to See My Movie!"

STUART BYRON/1977

DEFENDING RESTORATION POETRY, W. H. Aùden wrote: "Those who condemn didactic poetry can only do so because they condemn didacticism and must disapprove *a fortiori* of didactic prose." One would hardly want to cast Robert Aldrich as the Alexander Pope of filmdom (for one thing, he has no taste for comedy), but the refreshing thing about his new film, *Twilight's Last Gleaming*, is its didactic bluntness. It is—and thus its Einsensteinian aspect—a film without a subtext. You don't leave it, as you leave *Kiss Me Deadly*, thinking: "It pretends to be just a thriller, but it's *really* about the atom bomb." You don't leave it, as you leave *Ulzana's Raid*, think-ing: "It pretends to be just a western, but it's *really* about Vietnam." *Twilight's Last Gleaming* pretends to be about the atom bomb and Vietnam, and it *is* about the atom bomb and Vietnam. As Elia Kazan once said, about another movie: "The thing's about what the thing's about."

Its style is as blunt and forceful as a Titan missile, and that is the style proper to it. The outrageous story of nuclear warheads and U.S. Presidents demands a crude grandeur. The *bigness* of *Twilight's Last Gleaming* subsumes petty objections. I can forgive Charles Durning's President being shocked by revelations about Vietnam no more current than the Pentagon Papers, because Aldrich has developed a context in which Durning stands in for the betrayed guilessness of the American people. The film, after all, culminates operatically, with the dead Durning being wept over by a distraught Gerald

From *Film Comment* XIII (March/April 1977): 46–52. Copyright © 1977 by the Film Society of Lincoln Center. All rights reserved. Reprinted by permission.

S. O'Loughlin. Its triumph is to have achieved the larger-than-life melodra-matics we associate with opera through the use of the most non-operatic material imaginable.

At the very least, *Twilight's Last Gleaming* should clear up any lingering doubts about the general thrust of Aldrich's politics. For despite his constant disclaimers to the contrary (he has always claimed that "luck" alone kept him off the black-list), it has been common to dismiss Aldrich as a fascist. In retrospect, the parabola of his whole career makes no sense unless he is viewed as a left-wing director. Where the confusion enters is with his belief that the forces of authority are so great that they can only be countered by an equal force that sometimes gets out of hand (e.g., *The Dirty Dozen*). Per-haps Sylvia Polonsky's suspicion that Aldrich is a Stalinist is perceptive. He is certainly a most pessimistic democrat.

Film Comment's last encounter with Robert Aldrich (Spring 1972) coincided with the demise of his production company-cum-studio, The Associates & Aldrich, following a string of costly flops (*Too Late the Hero, The Grissom Gang*). He no longer is in a position to develop projects from the seed level. Rather, he chooses from among what's "going around" in Hollywood—which means that a project exists at least as a first-draft screenplay before Aldrich brings his talents to bear upon it. I don't think it can be claimed that the five movies since *Ulzana's Raid* are less personal than those before; as Aldrich makes clear below, he has altered each of these projects considerably by the time he filmed it. But it is probably true that he is more restricted to the male action film than he would be otherwise. Such films have always been an Aldrich specialty, but only one of them; it's easy to forget that in the sixties Aldrich was something of a women's director, making films both com-mercially successful (*What Ever Happened to Baby Jane?*) and unsuccessful (*The Killing of Sister George*). Hollywood has forgotten, however, and it seems unlikely to be reminded until Aldrich is again in a position to control totally his own career. That time may not be far away: while Lorimar, the producers of *Twilight's Last Gleaming*, is not owned by Aldrich, he has clearly formed a continuing relationship with it which might result in greater freedom of action for the fifty-eight-year-old director after completion of his next film, *The Choirboys*.

Q: *At what stage did you enter* Twilight's Last Gleaming?

A: Lorimar—the production company I'm now associated with—had had this project for a long time, and they couldn't get it financed. Every actor in town had seen it—including Burt Lancaster, a couple of years ago.

It was an action melodrama—and if you hadn't already seen it, you were going to see it. Or you knew one or two pictures that were kind of like it. Two guys hijack the President, they hold him up for some money, they get killed and the President gets off free. There was no social impact. The kidnappers had no interesting motivation. The reasons they wanted to get the President weren't even PLO-type reasons. They just wanted the money. That didn't seem to me to make much sense.

I wondered what would happen if you had an Ellsberg mentality, if you had some command officer who came out of Vietnam and who was soured not by war protestors but by the misuse of the military. The military, really, has had a unique relationship with this country; they've really done what they were supposed to do—stayed out of politics, and protected the country. Now in Vietnam, they were there for political and not defensive reasons; they weren't there for the protection of our citizens. What would happen if you had a general who was angry at the political use of the armed forces?

So I told Lorimar that I would only do it if I could turn that story upside down. And if Lancaster would agree to do it, I would agree to do it on those terms. Now I get along pretty well with Burt. He's a strange, strange man—not a guy you want to spend your life in a cocktail bar with. But when you can arouse enthusiasm in a project in Burt, he's a man you can work with—particularly the older he gets, because he tends now to be more concerned about how good he is rather than whether he's right or wrong. I think he's becoming a better actor every year.

So I told him my version of the story—it wasn't written yet—and Burt agreed to do it. And Lorimar was so glad to get anybody that the Germans would buy—because the Germans had agreed to come up with two-thirds of the budget if they liked the elements. The Germans—they have all the money in the world. We gotta lose the next war so that we end up like Germany or Japan, because they got everything! In any case, the Germans said, "Fine. You bring us Lancaster and that movie, we'll finance sixty-six and two-thirds percent of it."

Q: *They didn't require as big a star in any other role?*
A: No, but the President could have been a Camelot kind of President. So Burt made a call to Paul Newman, and I made a call to Paul, and he was

frosty polite but that's about all. So then we thought, "Hell, we'll write the picture the way it should be and worry about casting it later." And my idea of the President was really that of a smart, classy, uptown Daley. Catholic origins. Maybe Holy Cross as a school. His mother wanted him to be a Jesuit, but he liked politics, became a lawyer, was really a pol, never pretended to be a statesman—very pragmatic man.

Q : *The writers, Ronald M. Cohen and Edward Huebsch—did they work together?*
A : Yes—the most unlikely marriage in the world. Huebsch's a little wizened old man, sixty-two, sixty-three years old, been in the political wars for forty years, probably the most knowledgeable political analyst in town—or at least up there with Abe Polonsky and Ring Lardner. And Cohen is a loud-mouthed, extroverted, young, smart-ass guy who knows that he votes Demo-cratic, and that's the extent of his political exposure. But Ron's an extraordi-narily gifted writer in terms of what people say and how they say it. And I put these two guys in a pressure cooker for about six weeks, and they came out with a very good first draft, though it was very long.

Q : *Did you visit them occasionally?*
A : Oh, I had an office just down the street. I visited them nine times a day, and they were screaming and throwing doughnuts at each other. But it worked.

Q : *What books did you read for the political aspects?*
A : What we read for the military analysis was . . . Kissinger and Lucius Clay both wrote books in '57—the Kissinger book was *Nuclear Weapons and Foreign Policy*—that said that we should embark on a venture of limited war to con-vince the Russians to stay within their sphere of influence while we stayed within ours. To hell with any human reasons. National security wasn't threatened. And Vietnam hadn't really come along. And if it hadn't been Vietnam, it could've been Colombia. It could've been Angola, it could've been anywhere. It happened to be Vietnam. I'm sure as hell that nobody ever understood that. Sure as hell I never understood it.

Q : *But is it credible that a President wouldn't understand it?*
A : I don't' care how smart Jimmy Carter is, or how cynical. There are going to be things that he never had an inkling of that he's going to learn in those

four years. They may not have anything to do with Vietnam; they may have to do with how C. Anhault Smith [the chairman of Coca-Cola] was protected from a $2 billion fraud. The depth of what they learn has got to surprise the shit out of those guys. They know maybe three layers, and you and I know maybe half a layer. But they're going to discover twenty layers. And I think they're all shocked; there's no way they could not be shocked.

Q : *Don't Carter's appointments of Cyrus Vance and Zbigniew Brzezinski demonstrate the continuity of foreign policy from administration to administration that* Twilight *condemns?*
A : Right! And I can't get him to come to the movie! You know, I met him three times when I was making *The Longest Yard* in Georgia and he was governor; I know some people who know him very well, and I was a modest contributor. And I can't get him to come to the picture!

Q : *Why all the split screen work?*
A : Well, they sold me on what they call multiple images and you call split screens and I call panels. The original script was 350 pages long—a four-and-a-half-hour picture. Now it's two hours and twenty-three minutes, and probably still twenty minutes too long. But if you're going to tell that story, there's no way without panels. I don't particularly like panels unless they're in a bread commercial. But I thought they fitted that particular movie. They cost me an extra half a year—*half a year.* But you couldn't tell that story in less than three hours without them. So I finally acquiesced.

Q : *Do you see the film as being "larger than life"?*
A : Oh, sure. Yeah. Mr. Aldrich has never been accused, even in a moment of anger, of understating anything. Also: Once you pick a date of 1981, you're not limited to what has happened. You're saying what *could* happen. Your guess is as good as mine or the guy's next door. The parameters of what you can do are not cast in cement.

Q : *Nobody's "crazy" in* Twilight's Last Gleaming. *Even the Widmark character seems a professional doing what he has to do; he's no Strangelove type. Was that what you wanted?*
A : Yeah, except for one thing. I think you have to understand that in the Lancaster character there is a degree of imbalance, because he's willing to do

an insane thing to prove a point. I don't think you prove a point with X millions of lives—you have to be a little crazy. My hope was that you gradually came to understand that Lancaster is crazy. But I don't think we did it. The audience is so much for those guys getting away with it that they don't quite realize how much Lancaster is over the edge.

Q: *Any other regrets?*

A: Well, every picture has one target or goal. With *Twilight,* the ambiguity is supposed to be that you could argue, equally forcefully, two propositions—first, that they really intended to kill the President all along, and second, that the President was killed by accident because it was more important that the terrorists not get away. I wanted to give equal substance to both those arguments. But my guess is that we tipped the thing in favor of the idea that the Security Council intended all along to kill the President. We shouldn't have. You should come out of the picture feeling a true ambivalence.

Q: *Why didn't you use your regular director of photography, Joseph Biroc, on* Twilight?

A: His wife got a very massive seizure about two weeks before we were starting the picture. He just couldn't leave for Germany. Fortunately, she's recovered; she walks five miles a day. He's working again: He did *The Moneychangers* for television and he's going to do my next picture, *The Choirboys.* But Robert Hauser did a very good job on *Twilight.*

Q: *Do you think you lost anything by shooting* Twilight *in a country other than the one where it was taking place?*

A: No. I had a great art director—Rolf Zehetbauer, who had done *Cabaret.* Maybe next to Ken Adam he's the best art director in the world. Those things all work in the goddamn silo, because they had better research than we have. They had all the photographs down to the minutist detail. I don't know if they got if from the East Germans or where they got it, but they had it!

Q: *In the era of* Baby Jane *and* Lylah Clare *you were known as a director who dealt a lot with women. Now you're sometimes called "Mr. Macho"? How did this happen?*

A: I don't know. I get asked that question all the time, not usually that politely. "Why do you downgrade women?" In point of fact, I always thought of myself as a guy who was very fond of ladies, and I thought I worked with them very well. I take a very tough view of ladies. Long before liberation, I thought they were to be reckoned with. They're not docile, they're not subservient, they're not secondary citizens. They kill you as much as you kill them!

We actually shot two scenes for *Twilight* with Vera Miles as the First Lady, and she was very very good. We did a domestic scene in which she realized that being the wife of the President was no fun at all. And we did a scene in which he says goodbye. I cut the first scene out because the picture was too long, and it didn't move the story. And I cut the goodbye scene out because it tipped the scales too much in terms of "Is he going to get killed?" I was very proud of both scenes. Now another Aldrich picture comes out and there are no ladies in it!

Lorimar bought a book last year all about a girl, *Who Is Killing the Great Chefs of Europe?* Now, even though my company bought it, they're going to make it without me, because I'm going to be doing *The Choirboys* for them. That's the way it happens.

Q: *Tell me about* Choirboys. *From the reviews, I gather that the novel is another one of Joseph Wambaugh's examinations of the frustrations of being a Los Angeles cop. As I recall, it's about a group of ten cops who call themselves "The Choirboys" and who eventually take out their frustrations by killing an innocent homosexual. Your own anti-authoritarianism would seem in conflict with Wambaugh's sympathetic view of the cop.*

A: Well, *Choirboys* is an enormous problem. It's a best-selling book, it has had an enormous circulation. And I think Mr. Wambaugh is going to be very unhappy with this film of his work. I haven't figured out yet how to correct some of the things that are in the book and still make people who read the book want to see the movie—but I do intend to figure it out. You see, I think Wambaugh's feelings for "the problems of the cop" are probably genuine, and I don't think they're phony, but I don't feel the same way. I don't find the fact that cops can't "cope" particularly rewarding; I can't relate to it. I don't know how to feel sorry for a cop. It's a volunteer force. You're not drafted to become a cop. So you've got to take some of the heat if you don't like what people think about you. After all, that's an extraordinary pension you get in twenty years; nobody else gets it. In fact, I disagree with Wambaugh to such an extent that I don't think people really *like* cops.

Q: *That would be hard to prove from the ratings of TV shows.*

A: Yeah, but *those* cops you see do humane and unlikely things. And in *The Choirboys,* they don't. All the more credit to Wambaugh. They're not card-board heroes; they don't do very nice things. But Wambaugh doesn't go far enough for me. For instance, he really doesn't touch the problem of white cops isolating the black cops and putting them in Watts and never using them. And he certainly wouldn't agree with me that the Los Angeles police force is murderous in terms of their attitude towards the public, particularly when the public is black or minority. In New York, cops are on the take. Out there, the cops aren't on the take, but they've traded that in for the opportu-nity to be stormtroopers. The SLA shootout wouldn't have happened in any other city in the country. Anywhere else, the cops would have surrounded the house, they would have sat there for three weeks, the SLA would have eventually given themselves up, and it would have been over. So I think you've got to show L.A. cops as brutal as they really are. And Wambaugh can't face that problem, so it's never touched in the book.

Q: *Do you have any other projects?*

A: Well, I'm trying to get Abe Polonsky to write a film for me. I *really* want to make a political picture, a *real* political picture, that says that the continu-ation of these kinds of governments we've been having can't solve our prob-lems, won't come to grips with them. And I'm having great difficulty convincing Abe to do the screenplay. He doesn't necessarily want to make a picture that is that bleak, or is that alarming. And he said, "Sylvia [Polonsky's wife] is gonna call you a Stalinist if you want to make that picture." I said, "Abe, you can call me anything you want to. The point is: Unless somebody admits that you got cancer, you're not going to cure it. Nobody says that these problems are insoluble, that they're not going to go away. Carter, Ford won't talk about them." Well, you can see the problems. Big problem to convince him; I don't blame Polonsky for being slow to want to do that picture. I don't know if I'm going to convince him or not.

The idea is for a big picture—not a little picture, bigger than *Twilight,* more athletic than *Twilight,* more trappings of suspense and such—that said to you that the American people lost control of the Revolution. And it doesn't look like they're going to control it. Those guys sitting in Philadelphia never fig-ured out that there are insoluble problems that 200 years of democracy don't let us resolve. And the only solution for this is some kind of benign "ism"—I don't care what you call it: socialism, fascism, statism—to take over for a ten-year period in order to get at the root causes of all our problems, such as the inner cities and the oppression of blacks. You set a conspiracy afoot of people who are going to take over the government, and they've given themselves a self-destruct mechanism that will put them out of business in ten years. They would say: "Look. There's no way the great things about this country can be preserved unless we can solve these problems. Our system of democracy doesn't *let* us solve these problems. So it all goes on unchecked. Well, we're going to put our system in the icebox for ten years. You're going to have to live with that. And here's the proof of our intentions: We're going to give it back to you in ten years. Meanwhile, we can't solve these problems by having different faces saying the same things."

I think some kind of picture like this should be made. If I don't make it, I think somebody should make it. I'm apprehensive that nobody's going to make it.

Q : *If somebody else makes it, that wouldn't be the first time that somebody else made something that you wanted to make. I'm referring to the well-publicized case of* The Yakuza.

A : I've always regretted not making that picture—one of the few pictures I really wanted to make. Even though I wasn't getting along with Paul Schrader, the scriptwriter, and it was clear that he wasn't going to make the changes in the script that I wanted. It was a *terrible* script, I thought, but a *sensational* idea. I said, "If I'm going to make this picture, I'm going to turn this script upside down." I saw it one particular way, and Paul didn't see it that way—and Warners didn't see it that way, either. Still, it might have happened my way if Lee Marvin had been cast in the lead. I'm not sure of that—because Marvin had been in the Marine Corps, and he had certain preconceived attitudes about the Japanese, so I'm not sure we would have agreed on the viewpoint in *Yakuza*. But things never reached that point with Marvin, because he got mad at Warner Brothers over—I think it was $10,000. $10,000 was between Lee and Warners and Marvin wouldn't give. He hanged himself on $10,000. So then they cast Mitchum, and my doing *Yakuza* or not came down to Mitchum's okay.

Well, Mitchum. I have a great admiration for Mitchum—not shared. When I was an assistant at RKO, and Mitchum was doing Zane Greys over there and was marvelous, I went over to be Wellman's assistant on *The Story of G.I. Joe,* and we couldn't find a guy for G.I. Joe. And I said, "You know, there's a cowboy actor at RKO and he's tremendous," and Wellman had Mitchum brought over, and Mitchum did a test and he was absolutely brilliant. He stole the picture from Burgess Meredith, which wasn't easy to do, and his career was off. Years later, we did a picture together in Greece, terrible picture, a Leon Uris novel, a joke, called *The Angry Hills.*

I really considered him my friend, and I admired him. I think he's a brilliant actor—a strange, convoluted guy. I knew I wasn't his favorite director, but I never really knew he disliked me. But when it came to discussing *The Yakuza,* we both assumed positions of power. He wouldn't come to my office; I wouldn't go to his office. Who's going to meet whom where to decide to make the picture? Finally Frank Wells, who was then president of Warners, said, "What if I get you two assholes a bungalow at the Beverly Hills Hotel? Would you meet there?" We each agreed to that, and from six o'clock to midnight that night we met at this bungalow. It was a Liz Taylor sort of bungalow—it wasn't two rooms, it was *ten rooms.* He finished off a whole bottle of Jack Daniels, so I felt obliged to finish off a Johnny Walker Black. I drink pretty well—but I don't drink like *that,* not any more.

And in those six hours, we never talked about the movie one minute. We talked about the days at RKO, we talked about our mutual friends, we talked about *G.I. Joe,* we talked about *Angry Hills.* Never mentioned *Yakuza.* Ten o'clock the next morning, which was a Sunday—naturally I had the world's worst hangover—Frank Wells called me. He said, "How do you think it went?" I said, "I don't know a fucking thing about how it went. I haven't the faintest idea." On Monday morning he called me and said, "Mitchum turned you down." Too bad. I think it was possible to make a marvelous movie out of *Yakuza.*

Q: *You were quoted at the time as feeling that Mitchum and Warners had been affected by the poor grosses for your then most recent films,* Ulzana's Raid *and* Emperor of the North.

A: I'll never understand exactly why *Emperor of the North* failed. I thought the symbols were so clear. It never occurred to me that the audience would miss the relationship—that Borgnine was the Establishment, that Marvin was the anti-Establishment individualistic character, and that Keith Carradine was the opportunistic youth who would sell out for whatever was most convenient. I never thought that people wouldn't root for the Marvin character. I thought everyone would say, "I understand what Marvin is. He's trying not to be regimented and suppressed, and denied his rights, and I'm for him." And nobody was. It just didn't happen. Nobody cared.

Q : *Some people think that the commercial problem derived from the Carradine character.*
A : I think that Keith Carradine, if he's careful—I don't think he *is* careful—and if he's prudent about the selection of his parts, can be a great big movie star. I think that whoever's advising him is making some terrible selections about material. Because I think the guy is gifted, he's talented, he's attractive. He was good in *Emperor.* He didn't care who won between Borgnine and Marvin; he was going to end up on the winning side. He represented the post-Vietnam era, when everyone went back to sleep and said, "I don't care. It's over. I'm gonna play melody."

Q : *But he was the only representative of youth in the film, and I don't think young people like to think of themselves that way.*
A : I don't care!

Q : *Young audiences wanted that character to be an "innocent."*
A : Yeah, but they're not innocent! Or I don't think they are—and I got four kids to prove it who are cynical and smart and *deadly.* They're *too* smart—a lot smarter than I ever was—and they're opportunistic. And their ideals? They left them in the closet!

Q : *How much input did you have into* Ulzana's Raid?
A : Oh, very much. From the time we started to the time we finished the picture, I'd say fifty, sixty percent of it was changed. Alan Sharp, the writer, was very amenable and terribly helpful. And terribly prolific. He can write twenty-five pages a day. He couldn't agree more with my political view-point—so that was no problem. And fortunately, Lancaster and I felt pretty much the same about the picture. It was good that I had support from Sharp and Lancaster, because I don't have the highest regard for Carter DeHaven, the producer.

Q : *How much were you and Lancaster aware of making a kind of updating of* Apache?

A: A lot. It was kind of an inside joke between Burt and me. In *Apache,* the Indian scout was played by an actor named John McIntire. And in *Ulzana* we named the Indian scout—the part Burt played—John McIntosh. I'm not sure that Alan Sharp ever knew just why we did that.

I was very proud of *Ulzana's Raid* and *Emperor of the North*. But you can make three or four of those in a row, and you'll be back doing television. No way you're going to make three or four million dollar pictures that *die*. I don't care how well they do critically; nobody wants to know you. We misjudged the audience, or misjudged the application of those stories. We misjudged something. Fortunately, I got lucky with *The Longest Yard*. People who are in my business—and I'm not in the Bergman-Fellini business, that's another business, I don't know how to do that—people who are in my business have to have a commercial success every two or three years, certainly every third picture, fourth at the most, or you're in terrible, terrible trouble.

Q: The Longest Yard *was a late starter. I remember that at first business wasn't so hot—perhaps as a result of bad reviews.*
A: It was a very nervous first few weeks. I don't have to defend Burt Reynolds, but I think that on occasion he's a much better actor than he's given credit for. Not always: sometimes he acts like a caricature of himself. I thought he was very good in *Longest Yard*—not so good in *Hustle*—but very good in *Longest Yard* for what he had to do. So, when *Longest Yard* opened in New York, Vince Canby was out of town, and Nora Sayre really cut the picture to ribbons in the *Times,* and jumped all over Burt.

Now I've known Vince well since he was on *Variety*. So I wrote to him: "I don't care what you say about the picture, what you say about me. But Burt worked his ass off, and he was really dismissed, and I'd really appreciate it if you'd take a look at him." So Vince took a look at the picture, and a couple of subsequent Sundays later he really kicked the shit out of Burt all over again! The moral of this story is: The smart thing to do is to keep your mouth shut and your head down.

Q: *What do you think of Reynolds in the Bogdanovich pictures?*
A: Bogdanovich can get him to do the telephone book! Anybody else has to persuade him to do something. He's *fascinated* by Bogdanovich. I can't understand it.

Q: *How was Catherine Deneuve cast in* Hustle?
A: Burt got the script from the writer, Steve Shagan. He came to me—we were in Georgia on *Longest Yard*—and I said, "I'll do this picture on one condition: that you help me get Miss Chanel." Because the woman's part had been written for an American, and I didn't think it worked that way. I think our middleclass mores just don't make it credible that a policeman have a love relationship with a prostitute. Because of some strange quirk in our backgrounds, the mass audience doesn't believe it. It's perfectly all right as long as she's not American. So Burt accepted this as a condition, and we put up our money and went to Paris, and waited on the great lady for a week, and she agreed to do the picture.

Q: *All of your recent films, all the ones we've been talking about, are about futile struggles. Nobody wins in your films.*
A: I disagree. Perhaps they don't "win." But I like to believe that my indelible trademark is my affection for the struggle to regain self-esteem. Now, the likelihood of doing that is remote. Still, it's the costs that make it into a gallant struggle. In *The Longest Yard,* perhaps Burt Reynolds is not going to have a happy prison life; perhaps he's not going to go on living at all. And in *Emperor,* perhaps Lee Marvin hasn't really prevailed over anything. But in each case a man has fallen from grace, done something he's ashamed of, and then struggled to recapture his opinion of himself. Now, I think the odds against succeeding in doing that are overwhelming. It's not in the cards that that's probably going to happen. But I think you admire the people beside you who say, "The hell with it. I'm not going to quit. I don't give a shit what other people think about me. I'm going to try and hold myself in esteem." That's what all these pictures are *really* about.

Q: *You know, it's always struck me that an impersonal director like J. Lee Thompson or Edward Dmytryk or Stuart Rosenberg . . .*
A: . . . or Richard Fleischer . . .

Q: *. . . or Richard Fleischer can have four or five flops in a row, and keep on getting films to make. The process you were talking about before doesn't seem to apply to them. Nobody blames them. But if you, or Sam Peckinpah, or Robert Altman— people who rewrite the scripts they're given, who alter the movies to their personal concepts—have two or three flops in a row, everybody gets scared.*

A: Well, they should. If you're capable of forcing your will, if you say, "I want to do it *this* way," and then it falls on its ass, you can't turn around and blame someone else. You made them do it that way. You can't keep on asking a series of guys to put up money after your last three films were disasters. If you want to take the bows, you also have to take the rejection.

Interview with Robert Aldrich

CHRIS PETIT AND RICHARD COMBS/
1977

THE FOLLOWING IS AN AMALGAMATION of two separate
interviews conducted with Robert Aldrich: one by Chris Petit in August 1977;
the second by Richard Combs in January 1978. We have tried to avoid topics
that have been extensively covered in the many interviews with Aldrich
already published, except where a comment may shed additional light on a
particular film or subject. The most useful of the existing interviews have
been quoted after each entry in the filmography, to provide a loose career
commentary. This piece therefore concentrates more on themes and attitudes, attempting to make connections between the films in terms of Aldrich's ideas on politics, his subject matter and filmmaking in general.

Q : Twilight's Last Gleaming, *which was certainly one of your best films in recent*
years, now seems to have disappeared altogether.
A : I just finished cutting the television version, which I think is really quite
good. They're going to run it full length, which is helpful. It's two hours and
twenty-three or twenty-four minutes—I think because of profanity we lost a
few minutes. I still think it's a marvellous movie; you're faced with the fact
that if nobody goes to see it, there's something wrong with it.

Q : *Were you consulted on the cuts that Hemdale made in England? They cut not*
only some of the consultation scenes between the President and his advisers, which

From *Robert Aldrich*, ed. Richard Combs (London: British Film Institute, 1978), 37–48.
Reprinted by permission.

they said held up the action, but such odd details as the moment at the beginning when the President cuts himself shaving. That was done, apparently, because they didn't think it proper that the President should be heard to say "shit."

A : I wouldn't have thought they would cut that. We thought that was rather important symbolically. Those kinds of things become capricious and cavalier, and you either jump out the window or you shrug and go on to the next thing.

Lorimar came to me and said look, you don't have final cut but you have consultation. Hemdale wants to cut approximately twenty-five or thirty minutes, and their position is, if they can't cut it they won't release it. We had died in America, in Italy, and Canada, and I said I won't, at this late date, stand in your way for a territorial sale, because if the point isn't made on Americans in two hours and twenty-seven minutes, you can't really expect it to be made on the English. So I waived my right to protest.

Q : *One problem with the film is that it begins very awkwardly. Although it would be difficult to get round in terms of the action, one feels that the film should begin with Dell and his men already in the silo.*

A : We thought about that question. Not put quite that way but basically the same misgivings about what kind of movie we were telling, and were we being misleading. But there is such a false conception about the security of those things that we thought people would say, this could never happen, this is a fairy-tale, this is just another science-fiction picture. Well, if you read the papers, it's not that imaginary and it's not that safe, and all countries should be worried about this. So we thought the lesser of two evils was to have the false start, or the athletic start, to establish the credibility, and then get into the story, rather than pick them up down in the silo and say, now fellers, we've got a problem.

Q : *The balance of the characters in* Twilight *was very interesting, and particularly the way the weight was gradually shifted from the Lancaster to the Durning character.*

A : There are some marvellous nuances in American politics, in American levels of political thinking, in that picture. What you discover is that there is no room for purity at either end of the spectrum. To survive you have to operate somewhere between the purity of the idealistic innocents at both ends. You're not going to get through the game if you don't find some middle ground. Also, treachery comes from the most unexpected quarters. You spend the whole film building up the Secretary of Defense as the last honourable man, then you see that under certain pressures he's not going to fulfill either. That's why Billy Preston sings "America." You realise that if people like the Secretary of Defense are betraying the national good, what happens to the black man who really wants to become integrated, to become part of the whole fabric. What real chance does he have—isn't he going to be fucked forever? You and I know that Billy Preston didn't sing that song for that picture, but it grew out of his total inability to join with what he wanted to join. It was uniquely identifiable with that picture. And that was totally missed.

Q : *The hope of the film seemed to be that the pragmatic characters and the idealistic ones might somehow pool their strengths and check each other's weaknesses.*
A : In the book, those guys were killed and the President lived. I found that unrealistic and, well, there was no social comment in the book at all.

I do think there has been a growing up process in this country. I don't want to pretend that it had been completed during the Kennedy administration, but I do think that the country, for one reason or another, had faith in the Kennedy brothers. I do think that we quickly learned, after Vienna anyway, that they weren't as smart as we hoped they were. But they were smart enough to know that they needed to grow. And you respected and/or loved them, and you had hope for that. I think the reverse is true with Carter; you really thought he was smart, now you find out that he's dumb and that he's getting dumber every day. I think there was a fundamental idealistic undercurrent, but the Kennedys were totally pragmatic politicians. To preach civil freedom in Argentina or Korea or Poland is a joke—a cruel joke, but a joke.

Q : *There is usually some sort of learning process in your films—characters are continually redressing each other's balance.*
A : But don't you find that true? I think history is filled with unwise martyrs. There's nothing wrong with being a martyr, if you know beforehand that being a martyr is going to advance the cause, which most martyrs don't. Life, it seems to me, is filled with knowing that you can rock the boat just so far; if you rock it beyond that, you're not really going to make any substantial change because they're going to get rid of you. I mean, they're not necessarily going to kill you, they're not necessarily going to have to send you to

Siberia. But they're going to find a way to excommunicate you from that society. So you've got to find—and it's very difficult—how far you can push and still stay in the ball game. You have to come right up to that edge. What I think you find in most countries, and certainly in most industries, is that people stop—not out of cowardice, out of a sense of survival—far short of the edge.

Q: *You have a particular affinity for characters who are prepared to go that far, even if it also seems to involve a dangerously unstable neurotic quality.*
A: True. But you wouldn't have said that a couple of years ago about Burt Reynolds, and he did it in *The Longest Yard.* It's the same character superimposed on another background. It's Palance in *Attack* and *The Big Knife*; it's Lancaster in *Apache* and *Ulzana's Raid.* Most of all, it's in the picture that I really feel responsible for—regardless of how badly it was done—the Gogol story that I sold to Hecht-Lancaster. The whole concept of *Taras Bulba* was how far can you push a society and not have the retribution be so terrible that . . . I think that's the most interesting thing in the political-social aspect of life: how far can you push? Certainly, it's stolen lock, stock, and barrel from what I perceive to be the wisdom of the Polonsky hero in *Body and Soul.* The people audiences really love or identify with are those who fall from grace. It's their own opinion of themselves that makes them function, not somebody else's, not outside society's. And to regain their image of themselves, to redeem their self-respect, they'll do anything. Therefore they're to be admired; you can accept failure on that level. If you don't stray too far from that central character the audience will understand, no matter what he does. They may not root for him, but they'll love him. When I failed to do that, as I did in *Ulzana,* it puts the audience in a position where they don't know how to judge.

Q: *Games crop up a lot in your films. But the use of football references in* Twilight *is particularly interesting.*
A: I think this country is given to that. Certainly I am. It's probably a middle-class attitude, but it's one that has instant communication, a shorthand, for ninety per cent of the people. They say, oh, that's who he is, now I know everything I need to know about him, I know how he's going to react. It's a vice, but a practical one. You should be bright enough to be able to sketch that character without that shorthand, but it's easier to do it that way.

Q : *But it also works in more complicated ways, when you realise that the frame of reference of the military aides is the same as that of the more obviously childish, anarchic Burt Young character.*

A : I think it works. I think what happens in both instances is that all the games turn out to be more serious. They can play them as third persons, but they never think they're going to be involved. It's always as if somebody else's going to die whether they lose the game or not. The thought was that Burt Young is the most surprised man in the world that the game is going to end up in his death. And the President's staff is never involved in first person singular death. Except for the President.

Q : Ulzana's Raid *actually begins with the soldiers playing baseball.*

A : At that end, you needed to know the strengths and weaknesses of the Jaeckel character right away. And what did they do in the middle of those goddamned camps?

Q : *With* Apache, *the Cherokee demonstrated a positive alternative for the Indian: the possibility of integration, the corn. In* Ulzana, *the only alternative to the reservation is death. Which do you think the truer picture?*

A : In *Apache* there was no white man to speak for the strength and integrity of the Indian. You only had a self-serving statement by Indians about Indians. In *Ulzana,* I hoped that by having Lancaster speak for the Indians you got an educated and experienced point of view on their culture and what that meant. It worked, but not for the audience. They sat there and knew what he was saying but didn't emotionally relate to it. They don't know whether he's the good guy or the bad guy. They're sorry to see him die but they don't really understand whether he represents good or evil.

Q : *But it seems a very futile film and not particularly to do with good and evil. The film seems more like a text on guerrilla tactics. Were we meant to pick up on the fairly obvious references to the white man's very uncertain hold on a hostile country?*

A : That was Alan Sharp, the writer. We had constant fights with the producer over it. Sharp, Lancaster, and I totally believed in the parallel with Vietnam. The producer thought the public would see it immediately and if they did that would lessen the film's chances of economic survival. We tried to do it all the same.

Q: *Was there originally more in the film about Lancaster's "Indian woman"?*
A: Yes.

Q: *Talking of political references, with the train sequences in* Apache *was there a deliberate parallel between the Apaches and the Jews?*
A: It came up very early in discussion. Harold Hecht, who produced the picture, was very sensitive about it. He wondered if anyone would be upset because the parallel was too close. The parallel wasn't in the book and crept into the picture a little bit because of the script, but on a very low level.

Q: *Describing* Kiss Me Deadly *as an anti-McCarthy picture is now something of a cliché, but could you elaborate?*
A: Fascinating thing, Bezzerides and I thought we were making a real important statement. We were very apprehensive because it was such an uncomfortable time and it would bring down a lot of heat on us. Nobody, but nobody in the United States picked up on it at all. When the picture got to Europe, the French in particular picked up on it immediately.

Q: *Did you contribute a lot to the script?*
A: Bezzerides and I worked very hard on it. We took an awful chance. In Spillane's book it was jewels, but what the hell are you going to do with another jewel heist? It seemed to us that the only way to inject any political significance—and that's already a heavy word—any uniqueness, was to say what if the secret were the atomic weapon? Once we made that decision everything fell into place.

Q: *All the art references?*
A: That's all Bezzerides.

Q: *And va-va-voom?*
A: Va-va-voom was Nick Dennis. He asked me if he could use it. I'd love to take credit for it because it's become part of the language.

Q: *It's odd that after doing something as cinematic as* Kiss Me Deadly *you did two rather stagebound play adaptations.*
A: For the young producer, plays present the easiest form for getting development money. Any idiot can read a play: that's the beginning, that's the

middle. I see what's going to happen. You tell somebody an idea and they're lost. They don't want to give you the money to develop it because it requires judgment.

Q : *Steiger's performance in* The Big Knife *was so outrageously "Method." Was that something designed between the two of you?*
A : Two things happened. We decided to steal from Mayer, Cohn, and Warner. Now Steiger has about as much humour as terminal cancer—fine actor, though. Warner's a very funny guy, tough as nails but funny. Because of Steiger's lack of humour we were reduced to using Cohn and Mayer as models. Secondly, Steiger's capacity to infuriate Palance was extraordinary. So I kept using that, and the more I used it, the more outrageous Steiger became through taking advantage. It helped the movie, though. One day I had to break off shooting and send everyone home early: I thought Palance was going to kill him because he was so outrageous and intent on stealing everything including the set. But it helped the acrimony and animosity between the two characters, so I let them go ahead.

Q : *Was Monty Ritt's party a private joke in* The Big Knife?
A : Yes.

Q : *What was the dispute over your work on* The Garment Jungle?
A : It was a very tough picture. It was about how the garment workers, who are predominantly Jewish, employed the Mafia, which is predominantly Italian, to protect them against the manufacturers, who are also Jewish. And so the manufacturers, to protect themselves against the Mafia protecting the workers, also hired the Mafia to protect them. And they were really ruthless, because they got different families of the Mafia. It was a marvellous conflict—racial, social, religious. Halfway through, Cohn realized it was going to be a very tough, bitter, nasty picture, and he got frightened. I got fired because I wanted to stay with what was there; Cohn wanted to change it. It was directed by a nice man, who was famous as a woman's director [Vincent Sherman]. It was very quiet and very mild; it became a love story, also about a father who wanted to give his business to his son, all that bullshit.

Q : *You then did two pictures in Europe, including* The Angry Hills *in Greece. Robert Mitchum would seem to be a natural actor for you to work with, yet you've only made this one film with him.*

A : It's a five hour story. I'm very fond of Mitchum. I was an assistant when he was doing those Zane Grey Westerns at RKO. I think he's a marvellous actor. But that opinion isn't mutually shared. We've missed doing a couple of pictures together because he doesn't think I'm a very good director.

We were about a week into the film [*The Angry Hills*] living in a sensational place outside Athens. The picture was going terribly. So one evening after dinner I walked down to Mitchum's cabaña at the other end of the beach. I told him, "We're making a lousy movie. I'm trying the best I can, and I sense you are, but it's not working and I don't know what to do." "Don't you understand what we're making?" he said. "We're making a gorilla picture." What was a gorilla picture, I asked. "A gorilla picture is when you get 250,000 dollars for doing all the wrong things for ten reels and in the last shot you get the girl and fade into the sunset. That's a gorilla picture. I don't care how well you make it, it's still going to be a gorilla picture. Now if you understand that, you'll be very happy. If you don't, you'll be very unhappy." "I don't understand that," I said. "So I'm going to be very unhappy. I don't want to make a gorilla picture."

Q : *Not just because of Deneuve, there seemed to be a definite influence of European cinema in* Hustle, *a mix of European and American.*
A : I spent a lot of time in Europe in the middle '50s. I lived in Italy for three years and there was nothing to do in time off. The American community is pretty small. You just run picture after picture. There aren't that many American ones so you run French and Italian ones. Maybe some of that rubbed off. It wasn't intentional.

Q : *None the less, the references to Lelouch and the feel of Deneuve's relationship with Reynolds are more what one is accustomed to seeing in European films.*
A : That was intentional. We have a whole section in this country, laughingly referred to as the Bible Belt, though it's bigger than that. It is very conservative and those people would find it hard to believe that an upright guy like Reynolds was in the film could fall in love with a prostitute. He might want to live with her, he might want to bang her, but not be in love with her. However, you move that prostitute 3,000 miles and give her foreign origins, they understand it immediately, because of two world wars. There's no moral gap.

I'd love to do another picture with Deneuve. She's a better actress than she was in that picture. I don't know why. I think probably we should have rehearsed more. But she didn't want to rehearse. She's not a stage actress, and felt uncomfortable rehearsing.

Q: *What was your disagreement with Joseph Wambaugh on* The Choirboys? *I notice that only Christopher Knopf gets script credit on the film.*
A: Knopf did the end. The book ends in MacArthur Park, with two police-man talking about the demise of the human soul, or whatever. I didn't think that was a very appropriate way to end the picture, and we asked Knopf to come in and do another ending. Wambaugh did six or seven scripts, and in the arbitration of the Writers Guild it was agreed that 90 percent of the work was Wambaugh's and 10 percent was Knopf's. But Knopf had changed the intent of the work, and that's why they allowed Wambaugh to take his name off. It's unusual, I think, that 10 percent of the work changes the intent. So all those things are written by Wambaugh; he wrote a dirty, tasteless, vulgar book, which I think I've managed to capture. But what he would like to have you think is that we changed the thrust of those scenes—those scenes are word for word from his screenplays. Knopf never even touched them. We changed the ending from pablum Sartre to something in connection with the episodic comedy we'd been telling. Wambaugh was furious. He wants to write the Great American Tragedy. As a matter of fact, we shot that ending of his. We didn't arbitrarily say, well it has no merit. We shot it with some very good actors. As I suspected, it turns the play around, it turns the whole piece into a philosophical diatribe about what life is all about and the meaningless-ness of it and how everybody's a piece of shit. It's nonsense. It went out of style twenty years ago, and if it ever was in style, it wasn't the style for this kind of a movie.

Q: *What did you want to achieve with the new ending? Was it to give more sub-stance to the Charles Durning character and in some way "rescue" him?*
A: The Indian, as you may remember in *One Flew Over the Cuckoo's Nest,* was an added thought. It was not in the play. And the Indian made that picture. I think if you stopped *Cuckoo's Nest* with the frontal lobotomy, it would have been a disaster. The Indian gave you your hope back. I discussed this many times with Wambaugh, and he wanted that ersatz Sartre ending. By extend-ing the picture to a hopeful resolution, certainly not a happy one, you have

a chance to expand the character of Durning and give him some redemption and self-esteem. There was no self-esteem in the book for anybody.

Q: *The main problem with the film, and the book, was the unjustified attempt to lend some coherence and significance to the anecdotal plot with the business of the MacArthur Park killing. The Vietnam prologue also seemed an inadequate way of giving the incident psychological validity.*
A: Everybody hated that, and I thought it worked. Wambaugh thought it worked. We fought off the philistines, as he's fond of saying. The problem is very simple. The story is basically a patrol story, but the way that book was set up structurally there was no place for anybody to fall on the hand grenade. Those pictures require *something* to coalesce the patrol around, usually a heroic act or a self-sacrificial act or a brotherly act, so that you bring all the dissidents into a single thrust for a goal. Now, the way that was written, there was no place to put those ten guys under a mutual jeopardy. So that there was no mutual goal, illicit or otherwise. That's what really makes it tough to root for those guys, because they are all a little shady or a little dicey. If you had seen one act of mutual courage, that they all exercised for the benefit of one another, then that would be a perfect balance, but we couldn't come up with that.

I made a mistake. In my contract, I have two previews. I always go to a very tough city for the second, so I went to Madison, Wisconsin, for the first one, because I really wanted to see what a youthful audience would think about this picture. And we didn't get the youthful audience, we got a lot of blue collar people, elderly people. I had the picture at about two hours and sixteen minutes, and it was obviously long for that audience. The distributors, and Lorimar, really started worrying about its length, and rightly so. But by cutting it to two hours, you lose a lot of the understanding of why some of those ten guys behave the way they do, because they're all expository and not action or comedy scenes. Now that's fine if you have a thematic story that has a beginning, a middle and an end. But in an episodic story you really need to know more about those people and what happens to them. And I made a mistake: I cut that expository material for the New York preview. Now the New York preview was sensational. As you could imagine, it was an urban audience, a lot of blacks, Puerto Ricans, blue collar, very few sophisticates. And they identified instantly with the anti-authoritarian theme; with their dislike for cops, they picked up on it immediately. Once having done that, there's no way you could make any logic in your head, let alone in anybody else's, for going back to two hours sixteen. So it's a trap I built for myself.

Q : *What was in the cut scenes?*
A : A marvellous scene between Don Stroud and his wife; two marvellous scenes between Bloomguard and his Vietnam buddy. And even more important, two long scenes with the eventual suicide, Perry King, to explain where his head was at, so you didn't think, as you do now in the picture, that he committed suicide only because he got caught in some deviant sex act. You realise that psychologically he was falling apart, that that happened to be the straw that broke the camel's back. But if it hadn't been that, it would have been something else. But without those character insights—and you knew much more about Spermwhale—it is truly episodic and just for laughs.

Q : *Did you see any relationship between the masochistic elements in Perry King's personality and Burt Reynolds in* Hustle?
A : Yeah, but he's in a cultural and social stratum, and comes from a snobbish, intellectual kind of background, that wasn't true of Reynolds. Reynolds was operating on a really pragmatic, day-to-day level, and the thing that really fucked up Perry King is that he couldn't make that adjustment from the idealistic to the practical.

Q : *How do you feel about the film now?*
A : I thought the screenplay, not the book, was hilarious. I thought it was outrageously funny. Now, obviously that view isn't shared by everybody, but that's why I did it. I realized the story-telling techniques were going to be difficult because they were jumpy and episodic; I thought it was funny enough to overcome that. I thought it was a broad-based audience picture; I didn't think it would ever be a "critic's picture" or a New York art picture. We aimed directly at a broad-based audience and I thought that they would react. Basically, they have.

Q : *Can we talk about something that isn't usually discussed: how much a film's style is determined by practical necessities rather than artistic intentions? And how much were you aware of an emerging style in your own work?*
A : A lot of people fail to understand how often practical considerations

intrude on what passes for style. I used a marvellous cameraman, Ernie Laszlo, for many years. I stopped using him because the rate at which we worked was too slow. I just couldn't get enough on film to allow me the latitude I like when editing. That, and an experience I had in Morocco and Italy, changed a lot of things. I made this terrible picture called *Sodom and Gomorrah* in the early '60s. Labour was very cheap, so I was using three and four cameras in an effort to speed up the production schedule because it was supposed to cost two million dollars and wound up costing six million. The picture was very, very long and we got into a legal hassle with the Italian government about who was the author of the film. Italy's a country like France which comes under the Napoleonic Code concept of authorship. So the producers were faced with a dilemma. If they accepted the Italian subsidy, which they needed to pay for the picture, that meant accepting Aldrich as author of the picture. This gave me a great deal of cutting prerogatives that I wouldn't have had if I'd just been hired in the States. We struck a compromise, rather than staying in court like that five-hour film of Bertolucci's. I agreed to reduce the film from something like four-and-a-half hours down to two hours twenty minutes. The only way it was possible to get any respectable movie out of it was because I had multiple coverage. If I had done that show like I had *Apache* or *Vera Cruz,* there wouldn't have been any way of truncating and compressing it. So I came back to this country convinced that trying to shoot a film with just one camera is nonsense. You're talking about shooting a lot of extra film and hiring an operating assistant, but these are more than balanced by your cutting latitude. Ever since then I've had as part of my contract a two-camera system. It's strange that an outrageous picture like *Sodom and Gomorrah* turned around the whole way that I shot pictures. With two or three cameras you can compress a sequence down to its essence. It also makes a picture move much better. Do it with one camera and you're going to have a four-hour movie. Then there's no way to compress it and you'd have to lift something out. So I think since *Sodom* most of my pictures—not all, *Lylah Clare* is a terrible example—have had much more energy and compression. That doesn't necessarily mean they're better, but they're different.

Q : *Some years ago you told Paul Mayersberg in* Movie *that you hated the process of editing because it's claustrophobic.*
A : I don't remember saying that. I don't like editing as much as I like shoot-

ing because it's more mechanical. But it's not because I don't like being closed in. It's more tedious and there's more drudgery involved. You sit there hour after hour and only occasionally can you be creative.

Q : *Shooting's the stage you like most?*
A : It's the most intense and the most rewarding. I've come to rely more than most on rehearsal. Everybody thinks they're rehearsing for their own benefit, which is good. In point of fact, what's happening is that I'm rehearsing. It's an obvious and overt brain-picking session when I get the final fix in my mind. Right down to the propman, somebody always contributes to these sessions. If there's one thing that separates the good director from the not-so-good, and this includes every director I've met, with the exception of Chaplin, it's that the good ones accept ideas regardless of where they come from. The others, either because they're insecure or for some reason that's totally unclear to me, won't accept them. They have a fix on a scene, a script, or a sequence, and stay with it. Somebody will always have a better idea for part of it, even a tiny part of it. It's nonsense not to accept those ideas or not to admit that they're better than yours.

Q : *On a number of occasions you've talked about what you learned working as an assistant to good directors. Were there any cautionary lessons you picked up from the bad ones?*
A : If you put Losey on one side and say that of all the people you've ever worked with he's probably the best with actors, then go to the other end of the spectrum, you realise that with the less talented or accomplished directors, some of their problems grow out of their inability or unwillingness to get along with actors. Granted, not many people can manufacture the kind of camaraderie of which Losey is capable. But the name of the game is trying to make the best film possible, and I don't know anyone who has made many movies if director and actor are constantly in adversary positions. Of course that's such a general statement that it doesn't mean much. Chaplin, for instance, is terrible with actors other than himself because he hasn't any patience, and with very good reason. They're not as quick or as malleable, or don't readily see the opportunity he does. So it's unfair to say that's always true. He just doesn't get along with actors! You also learn that there's no way not to do your homework. It really shows up. Among the good directors too, unfortunately. But there is a consistency: better directors are better prepared.

It doesn't mean they've figured out every shot, but they've worked out what scenes should say, maybe even down to individual set-ups. Again there are exceptions. Milestone, for instance, used to sketch a picture before he met any of the actors. This builds in a rigidity, and it was very tough to move with or to get him off that. Now I'm sure that people can neither afford nor want the kind of painstaking care that Zinnemann exercises; but by and large the guy who has prepared has a better chance to do his best. Maybe his best doesn't measure up. Very strangely, this has nothing to do with economics. Cheap director, expensive director, it's just what they think.

Q: *You worked with Enterprise Studios in the '40s. It was run on very enlightened lines compared with other studios.*
A: Extraordinary undertaking. All the sentimental and emotional reasons for wanting it to survive prevailed because they had a very populist concept about how pictures should be made. David Loew was the money, from the Loew family. Charlie Einfeld was head of publicity and public relations at Warners. They formed a joint company called Enterprise and got a release from MGM, later through United Artists. We made twelve or thirteen pictures. It was a great idea. Everybody got life insurance, the barber was free, so were coffee and doughnuts. You could park on the lot which you couldn't on any of the others. All the marginal unimportant things but they soon add up. There was a great deal of employee participation. Unfortunately there was no real production supervisor. There was no poor man's Mayer or Warner or Cohn. Consequently they'd bring in producers—good, not so good, terrible—and there was nobody to whom they should report. There were two guys, a businessman and a public relations expert. They made no pretense at being able to make those kinds of terrible decisions. But they were called upon to do so, and almost always were wrong. Out of all the pictures, only one was moderately successful, *Body and Soul,* with John Garfield. And that cost too much because Rossen was afraid of Jimmy Wong Howe and the picture took too long. The other pictures were disasters. I was Milestone's assistant on *Arch of Triumph* which cost four million dollars. That's equivalent to sixteen or seventeen million dollars today. It was a marvellous place to work but the pictures were terrible!

Q: *A long time ago, Ida Lupino referred to you as the best director of women that she'd come across. This raises the inevitable question about women in your films. Apart from Deneuve in* Hustle, *there's been a noticeable absence.*

A : In this town, it's not how you perceive yourself, it's how others perceive you. I'm thoroughly proud of my ability to get along with women. I think they're much easier to direct than men: they're more malleable, they're more giving and, strangely, they're not as vain. I thought, regardless of its economic success, that *Sister George* was maybe the best directing job I ever did. One I badly botched up was *Lylah Clare* and that wasn't Kim Novak's fault. I just could never convince myself, and therefore the audience, of the credibility of the situation. I never got the script right, *ergo* I never got the picture right. That's why the picture failed, it had nothing to do with my rapport with Kim and her performance. She was marvellous. I think I do very well with women. I'm involved in a project now which I like very much; it concerns two women.

Q : *Was* Billy Two Hats *once your project?*
A : I hadn't met the writer Alan Sharp then, but I loved the script. I thought it was one of the best Western scripts I'd read. We optioned it originally for six months, then for a further nine, but I couldn't get anyone to take it. I intentionally stayed away from the film, Gregory Peck being in it. Terrible casting. I had such high hopes for that film and I couldn't get anyone behind it.

Q : *What happened to* The Biggest Mother of Them All?
A : I have it around for the rare occasion somebody wants to see it. The goddamned thing ended up costing about 150,000 dollars. A thirty-minute monument to my misjudgment of who can act and who can't, so I'm understandably reluctant to show it. It's a marvellous piece of film in terms of wouldn't this make a great movie, if we could find the right girl. Maybe there are girls now, but this new Californian child pornography law would need very careful examination.

Q : *What projects are you involved in at the moment?*
A : I'm trying to find a big athletic picture that has to do with revolution—in some other country, you couldn't do it here, but where people will be able to read in that it could happen here, if it was a truly idealistic revolution. A revolution that really only benefited the people, that wasn't for the usual purposes of power or privilege. A real revolution in which the hero again asserts his self-esteem, in the view not only of himself but also, quote, the

people. And that picture I think would do wonderfully well. I don't know what it is yet, but I think that's the kind of picture to make. You can tell the story in action rather than in dialogue, but you could make the same point.

Q : *Is this the project you wanted to work on with Polonsky?*
A : No. Polonsky and I were going to do a picture about the South Seas that dealt with the same problem. It dealt with how to nationalise the remaining islands in the trust territories. Some of them have accepted the kind of supervision that Puerto Rico has. But there's a whole bunch of islands that haven't decided, and it's fascinating what is making them make the choice between becoming in essence a colony or staying independent. The story has a modern background—I mean, it's not Captain Bligh—it's 1978, '79. I don't know if it's going to go through or not. Polonsky has developed a concept from a book that I bought, a dull book but which has the seeds of a marvellous idea. He's a consummate storyteller anyway, and when he goes and tells that story to the people who will have to put up the money for the development of a very expensive picture, they're spellbound, but they say, that's such eloquent bullshit I wonder if I'm really being conned. Sure they're being conned a little, but not much. It's sad, because it's a tremendous story, and terribly cinematic. It's all visual, and nobody's ever seen the modern culture clash in those islands. We reward guys by sending them to the University of Hawaii, so that they can go back and do what? What are they going to do with a college education—pick more coconuts? There's nothing for them to do. It's a tragic situation. You see all these young kids on mopeds, and the children get all kinds of diseases from improper nutrition. And we're not doing anything. We're just sitting there. Because eventually, when we leave the Philippines, we're going to want them for military bases. But that doesn't have to be in this generation. In the meantime, the islands are not going to go away as long as we can control them.

Q : *Was there any real political figure behind the Durning character in* Twilight?
A : The mayor of Chicago who died last year. We said what would have happened if he had been a lawyer and a civil servant and had finally got to be on the city council, and that's how he got to be mayor. A compromise: in the convention, they picked this guy, who was not intellectual but was at least educated, and put him in that spot. How would he react? Strangely, what makes them such successful politicians, those guys have very idealistic

views of good and bad. They can't exist on the grey. They don't call it grey when they pay off a guy to take care of the ward. Old-fashioned, political, pragmatic people. I don't think there's any doubt in the world that Kennedy wouldn't have been president if it hadn't been for the Chicago mayor. I think that convention was controlled by Daley. There wasn't a chance that Johnson was going to win; without Daley they wouldn't have made the compromise, Johnson wouldn't have been vice-president. The whole thing at the Chicago convention with the anti-war protest was terrible, but there was no doubt who was running the store. That guy sitting at the convention shouting back at 18,000 people was a ludicrous but powerful figure. The people who were screaming were truly impotent, and the guy who was screaming back was truly Hitler. And we said, what would happen if you put one of those guys in the presidency, rather than just start off with nobody. And Durning was perfect for that.

Q : *There haven't been many good films about politics in America, especially about labour, the sort of subject you were dealing with in* Garment Jungle.
A : We've made two or three pictures on labour, and they're really awful. There have been three or four very good scripts, most of which haven't been made. Budd Schulberg wrote one a couple of years ago about a Walter Reuther character; nobody's ever made it. I'm very anxious to see what they do with *F.I.S.T.*, though I don't think Jewison has the kind of credentials to make that picture. Marty Ritt is trying to make one now about a big set of mills in North or South Carolina that refuses to be unionised. And he can't get it financed. But Marty made another one with the coal miners [*The Molly Maguires*], a terrible picture. That may have been Marty's fault, but we just haven't been successful making labour pictures.

I don't know if you've seen the picture that Ford did towards the end of his life, with Tracy on Mayor Curley [*The Last Hurrah*]. The Irish have a marvellous way of understanding that about America. If Ford had done that ten years earlier when he had the vitality, and Tracy were ten years younger, that would have been some picture. Because they knew; the picture contained all the weaknesses of the American perception of power, but they knew how it should be applied. The fact that you take care of the widow, the fact that you take care of the family; that's really how the political machinery in the urban centers of this country works. There is a mutual responsibility. It's really what happens in parts of the American labour movement. It happened with Lewis, it happened with Gompers, it's happened with the guy in the Teamsters who has disappeared. Did he steal? Of course. But did he take care of those guys, and did they get extraordinary wages, extraordinary benefits? Yes. Do they know he was stealing from them? Absolutely. But the prime requirement of the job is that he take care of the members, and if he does that he's entitled to steal, and everybody is going to look the other way. People talk about *Stagecoach* and those pictures. Yes, they're marvellous pictures, but what Ford really understood was the Irish political mentality of this country. And he just never really attacked it, or dealt with it.

A funny thing has happened. In this country there are a few voices in the wilderness saying, now come on, that's not right. But there is no real militant—I don't mean Left—opposition. We're so fucked up we're not going to have it. You hear it in reflections in pictures like *Network*—we're mad and we're not going to put up with it any more—but that's fictitious, it's not real. If you really look to who is the heavy in American politics, it's Eugene McCarthy. McCarthy thought that there was a group of persons in the country, large enough and unhappy enough to have its will in national politics. And he was so wrong that it gave us Nixon. Without McCarthy there wouldn't have been Nixon. Because there isn't that body politic out there. There's an apathy that people have accepted in this country that says, I can't change it and therefore it's not going to be changed. Now that's not true in Great Britain. Maybe they can't change it, but there are a lot of people who are going to continue to try. I'd say that in England they're doing it for the best; I don't mean that I endorse that, but I say that there's a body out there you're going to hear from if you don't play responsible politics. Those people are going to make their opinions known. That's not true here.

Dialogue on Film: Robert Aldrich

THE AMERICAN FILM INSTITUTE / 1978

MOST FILMMAKERS RISE from obscurity. Robert Aldrich rose from a family of illustrious names—a vice-president, an outspoken senator, an ambassador, assorted governors and tycoons. Family background, though, is an accident of birth. But the illustrious names that form the background of Aldrich's early career in Hollywood had to do more with talent than with accident. He was an assistant to Jean Renoir, Charles Chaplin, William Wellman, Lewis Milestone, and Joseph Losey. There are worse ways to start out in the movies.

Aldrich watched and listened; soon he launched his own career as a director. In twenty-five years of moviemaking he has turned out close to thirty films. They are marked by energy and immediacy and a wide range. They have included rousing Westerns like *Apache* and *Vera Cruz*; gothic melodramas like *What Ever Happened to Baby Jane?* and *Hush . . . Hush, Sweet Charlotte*; war films like *Attack*; thrillers like *Kiss Me Deadly*; and even a comedy, *4 for Texas* (the party includes Dean Martin and Anita Ekberg).

Despite the range of subjects, Aldrich is mainly known as a director of action pictures—the kind represented by *The Dirty Dozen, The Longest Yard,* and *Hustle*. They are set in a man's world, the talk is rough, the camaraderie close, and the action violent and heroic. It is the character who unexpectedly rises to heroic action that strongly appeals to Aldrich. Labels dismay him, but he acknowledges a basic theme throughout his movies—a heroic quest for redemption. The tendency to independence and strong will that marks his characters has marked Aldrich's own career.

From *American Film* IV (November 1978): 51–62. Reprinted by permission of the American Film Institute.

Born sixty years ago in Rhode Island, Aldrich followed a well-worn family path. He studied economics; a career in business seemed to lie ahead, but in his last year of college, the heir of a powerful family abruptly left for Hollywood. He started as a production clerk at RKO in 1943 and rose to an assistant director, working with Renoir on *The Southerner,* with Chaplin on *Limelight,* and with a dozen other leading directors.

But Aldrich's first chance to direct came in television. He worked on series like *The Doctor, China Smith,* and *Four Star Playhouse* and finally turned to the screen in 1953. In the Dialogue, Aldrich recalls the television days, what he learned from Renoir and Abraham Polonsky, discusses the ins and outs of working in Hollywood, and talks about the varied work of the Directors Guild. He happens to be its president.

QUESTION: *I don't think it's commonly known that though you were once an assistant director to Jean Renoir and Charles Chaplin, you actually got your start as a director on television. How did that come about?*
ALDRICH: Around 1950 was the so-called golden age of live television, but soap operas were being made on film. Somebody at Procter and Gamble heard I had been Chaplin's assistant on *Limelight,* and I was asked to direct a soap opera series called *The Doctor.* The pay scale then, I think, was $450. If you kept your family here when you moved to New York, you could just about get by. So I went and worked two years in soap opera and then came back to California and did an awful lot of television.

QUESTION: *When did you turn to directing movies?*
ALDRICH: That part is amusing. There was once a Western singing group called the Sons of the Pioneers. Now, again around 1950, Dore Schary was put in charge of Metro-Goldwyn-Mayer. His predecessor had formed a unit called the Sons of the Pioneers, who were the sons of the people who had helped him. Schary thought the unit was a great way to bring along new talent; the Sons of the Pioneers would go out and find brand-new directors. So I was invited to do a picture—a nineteen-day marvel called *Big Leaguer,* with Edward G. Robinson as a baseball manager. Eddie Robinson was a marvelous actor and a brilliant man, but he was not physically coordinated. He would walk to first base and trip over home plate.

QUESTION: *After a number of movies, you started your own studio. What brought that about?*

ALDRICH: Everybody has a dream. I had always dreamed to get enough money to have my own studio. When I made *The Big Knife,* in sixteen days, I made it in a little studio down on Occidental Street. It was built by Mary Pickford's brother. It had two stages, a few offices, and a few cutting rooms. It was run-down, but it was a marvelous little studio. It cost nothing to shoot there—I think it was about $100 a day. I made a lot of money on *The Dirty Dozen,* and so I took all the money, and I bought it.

I put in some more cutting rooms, I built another stage, and I bought a lot of small Arriflex equipment, a small boom, a small crane. It was a sensational operation. We only needed around sixty-five production days a year to break even. Then I followed that classy act by making four dogs in a row. Nobody is going to finance you after four dogs. It makes no difference that you can prove that in your own studio you can make a picture literally two-thirds cheaper. So the sheriff came and took the studio. But it was an experience I would go through again. I enjoyed every minute of it. I'm sorry the pictures weren't better.

QUESTION: *How did you recover?*
ALDRICH: Expensively. You go and work for about a quarter of what you worked for before. You work for fewer prerogatives. If before you could write a shopping list and say, "I want this cameraman and that musician and that grip," you forgo that. Take a director who is moderately successful and who occasionally has good films and really knows what he's doing and who then has run of terrible luck. If you look at his pictures later, you find they weren't that bad. Something happened, and they weren't accepted. Everybody I know has a saying: You jump on a bottle of whiskey for about six months, and then you've got to go back to work. How? You cut your price, and you take pictures you wouldn't have taken before.

The name of the game is to stay at the table. You've got to stay at the table. You cut your price or your demands or your contracts or your obligations. You cut them and stay at the table. But you can't win staying in the other room. Then if you are really lucky, you'll find the right script. Someone else will have turned it down. The people at the studio will need somebody, and they get you. It will be a good picture, and you're off to the races again. But you can't sulk in the other room and wait five years between movies.

QUESTION: *Do you have any particular directors in mind?*
ALDRICH: I haven't seen any Peter Bogdanovich work lately. He happens

to come to mind quickly, because his pictures were bigger. There are a lot of fine directors just as qualified today as they were the day they finished their hit pictures. John Sturges hasn't worked lately. *McQ* was a terrible picture, but there are moments with Colleen Dewhurst that are maybe the best moments of acting you've ever seen in a movie. There is a car chase on a beach at the end as good as anything in *The French Connection.* But nobody is going to remember that picture. If you get that kind of picture when you're trying to struggle back, it's going to put you down the tube. John Sturges hasn't been able to stay at the table. Last year Sturges had a chance to do a picture in Germany called "The Boat." It was a terrible script. He thought he could fix it. When he got to Germany, there were restrictions on what he could do to fix the script. The author of the book had final script approval. So Sturges had to walk away.

Marty Ritt had a very bad time, even after all those marvelous pictures. Then he made *Sounder,* and he was off again. Richard Brooks worked for almost nothing for two years on *Looking for Mr. Goodbar.* Now, I don't care if you like him or don't like him, he is a marvelous director. But he's fallen on bad times. People haven't been coming to see his movies. He is just as good a director as he ever was. He knows more about directing than half of those who are now doing pictures. He took a crap shoot and stayed at the table and did *Looking for Mr. Goodbar* for next to nothing, because he thought it was going to be a big hit. The picture is doing pretty well around the world, but this town thinks it is a terrible picture. He made, I think, a mistake in showing it to the academy. People booed, hissed, all those ladies with lavender hair screamed, and they got up and walked out of the theater. Everybody thought it was a terrible movie. Well, it's not. Either you like it, or you don't like it, but it's not a terrible movie.

Then there are the directors who wait five years for the single great script. I question the wisdom of that. I can't believe you get to be any better while you wait five years between scripts. What we directors do is not only creative, it's a craft. You can't become better at a craft without practicing that craft. You can't go home and direct a picture. It doesn't work that way. I can't believe the guy who directs a picture every year doesn't know more at the end of five years than the guy who doesn't direct a picture every year.

QUESTION: *And then there's a director like Fred Zinnemann who four years after* The Day of the Jackal *comes out with* Julia.

A L D R I C H : The fascinating thing about Zinnemann is that his style has never changed. In my opinion, what has happened is that the acceptance of that style goes back and forth. He's always been terribly deliberate, terribly slow, in the pace of his films. But there are periods when people don't want that. *The Nun's Story* is done just the way *Julia* is, just as well, with just as much great imagination. But nobody would ever say his films are fast. He's a marvelous director but the style is always that way. If that style is out of tune, then you're in terrible trouble. You can say, "I'm going to do it differently," but how can you do it differently? The material may be different, but I suspect you do it the same way.

This is going to sound like a knock on Zinnemann, but I don't mean it that way. He's a fine, fine director. But I don't think Zinnemann could do a picture like *Saturday Night Fever*. Some people are more malleable. For example, I think Brooks could do *Saturday Night Fever*. I don't think it would be as good as it is, but I think he could do it. Zinnemann just couldn't do that picture.

Q U E S T I O N : *He comes out of a different tradition.*
A L D R I C H : Also, he's God's patient man. He'll stay there forever until it works. I think what makes his pictures important is the care with which they're done. What killed some of his pictures is the lack of energy. If you get pictures that don't require energy, he probably does them better than anybody in the world. But there are directors and actors who will tell you they don't know how he did *From Here to Eternity*. That picture is so unlike him. It has energy, it has drive. You can look at ten pictures before and ten pictures since, and they have a steady, considerate, thoughtful pace. But there's no drive to them.

Q U E S T I O N : *Do you see yourself as typed with a certain style or a certain kind of picture?*
A L D R I C H : I'm perceived to be an action-adventure director. But you don't want to type yourself, because everybody else types you. When you're looking for your own material, you look for material different from what is usually sent to you. You try not to finance the kinds of scripts you know you're going to get from other people anyway. It doesn't always work. I financed a variety of comedies, but nobody has ever said, "Wouldn't it be great to have Aldrich do a comedy?" But the idea is to try not to get typecast.

QUESTION: *You'll never be an auteur that way.*

ALDRICH: My hunch is that any director would trade in that label in a minute for the ability to do all kinds of movies. I don't know a single director who wouldn't say, "I would like to do every kind of movie, rather than make the same one over." Maybe Hitchcock wouldn't say that, but everybody else would. By the way, here's a bit of enlightenment. When the Directors Guild had its fight with the writers, we spent a great deal of money for lawyers to define the concept of auteur and to find out where it came from and when. In 1937 there was a trial in France in which the court came down on the side of the writer, the director, and the composer as the artistic controllers of a picture. They were, therefore, the auteurs of a picture and had certain rights. The Italians, during Mussolini's heyday before the war, took that one step further and said that, while that might be true in France, in Italy only the director was the artistic controller. Under Italian law, the director truly is the author. You will find much more freedom under Italian jurisdiction, in terms of the director's final authority over a film, than anywhere else in the world.

QUESTION: *Do you see a recurring theme in your work?*

ALDRICH: I think if you look at my pictures you'll see that not only am I a friend of Abraham Polonsky, but I'm a fan of Polonsky. I think there are no formulas, but there is a concept, it seems to me, of a man struggling to redeem his self-esteem. I think that is thematically recurrent in all the pictures, regardless of whether it's *The Legend of Lylah Clare* or *The Killing of Sister George.*

QUESTION: *Or* The Longest Yard.

ALDRICH: *The Longest Yard* was a marvelous story about an ex-pro football player who got sent to jail and was then asked to play competitive football. But the writer couldn't apply Polonsky's concept of self-redemption or the effort to regain self-esteem. *Rocky* is a case in point. Polonsky said in 1945 that to tell that kind of story you need to establish a heroic figure who falls from grace and spends the rest of the picture trying to regain his self-esteem. It doesn't make any difference whether he's successful or not. From the fact that he struggles to regain his opinion of himself, he will prove to be a heroic figure. That concept doesn't necessarily originate with Polonsky, but in his pictures, like *Body and Soul,* it is more clearly pronounced. So in *The Longest Yard* I simply introduced that element.

The writer had put on page 76, "And then came the game." My contention was that the game was very important; it was an artistic contribution. The game is the last forty-five minutes of the picture. I never asked for the credit, nor did I want the credit. I think the business of who writes what is unfair in many instances. Nowadays, the director must write more than fifty percent of the script, or he's not entitled to share the credit. Well, what if he writes forty-nine percent? Does that mean he doesn't get a credit? But if it's another writer, and he writes 49 percent, the picture will give two credits. I think the writers' arbitration system is not equitable, but I don't mean to demean their contributions. You know the old line, "It starts with the word." I think that's valid.

QUESTION: *How do you go about finding material for a movie?*
ALDRICH: Ideally, you find a piece of material you like. By definition, something that everybody else has passed over, that everybody else has been unable to solve. There is no way a small independent production company can pay $250,000 or $500,000 or $1 million for a best-seller or a play. You really can't buy the competitive material. So you're a vulture. You find out when the contract expires. You wait until the first or second option doesn't get exercised because nobody will pay the $250,000. Or you see the offbeat play that you *think*—the operative word—that you think you know how to solve. Often you don't know how, but you think you do.

Then you spend the money you do have on finding the writer you think is the best qualified to develop the script from your overlay of that property—because if the property were right, somebody else would have made it. You take the property, you write an overlay that you think corrects the damage or corrects the interpretation, and you give it to the writer. You work with the writer so that when the screenplay is finished, you own the material and the screenplay. It allows you the bargaining leverage when you go to a major studio, hopefully with a star, so that the studio can't make you an employee. The studio has to make you a true partner, because you own the material, you have a contract or the agreement of a contract with the actor.

Now, sometimes that is very successful, sometimes it isn't. You're betting on your judgment, and nobody's infallible. I've had some marvelous luck with plays. I had some luck with *The Big Knife,* which was a Clifford Odets play. *The Fragile Fox,* by Norman Brooks, was made into a picture called *Attack.* I haven't been that lucky with novels. The *Dirty Dozen* was not a very successful novel, but it was a very successful movie. I would love to tell you it is all inside the brain. It just isn't. It really is luck. You catch the public in a receptive mood for that kind of picture, or you misgauge the public's receptivity, and it doesn't want to see that picture that year. You'll find, quite often, that you're ahead of the mood. You may be one year or two years ahead of it. *The Killing of Sister George,* made in 1975 instead of in 1968, I think would have been a successful picture. *Sister George* may break even—may—in another five years. That means it will have taken fifteen years to break even.

QUESTION: *In presenting a project to a studio, how careful a consideration do you give to picking your players?*

ALDRICH: Different directors do it in different ways. I keep certain players in mind who I think, hope, pray, are receptive to me. I buy material hoping I'm going to sign them. But to show you how everybody's pretty stupid, I bought a very bad biography of Sophie Tucker. Now, if you read it, you know up front there are only two ladies who can play it, and you can't afford either one of them. It's either Bette Midler or Barbra Streisand. If you go to one, you're going to lose the other, because she's going to hear about it. Anyway we got a marvelous script, our first draft. So, thinking that Midler was more interested than Streisand—only because she hadn't done anything yet—we took it to Midler. Well, Midler didn't want to do it. There was a very good reason for her not wanting to do it. I suspect the picture should probably be her second or third picture, not her first. But that precluded the chance that I would ever get Streisand. So if you find material you really like, sometimes you have to go against your own best judgment.

QUESTION: *Is the script you present to a studio the finished, polished screenplay?*

ALDRICH: Most small companies usually can't carry it that far. You can't afford, at that stage, to have a writer do a third or fourth draft. You usually pay for the first draft and the second draft, and you hope the second draft is satisfactory enough to entice a star and a distributor. You assure both of them that the changes everybody knows have to be made will be made. It's all risk capital. My guess is that the very good companies—translate successful companies—get one in four of those projects made. I guess I get one out of five. I know a lot of people who get one of ten. You know you're going to eat six scripts or ten scripts to get one made.

QUESTION: *Do you deal at some point with a producer?*
ALDRICH: If you're any kind of filmmaker, you have to remove the word "producer." Although there is one, you function as one in finding the material, bringing in a writer, and financing it. If your film is in in good time and you meet your contract, the producer doesn't really exist. He's there on the project, but all you say to him is, "Good morning. How are you?" He doesn't do much for you, and he can't interfere with the way you make the movie. You consult with him, but he doesn't effectively bar you from making the movie you want to make. But if you fall on hard times, then you've got to listen to him.

QUESTION: *When you've got backing for a film, what sort of preparations do you make before you start shooting?*
ALDRICH: I'd like to preface this by going back to when I worked as an assistant for Renoir. Renoir truly believed that a transfusion takes place from the physical surroundings to the performances and the picture itself. We would go on location, and he would walk up and down a riverside, for example, where we were to build the set, for two or three days. He would bring the actors there a week early, get them into costumes, and have them walk around barefoot. I found, as I grew older and directed pictures, that I didn't really have to walk barefoot on the land to appreciate how to shoot or not to shoot. But getting the actors there, on location or on the set—or on the stage, for that matter—and having them in costume, in their parts, seemed to me to make great sense.

I go on location like an assistant director, to see how the logistics are going to be. Is there a piece of rock outcropping, or a place where I can put the house, the barn, the corral, or the chase, so that it will work photographically? Could a guy come around the corner? Could he fall off the rock? I look for the practical things on location first, the artistic things second.

Ever since *The Big Knife*, I guess, I've taken less money for the privilege of rehearsing for two weeks before every picture. Actors really welcome it, and they very rarely will raise their prices for that extra two weeks, because it lets them familiarize themselves with their roles. Not only that, but it gives them advance education about what the other actors are going to do and how they can be nourished by other actors' performances.

While they're rehearsing, the director's rehearsing, too. You pick up vibrations from them. You've already conceived 80 to 85 percent of what they're going to do, but that other 15 percent comes from the feedback at the rehearsal. If you've really done your homework and conceived 100 percent, you may get 105 or 110, because the actors give you ideas you never would have thought of if you hadn't had that rehearsal. The problem of getting three or four pages shot in one day wouldn't have given you the creating time to get the 110 percent. You might have got 80 and been lucky to have got 80.

QUESTION: *Those two weeks, then, are time well spent for you.*
ALDRICH: In my opinion, they're the most valuable two weeks in the picture, more valuable than polishing the script, more valuable than an extra month in the cutting room. In that two weeks, you can shape the performances, you can shape the thrust, you can shape the picture. You also see what doesn't work. You can see why something on page 110 doesn't play as it should—because something doesn't play on page 45. You can read it a hundred times to yourself and never understand why that connection doesn't go from page 45 to page 110. But if somebody acts it, by the second day you say, "That doesn't work. I'll tell you why it doesn't. She didn't say so-and-so. We didn't understand that." The value of rehearsal, I think, is greatly underestimated in the making of feature films. Nobody does it enough.

QUESTION: *Is the screenwriter helpful at rehearsals?*
ALDRICH: I work a great deal with Lukas Heller. I think we've done about four of five pictures, and I always ask Lukas to be there. He's responsive, he's quick, he understands, and he's very helpful. That leaves about twenty-five pictures or so. I guess of those, I would like to have had about twelve of the writers there and twelve of them not there. It depends on the rapport you have with the writer. Is it a friendly relationship? Is it competitive? Some people truly contribute. Other people are obstructionists. They say that a word is great and we shouldn't change it. In the first three or four days of rehearsals, you give actors liberty. You say, "Please try it. If it doesn't work for you, how would you like it better?" Well, some writers say, "Don't change that! That came out of the Bible." It's very tough, then, to have an actor feel at ease.

QUESTION: *Directors today have a good deal more to say about the first cut of their films than they once did. How were things done before?*

ALDRICH: If a director said, "I want to make the first cut," in theory, he had that right. But there were cutters at the major studios who would have your picture cut before you finished your last day. Then you were asked to come in and view what was called "the assembly." But it wasn't the assembly. It was the way the picture was going to go out. You would make one or two comments: "Wouldn't it be nice if you stayed here on the long shot and came here with the close-up?" Somebody would tell somebody else, "He said so-and-so on the long shot," and that would be the end of the conversation. You saw your picture four or five months later in the theater exactly the way you first saw it. Directors on television series today are in a not unsimilar position to the "nonstar" directors of 1940 or 1950. They do a show, and the organization that hired them knows they are going to have to move on to make a living, they're not going to be there for the cut, and no one could care less for their opinion about the cutting or the music.

QUESTION: *But the first cut of a movie, at least, is now in the hands of the director, and he has the Directors Guild to thank for it.*
ALDRICH: Nobody can touch the film until the director has finished the cut. It's not that there isn't more than one way to skin a cat. But the first time, you should skin the cat the director's way. In other words, the director's cut may be the way that he conceived it. That's possible. In the latest contract, we have a provision whereby the studio cannot dispense with the director's physical presence. If the studio's going to cut the picture, you've got to be there. If somebody is going to dub it, you've got to be there. If somebody is going to score it, you've got to be there. If somebody is going to take it to preview, you've got to be there. That's a minimum contract. As you move up to become somebody the studio wants, rather than somebody looking for a job, you write into your contract other prerequisites: "I want not only the first cut, I want the second cut. I want not only one preview, I want two previews. I want the changes in between those two previews. I want public previews." The stronger you get, the better contract you get. The better contract you get, the better chance you have to make a good movie—if there is a chance.

I've had many opportunities to have final cut, but final cut is an ego trip that doesn't mean final cut. If Kubrick makes a picture that's an hour too long, the studio's going to take the hour out of the picture and say, "Sue me." The concept, it seems to me, that always made sense is, if a director makes a picture as well as he knows how to make it, with two previews and the corrections from those two previews, and then can't convince the people who financed it or distribute it that that's the form it should be in, he's a schmuck, and he should be in the shoe business. If you really can't prove that after two trips to the plate, it doesn't make any difference who you are, you're not going to get final cut. Your contract may say you have final cut, you can tell the press and *Film Quarterly* that you have final cut, but you don't have final cut. If that picture is going to lose $10 million and the studio can make it lose only $5 million by taking out forty-five minutes, the studio's going to take out forty-five minutes.

QUESTION: *Did the older, classic directors spend as much time cutting as they're said to have?*
ALDRICH: They really didn't, though Chaplin did, Lewis Milestone did. I was Milestone's assistant on four pictures. But people worked at a faster tempo then. You used to be able to get thirty or forty setups in an A-picture. Today, if you get ten setups in an A-picture, that's batting a thousand. People worked harder and worked longer. Nobody went home at six o'clock. Good pictures were shot in twenty days or twenty-four days. Now pictures take fifty-five, sixty, seventy days, and I think we spend too long in the cutting room.

QUESTION: *Do you get involved with the distribution of your films?*
ALDRICH: Yes. The contracts call for "consultation" with a director. The studio has to tell you what theaters the picture is going to go into, what campaign is planned. But consultation is all it is. You can make yourself a nuisance and sit there and say, "Why not this theater or that theater?" There are always ten answers. If you're difficult, the studio will take the time to explain and argue, but you don't win those arguments, or you very rarely do. I used to spend my own money to come up with an ad concept or maybe a logo that was central to the theme of the picture. I don't any more.

The studio's ad on *The Longest Yard* was unbelievable. It was Burt Reynolds in a helmet with bars in front and a lock on it. Nobody understood what it meant, but we were assured by Paramount that the public would understand what it meant. Well, the picture opened in New York with that ad, and nobody went to see it. The picture opened in the rest of the country *without* the ad, and everybody went to see it. Finally word came back, "Gee, maybe there was something wrong with that ad."

QUESTION: *Have you noted a change in the pattern of how people enter directing over the last few decades?*
ALDRICH: I'm the wrong person to ask. I've always thought that working your way up from third or fourth or fifth assistant is like getting paid to go to college. Working with great directors—and terrible directors—is the greatest education possible. But that is not a popular belief any more. For a while in the forties, the concept was to bring stage directors to California. They became directors, some pretty good, some not so good. Then, with the success of Bobby Wise and Mark Robson and John Sturges, there was the idea of making cutters directors. It became an instant trend. But if someone asks me, I always say, "I truly believe that being an assistant is the best way."

When I was an assistant, in the forties, you really were the director's assistant. You worked for him and because of him. Quite often, he took you from job to job. You weren't an extension of the production office. But today, with the economics of film and particularly of television, that is not necessarily true. In television the directors rotate, but the assistants stay on the show. The assistants' loyalty, for their own survival, happens to be more to the production office than to the director. Consequently, the director is not as friendly and not as willing to share his time and ideas as he was previously.

QUESTION: *How do you manage to divide your time between directing movies and heading the Directors Guild?*
ALDRICH: I hadn't been that busy. The only picture I've done since *Twilight's Last Gleaming,* in Germany, was *The Choirboys,* and that was done locally. If you go on location, it's very difficult, if not impossible. You have to let somebody else do it. If you're working locally, it really isn't difficult: It means you work a lot of nights that you shouldn't.

QUESTION: *A little history. How did the Directors Guild come about?*
ALDRICH: Twelve directors got together in 1936 and said the major companies were exploiting them, and they thought they needed a collective bargaining instrument. But they weren't recognized until March 13, 1939. At the end of the first year, there were 135 members. At the end of December last

year, there were 5,025. Now it is directors, production managers, first assistants, second assistants, and others.

QUESTION: *Which guild presidents have been particularly political—that is, involved in advocacy?*
ALDRICH: I would think King Vidor, the first president, was a political president. He knew the directors were getting exploited, and asked, "What do we do about it?" I think George Stevens was a political president in that he understood that power was necessary in order to organize the television people into the Directors Guild. He brought the New York radio directors and television directors into the union. I consider myself a political president. The other ones have been very loyal, helpful, dedicated men, but they have not thought of the guild as a political instrument for the betterment of the members.

For a long time it was run by big-name directors in a benign, thoughtful, conservative way, but for their best interests. It was very difficult to make them understand that it was a vertical union, that they had to consider the welfare of a second assistant who was being exploited, who was not being paid proportionately to other craftsmen. It was very hard for them to come by the fact that, having involved the assistants, it was their responsibility to care for the assistants' concerns and welfare just as they cared for their own.

QUESTION: *I understand there aren't very many women in the guild.*
ALDRICH: There are more than there used to be. For all of the faults of the name presidents—I don't mean faults, but rather their union concepts—they saw the movement coming a little sooner than others. They demanded the guild's training program open up. I would like to say that it's because of an honest, liberal attitude. I think it's really because they've been afraid of government reaction if there isn't a reasonable proportion of women.

QUESTION: *The guild is sponsoring a number of useful programs. How did they come about?*
ALDRICH: Do you have time, first, for an anecdote? Elia Kazan is a favorite person of mine and, I think, an absolutely tremendous director. It was reported that he made a mistake in the fifties in going before the House Committee on Un-American Activities. People who didn't go before the committee obviously felt very strongly about it. Last year, when it was necessary for

us to prepare for a strike, it was up to me to appoint strike captains. I appointed Marty Ritt and Richard Brooks in the West, and Kazan in the East. We had a general strike committee meeting in California, and Ritt and Kazan had not seen each other in twenty-eight years. Everybody was terribly apprehensive of what would happen at that meeting, and rightfully so. Ritt was early, and Kazan was a couple of minutes late. Kazan came into the room, and nothing was said. Then all of a sudden, they walked across to each other and started to shake hands. But instead of shaking hands, they embraced. It was a very touching moment. Nobody said anything, we sat down, and we went on with our work.

To get back to your question: Five or six years ago, Kazan wrote a paper to the guild about the lack of creative and cultural projects in the Directors Guild. He proposed that programs and retrospectives be done, and that discussions and seminars be held to discuss directing and its problems. Under Bobby Wise's astute presidency, the projects were inaugurated, and when Mrs. Wise died, she left, I think, $125,000 to the special projects fund to get them started. Then other members made more modest contributions. But it all came out of Kazan's proposal.

QUESTION: *To return to your movies, some of them*—The Dirty Dozen, *for example—have been very successful. Have you generally been able to foresee which movies would find a large audience?*
ALDRICH: The pictures I thought would make a fortune—pictures like *The Flight of the Phoenix*—were not successful. Yet on television it gets extraordinary ratings. And much to everybody's surprise, a picture like *Hustle* made a great deal of money. It's always very hard to tell.

QUESTION: *Are there films dear to your heart that didn't find an audience?*
ALDRICH: The question is asked a lot. I think the really good directors have one illness in common: To be as good as they are, they really *have* to think they're always making a very fine movie and they're going to be proud of it. I never met a director whom I felt was any good who didn't think he was making a good movie, though the movie might turn out to be a dog. The good directors don't say, "It's a piece of crap. But I'm doing it to pay off the mortgage, or to get the kids through school." But three or four years later you may look back and say, "Why was I so dumb? How could I have thought that was good?" I was in Italy two years cutting *Sodom and Gomorrah*. Now,

you know you've got to be an idiot to sit there two years cutting *Sodom and Gomorrah.* But I thought it was going to be the best movie ever made. Well, it wasn't. But you don't make a movie—no matter how bad it is—without thinking it's going to be very good.

QUESTION: *It's been a good talk.*

ALDRICH: I'm sorry I haven't been funny, and I wish I was more profound. But you got the wrong fellow.

Robert Aldrich: No More Mister Nice Guy

RODERICK MANN/1981

ROBERT ALDRICH WAS DUE TO ATTEND an important meeting the other day—one at which there were bound to be strong differences of opinion—and his family was concerned that the feisty director should keep his temper.

"It's bound to be a rough meeting," they told him. "So you can't afford to be outspoken." For some time they drilled into him the importance of staying cool.

"And for the first time in my life," the burly director said the other day, "I tried to stay calm. You see, I thought my family was right."

Pause.

"Well, I'll never do it again. They were not right. Sitting there I got so frustrated I nearly had a heart attack. Usually if someone treats me badly I tell them—and that's that. So I've made another enemy. Yet, here I was trying to stay in control and be charming—charming? No, I'm never charming—be convivial and nearly having a heart attack when I should have been throwing the guy out of the window."

Having now tried once to keep his cool, Aldrich had decided the hell with it. He will not go back to the good old ways in the hopes of living longer.

And those who in the past have tangled with this maverick director—the man who was fired by both Louis B. Mayer and Harry Cohn and who once made a movie with Frank Sinatra and spoke not one word to him—will hardly be surprised.

From *Los Angeles Times Calendar*, 11 October 1981, 25. Reprinted by permission.

"Of course," said Aldrich the other afternoon, sitting in his office, his loosely knotted tied draped like a hangman's noose around his neck, "there just isn't enough time to get mad at everybody. So you've got to figure out who it is you really want to get mad at. Otherwise there'd be no time to make movies."

Aldrich has made a lot of films since he started in 1941 and worked with such giants as Chaplin, Renoir, and Milestone. And he has had a hit film (sometimes two) in every decade since. In the '50s it was *Vera Cruz*. In the '60s it was *The Dirty Dozen*. In the '70s it was *The Longest Yard*.

"And in the '80s, he said, "I hope it's going to be . . . *All the Marbles*."

. . . *All the Marbles,* his new film, tells the story of two women wrestlers struggling around the small-town wrestling circuit in search of fame and fortune, assisted and encouraged by their manager (played by Peter Falk).

A curious choice of a movie to make, you might think. But Aldrich, who used to wrestle on his school team, thinks not.

"I perceive the marketplace to be looking for pure entertainment and not message this year," he said, "and it's a good story, stolen from a past success."

How's that again?

"I used the Abe Polonsky screenplay for *Body and Soul* as the basis for this film," he said. "I was lucky enough to be assistant director on the film which had Robert Rossen directing and John Garfield starring. If you remember the film it had as its concept a man struggling to redeem his self-esteem.

"It always works. I know. I stole from it before. *The Longest Yard* had a fine first and second act but no third. So I called Polonsky and said: "I'm going to steal from *Body and Soul* and have my character fall from grace and try to redeem himself." And I did just that.

"So when this writer (Mel Frohman) came in with a story about two struggling girl wrestlers and their manager I thought, why not reconstruct *Body and Soul* from frame one to tag? So we did.

"We took that simple concept and superimposed on it the story of two girl wrestlers whose life would be changed completely if they win the title. Instead of the Garfield character we now have these two girls."

To find his wrestlers Aldrich saw 900 women and tested twenty. From those he picked his two main characters—Vicki Frederick and Laurene Landon—and sent them off for three months to work with a former world champion wrestler, Mildred Burke.

"We had two choices," he said. "We could pick wrestlers and teach them to act or we could pick actresses and teach them to wrestle. We elected to do the second. And when you do see the film I think you'll find it extraordinary that two girls who've never wrestled before should subject themselves to such punishment.

"Peter Falk was the guy we wanted to play the girls' manager. So I gave him the Bette Davis speech—a great hook for any actor. It goes like this: "Peter, if this isn't the best script ever written for you put it in a envelope and send it right back. But if it is the best let's make it. I don't want to hear that you don't like the speech on page 16. It's either the best or it isn't.

"That rarely fails. You don't always get the picture made but you always get a positive reaction. Nobody's ego can withstand that sort of flattery."

Why did he call it the Bette Davis speech?

"Because when I wanted her for *What Ever Happened to Baby Jane?* I wrote her a long letter with that same speech. For six weeks nothing happened and I thought, well, maybe this is one person it doesn't work with. Then I received a long, hand written letter in which she said, 'Mr. Aldrich. That is not the best script I have ever read though it's an interesting sales approach. However, it is the second best script I've read and I'd be pleased to talk with you about it.'

"When I had Davis and (Joan) Crawford signed I took that script to every studio in town before finally getting it made and the language about those two ladies—difficult, yes; talented, definitely—was not to be believed.

"But then the big problem of all us independent producers is finding out who to talk to at the studios; who has the power to say yes as well as no. I can talk to David Begelman (then at MGM, now at UA) direct. But he's the only one. Who do I talk to at the other studios. I don't know. I really don't."

Reaching for diet drink he continued. "I'm sixty-three and I've had hits every ten years and I just hope I can function long enough to have one in the '90s.

"But you have to be lucky. Those guys who come along and catch lightning in a bottle with one hit film and become overnight geniuses, they make me laugh. If they don't tell you that success has to do with timing, over which they have no control, selling, over which they have no control and the mood of audiences around the world, over which they have no control—then they're idiots.

"When we planned *The Dirty Dozen* in 1965 do you think for one moment we knew that by the time the film came out the French kids would be in revolt and Americans would be sick of Vietnam so the mood would be just right for our picture? Rubbish. The fact that the film grossed $80 million was luck. Pure luck.

"It seems to me there are more amateurs in this business than there were when I started. Harry Cohn and Louis B. Mayer may not have been guys you wanted to spend much time with but at least you knew where you were with them.

"Today there's no way you can tell someone who has the power to give $10 million that he doesn't know what he's talking about. With those old guys you could at least say, 'You're wrong and here's why.' They might throw you out of their office but next day you'd probably get a call saying, 'Come back and discuss it.'

"It's a tough business. And one thing I do know—unless I believe in a picture I can't make it. I'm the guy, remember, who spent two years making *Sodom and Gomorrah*. You've got to be an idiot to pretend to yourself that a film like that was worthwhile. But I did.

"I even went to court in Italy and sued the producer for not giving me cutting rights. What was I thinking of—arguing in an Italian court for cutting rights to a film like *Sodom and Gomorrah?* I had to be a jerk. But the film was my child. And if I hadn't thought that it was worthwhile I wouldn't have made it. And having made it I had to try to protect it. For me it's as simple as that. . . ."

Robert Aldrich

PATRICK BRION, MICHEL MAHÉO, DOMINIQUE RABOURDIN, NOËL SIMSOLO/1983

LEAVING ROBERT ALDRICH IN La Rochelle on July 4, 1983, we had no idea that this smiling, uncomplicated, considerate, and dynamic man had only a few months to live. Full of energy and new ideas, still quick-witted at sixty-five, he showed no interest in nostalgia or the past. He lived completely in the present, fully aware of the difficulties he would face in order to complete his favorite projects. Still, he was not at all ready to slow down. His energy and liveliness shine through every level of his work—even in his least ambitious films. Aldrich incarnated a certain archetype of American cinema.

The press conference held at La Rochelle is transcribed here almost in its entirety. In a personal interview with Aldrich following the press conference, we explored some topics in more detail. Our questions did not follow the chronology of his films, which explains the sometimes disconnected aspect of this interview, and also certain repetitions. Obviously this is not an exhaustive interview: Aldrich never worked from set formula; he was quite simply an American professional. Few filmmakers are capable of saying, candidly, "There is no such thing as a personal film." Coming from a man who made such films as *Vera Cruz, Kiss Me Deadly, The Dirty Dozen,* and *Hustle,* such modesty contrasts sharply with the pretensions and megalomania of many young contemporary cinematographers. In his art and his life, Al-

From *Cinéma 84* 302 (February 1984): 15–24. Transcribed and translated from English to French by Dominique Rabourdin. Retranslated from French to English by William C. Griffin.

drich's concern for realism, for exactitude and for honesty, lends authenticity and worth to everything he says.

Q: *What's the most important project you have right now?*
A: Finding work, as quickly as possible.

Q: *You've been working a long time on the adaptation of a novel you bought the rights to several years back.*
A: Yes, I finished the adaptation just before leaving for La Rochelle, and the studio now has thirty days to make its decision. In 1958, I took an option on a book entitled *Kinder Spiel (Children's Games)*. It takes place at the end of the Cold War in small-town America—it's about the events that frightened children then. I've yet to be able to make the film. But after seeing *E.T.* last year, I realized I needed to shift things around and adopt the children's point of view. So we reworked the script. Rather than setting the action in a New England small town, we moved it to a small German village, occupied by American, British, and French troops. To give it a more international flavor. But for now, we don't have a backer for the new version.

Q: *Can you tell us about the script that you just finished?*
A: It's sort of a wacky comedy about a dozen or so small-time Mafiosi, mostly young guys, who were going to be repatriated to Italy in 1960. Of course they think they're going to live the good life in Naples, but they forget that the Neapolitans are much more savvy than they are and years ahead of them in experience.

Q: *For a long time you've seemed to prefer to work with the same lead actors, Burt Lancaster for example, Lee Marvin, Charles Bronson. In the supporting roles you often use Wesley Addy and Richard Jaeckel. How do you cast your films?*
A: That's not entirely true about the casting, but it is true about the technical people I work with. As often as possible I work with the same photographer, the same sound engineer, the same editor. As for the actors who aren't big stars—you know, actors who can play a lot of different roles and who are less expensive than the big guys—it's true that I tend to use the same ones fairly regularly. In the U.S., in order to find financing for a film, you almost always have to have a star, but the stars change pretty often. There are several ways to get a film financed. The easiest goes like this: find a script and an

actor who's interested in it, then take the actor to the production and distribution company to get their agreement. If that works, they'll give you forty-
eight days to make the film. That's how most films are made. But since no
one would agree to finance *Baby Jane*, I had to find independent financing.
My company produced it, but with my own money.

Q : *Your company has been quite productive for a long time. What was your*
financial relationship with the big studios like?
A : If you have a very successful star and a good script, you won't have any
problems finding at least 50 percent of the financing. Then 10 percent to 15
percent goes for the star. That leaves you with about 30 percent. But if you
get an agreement to do two films at the same time, the person who's going
to finance your two films will ask you for that 30 percent as a guarantee. So,
if he loses money on one film, he makes it up on the successful one. Of
course, if the backers are afraid the film won't make any money, they'll just
make you pay for everything. When I did *Baby Jane*, I paid for the adaptation
rights and the script. Even though I directed and produced it, I didn't make
any money until the film started to turn a profit.

Q : *Who are the directors of photography who best understand how you like to use*
light? How do you explain to them what you're looking for? Do you work with a
story-board?
A : Whenever possible I work with Joseph Biroc and also with Ernest Laszlo.
But Laszlo has had some health problems, so I can't work with him any
more. I've been an assistant for lots of very talented directors over the past
eleven years: Renoir, Chaplin, Wellman, Milestone. After working with these
men, you either know what you want to do, or you know nothing at all. So
you tell the photographer where you want the first camera placed, that you
want to use a 40mm lens. Then you tell him where to place the second camera and what size lens to use. You tell him you want blacks that are very
black, not gray. That you want to see such and such colors. At first it's always
a very friendly conversation, but it's never a dialog where we decide together.
I tell my photographer exactly what he should do. Usually I don't use a story-
board. I always rehearse all the scenes for two weeks, carefully preparing
everything. For the action scenes that you can't rehearse in advance, I go
home, I make my own story-board, I make a copy for myself and I give two
or three copies to the people who need them, to the assistant director, the

cameraman, and so forth. From then on we follow a story-board, but only for the action scenes. In *The Dirty Dozen,* for example, I only had a story-board for the attack on the castle. All the other scenes had been rehearsed.

Q : *What role did Sergio Leone play in filming* Sodom and Gomorrah?
A : Not much . . . Sergio Leone was in charge of the second team filming in Marrakech . . . One Saturday when I wasn't filming, I went to watch him work. He was using the entire Moroccan Calvary, 1,700 men and horses. He was supposed to start filming at ten in the morning. When I arrived at 10:30 he hadn't gotten a first shot. Eleven o'clock, still no shot. Noon, still no shot. At half past noon, he took off two hours for lunch. So I sent my chauffer to get him, and I asked him what was going on. He said, "I just got a great shot." "When?" I asked. "About a half-hour ago," he said. So I told him, "Great. You're fired." He went back to Rome. That was Saturday. The next Monday, he started filming his first spaghetti Western.

Q : *So, in the end, how much did he actually film?*
A : A couple of days worth, but [laughing] nothing that day . . .

Q : *You had the same kind of problem when Vincent Sherman replaced you during the filming of* Garment Jungle.
A : I've never seen that film. What isn't good was done by Sherman. I'd already completed about 60 percent of the film. Harry Cohn, the producer, wanted to soften the film because he was wary of all the violence. Plus the fact that I had the Mafia playing a very active role in the story. So, I just left.

Q : *Have you always chosen the films that you've directed?*
A : After being fired by Harry Cohn in 1956–1957, I couldn't find work in the U.S., so I left and went to Europe where I made four very bad films, just so I could eat. But luckily no one ever saw them.

Q : *They couldn't really be that bad . . .*
A : Oh yes, they were very bad.

Q : *How do you work on your scripts? You are never credited as screenwriter, but you almost always collaborate on the screenplay.*
A : Since I don't write very well, I hire the best writers I can find and then I

work very closely with them. I insist that the screenwriter attend rehearsals, but after that, I don't want to see him for a year!

Q : *Most of your films are adaptations of novels. You rarely use original screenplays.*
A : Some of my films were made from original screenplays, unfortunately. My last film, . . . *All the Marbles,* is from an original screenplay. Again, unfortunately! But that's not really being fair. After all, if you make a film, you think it's good. It's only after you finish it that you realize it's not good.

Q : *You worked on a script in 1952.*
A : Yes, I worked several times on scripts, but the results weren't very satisfying. I wrote *Too Late the Heroes, 4 for Texas, Ten Seconds to Hell,* all of them very memorable films. The best thing that happened to me during the filming of *Ten Seconds to Hell* was that I met my wife!

Q : *What are your favorite films, or the most personal?*
A : There is no such thing as a personal film. However, there are films that have an impact on your career. For me in my early years, those films were *Kiss Me Deadly, The Big Knife,* and *Attack.* Then came *What Ever Happened to Baby Jane?* Ten years later, both *The Dirty Dozen* and *The Mean Machine* [*The Longest Yard*] really bumped my career ahead. But since doing those films, I haven't had any spectacular successes.

Q : Hustle *is a very good film, but underestimated.*
A : True, but also "under attended" . . . But I like the film a lot.

Q : *The style of* The Emperor of the North Pole *makes me think of certain silent films.*
A : In 1959 I was lucky enough to be a judge on a panel in Brussels selecting the best films in the world. A number of silent films were proposed for the list. Sure, the images, the movement, the choreography of the images in these films are all really beautiful. It's almost impossible to do those same kinds of things today. But when you watch those films today, you really miss the sound . . . I'm not sure I've answered the question you asked.

Q : *Since we're talking about silent movies, what was the nature of your collaboration with Chaplin?*

A : I never really collaborated with Chaplin. To me, he's Mr. Chaplin. A brilliant man. He's the boss and knows what he wants. The only sort of collaboration you can have with him, or rather, the only influence you can have on
him, comes from the look on your face when you're filming him. When he
turns and looks at you, and you make a funny face, he simply asks what's
not working. So you say, "I think you're going just a bit too far with that. It's
not quite subtle enough." He'll think a minute and do it again, adding just
the right nuances. He's a true genius. But he has very little interest in technique and knows very little about how to set up a scene. From time to time
I'd ask him, very politely, "Don't you think we should take a long shot of
you now?" He was used to putting the camera in the middle of the set and
saying, "OK, we'll film from here." One Sunday, after two weeks of shooting,
he went to see John Huston's *The African Queen*. The next day he told me,
"Huston uses lots of long shots. . . ." "Yes, yes, yes," I said, "that's how it's
done now." So he decided to start using more long shots. But it was Huston
who influenced him, [laughing] not me!

Q : *So, exactly, what kind of collaboration did you do with Chaplin?*
A : I was his assistant, with the title "assistant director," on *Limelight*. I had
a lot of responsibility, supervising the work of the technicians, the set decora-
tors, the carpenters, the cameramen. Generally overseeing all phases of production.

Q : *When you were talking about silent films, you said that it's almost impossible
today to recreate the technical perfection of those films. Why?*
A : Money! Except in the USSR if you're making *The Battleship Potemkin*, I
don't know of any country in the world where you can get 200 million dollars to make a film.

Q : *What's happening with your production company now?*
A : It's very close to being bankrupt.

Q : *Your son produced . . .* All the Marbles. *Did he use your money?*
A : I used all the profits from *The Dirty Dozen* to buy a studio. My company,
The Associates and Aldrich, made four films: *Too Late the Heroes, The Killing
of Sister George, The Grissom Gang,* and *Whatever Happened to Aunt Alice,* done
by Lee H. Katzin. Then they took away the studio and changed the corpora-

tion's name to The Aldrich Company. In fact, it's still the same company, just with no money.

Q : Kiss Me Deadly *has been a highly influential film in France, for a whole generation of critics and future directors. Has it been equally influential in the U.S.?*
A : When it first came out, *Kiss Me Deadly* went practically unnoticed. Its current reputation came from France. The New Wave critics were fascinated. After the French success, the film was more appreciated in the U.S. Now it's a cult film here, but all that occurred after the positive reception in France.

Q : *Why are there no more Westerns being made in the U.S.?*
A : Because too many of them were shown on television. In 1958–1959 you could watch a Western five nights a week. The audience was saturated with them. So, the real answer to your question is that no one wants to pay to make Westerns anymore. Now there's something I want to tell you. A man named Gene Moskovitz died last year. You probably don't know him but he wrote for the French edition of *Variety*. He came to France during the Liberation and stayed. No one knew more than he did about films and filmmaking. [With tears in his eyes] Gene Moskovitz bridged the gap between film-lovers and filmmakers in America.

Q : *How would you describe your style of directing?*
A : I don't know! [Laughs] I guess I'd like for people to think of me as someone who tells a good story, who has something to say. That's not true of all directors.

Q : *Is Lee Marvin difficult to direct?*
A : Lee's a charming man, very friendly, an excellent actor, very professional. But he can get incredibly drunk. Not everyday, thankfully, but two or three times during filming. It can get really awful.

Q : *Is he better drunk or sober?*
A : Sober. When he drinks too much, all you can do is send him home. But that doesn't happen often, really.

Q : *And Bette Davis?*
A : If you like, you can compare Bette Davis and Chaplin. Davis is a true

genius. The difference between the two is that Davis knows her limits, she knows what she can and can't do. She knows more than almost anyone about what goes into making a film—where the camera should go, where the light should come from, where her co-star should stand. She's extremely intelligent. Very tough, too. It's difficult to work with her. But rewarding. She's a great artist.

Q : *You took a risk in giving the lead role in* Kiss Me Deadly *to someone who wasn't yet a star, Ralph Meeker.*
A : Ralph Meeker had just finished a successful run as the lead in a Broadway play. When he quit the play to do *Kiss Me Deadly*, Paul Newman replaced him. I thought he was a very exciting actor, new and fresh. Plus, I didn't need a real star to get the money for the film. The name "Mickey Spillane," who wrote the book, was enough.

Q : *Did you come up with the idea of changing a story about drugs into a story about stealing the "secret of the atom"?*
A : The book is very different from the film. Bezzerides, who wrote the screenplay, suggested the idea of an atomic explosion. That completely changed the perspective of the film. I just put Bezzerides' wonderful idea on film. As usual, Bezzerides came to the two weeks of rehearsals and then went home. I didn't see him again for a year. I chose him because he'd written several marvelous films during the '40s, like *They Drive by Night* (by Raoul Walsh) and a couple of really good police films for Warner Brothers. He did some great work on *Kiss Me Deadly*, so I hired him again to help on a film I made in Greece, *The Angry Hills*. But he fell in love with the star and never finished the screenplay. He's a funny guy—a tough Armenian who hates the Turks. And, just about everyone else. I'm happy to say he's still alive . . . Screenwriters are a bit more appreciated now than they were in the past. But they're still far from being at the top of the profession. You have to remember that the whole black-listing episode ended the careers of an entire generation of writers. It literally killed three hundred of them.

Q : *During the famous quarrel between Joseph Mankiewicz and Cecil B. De Mille as president of the Guild of Assistant Directors, you took Mankiewicz's side.*
A : Mankiewicz refused to sign a loyalty oath. As president of a union, you have to sign a legal document that is completely apolitical. Mankiewicz

signed that document, but he refused to sign another one, at De Mille's insistence, that was highly charged politically. And that's why nineteen directors and one assistant director signed still another legal document trying to keep Mankiewicz from being ousted. At the Director's Guild general meeting, even men you'd never suspect of having the same political views as Mankiewicz—like George Stevens and John Ford—spoke out for him.

Q: *During the time of the black-lists, you worked with Joseph Losey and many others who were on the lists. Did that worry you personally?*
A: Since I was a very good assistant director, I was one of the busiest. In truth, there weren't many good ones. I also worked for the best and brightest directors, the same ones who were black-listed. If I'd been five years older, I think I would have been on the list, too. The people whose names appeared on those lists never recovered from the damage. Their careers were ruined. When Dalton Trumbo came back to Hollywood, I was the one who asked him to write the screenplay for *The Last Sunset*. But he still wasn't able to sign his name on the contract. In the middle of filming, he told me, "I'm leaving." "But we haven't finished the film," I said. "Doesn't matter," he said, "because Otto Preminger has asked me to write a screenplay that I can put my name on." He left and wrote *Exodus*. That was the first film that someone who had been black-listed could put his name on.

Q: *What's the story behind* Twilight's Last Gleaming? *The French version was severely cut.*
A: First off, I should never have made that film. It was well shot, and well acted, but it was a flop because at the time no one wanted to hear about Vietnam.

Q: *Your films are often very ambiguous—they can be very violent and at the same time denounce violence. And you've also been criticized for your use of violence.*
A: This isn't the first time I've been asked this question. But every time I answer it, I try to give a different response. To start, the world is violent. Whether you like it or not, violence is more successful than non-violence. Whether we like that truth or not, people we admire use violence to solve their problems. If I had to choose between attracting attention through violence or not attracting attention at all, I'd choose violence. Enough on that. A critic once told me that maybe I was getting rid of all my aggressiveness,

all my frustrations by putting it into my films. I said if that were true, I would already have killed a few critics . . . I don't know . . . It's a good question, though. But I really don't have a good answer.

Q: *You've made Westerns, police films, war films, and two films about the cinema. Which genre do you like best?*
A: I refuse to answer! I look first of all at the stories—stories involving men more so than women, men who've fallen from a certain state of grace, who've lost their honor, who don't really care about the world around them or their work, but who want to be better in their own eyes, to recover their lost honor. They could care less about being heroes or about being liked. At the same time, they want to get their self-respect back. "I can like myself again," that's what counts for them. But to get back your self-respect, you almost always have to resort to violence. No matter what the subject of the film is, the main character will have to deal with violent situations.

Q: *Do you have much contact with the young American filmmakers? Lucas, Spielberg, Coppola?*
A: "Hello, how are you?" That's about all. That's not meant as a joke. There's simply not much opportunity for contact, but there's no lack of respect. All those guys are products of film schools. They're quite brilliant. Spielberg is clearly the most brilliant. In my day, there were no film schools. You learned by working as an assistant director on three films with Milestone, two with Losey, two with Wellman, and one with Chaplin. Even when you worked with a very bad director, you learned what not to do. Filmmakers today learned their craft differently. You're talking about two entirely different ways of thinking. Maybe that's why there's so little contact between the two generations.

Q: *Why do American audiences only like American films?*
A: American audiences are very young. The kids hardly know their own country so it's useless to expect them to be curious about other countries. That may change as more people start paying for cable TV because the viewers tend to be older.

Q: *What do you think of French cinema?*
A: French and American cinema face the same problems. France went

through the New Wave era but the U.S. hasn't experienced that yet. Except for the sort of "New Wave" a few years back that centered around cartoons—films that really were "cartoons," made for a very young audience. Things need to be shaken up a bit in the countries that are producing major films. But I don't see that happening yet, although you can already see it coming in Australia and Great Britain.

Q : *Do technical problems interest you much?*
A : You learn from experience. I've been in this business for thirty years. I'm beginning to understand it. It's almost second nature to me. The technical stuff is the easiest part of the job. But in the end, the most important things are the story and the characters—and that's what counts for the audience.

Q : *What is your best screenplay? Is* Vera Cruz *one of the best?*
A : The screenplay for *The Dirty Dozen* was really bad the first time I read it. It was just an adventure story. But I reworked it with Lukas Heller, and the film turned out really well—because it's funny. It's got adventure and a feeling of openness, but it's also funny. Quite different from what we started with. Heller did a terrific job, like James Poe did on *The Big Knife* based on Clifford Odets's play. Poe also wrote *Attack* for me. He's one of my favorite screenwriters.

Q : *In* The Dirty Dozen *some of the gags seem to come right out of the world of cartoons. All the stuff that goes on between Ernest Borgnine and Robert Ryan, for example.*
A : I'm sure I'm responsible for that. In the beginning there was nothing funny in the script. It was simply an action film. But I thought that here and there it needed to be funny. Otherwise it would have felt just like the kind of film you'd seen fifty times before.

Q : *Why have you never directed a real comedy? Neither* 4 for Texas *or* The Frisco Kid *are really comedies.*
A : *4 for Texas* was a real disaster! Directors are like actors—we're chosen. We're catalogued and pigeon-holed. If you've only done gangster films, or Westerns, it's hard to convince someone to give you the money to make a comedy. That's how the system works. You get paid to do what someone else thinks you're able to do.

Q : *Wasn't it Burt Lancaster who gave you your first real break in an important film,* Bronco Apache?

A : Yeah, I met him while I was working as the production manager on *Ten Tall Men.* Willis Goldbeck directed and Harold Hecht was the producer. Hecht and Lancaster wanted to do *Bronco Apache* cheap. They knew that I'd done a film for Metro in sixteen days, *The Big Leaguer.* My next film, *World for Ransom,* only took eleven days! They asked me to do *Bronco Apache* in thirty-five days. They weren't the least bit interested in whether or not I was a great director. But, I was young, smart and understood the production and technical sides of making a film. And I'd already made forty-eight hours worth of TV programs. They offered me the union minimum wage and I accepted. It was a great chance not to fail. So I made *Bronco Apache* just like they wanted it, fast and cheap. They were pleasantly surprised, so much so that they offered me *Vera Cruz.* I might've had to wait a hundred years to make a film as important as *Vera Cruz,* if I hadn't started with *Bronco Apache.*

Q : *You often use the same actors in your films, especially character actors like Wesley Addy, Richard Jaeckel . . .*

A : I like to use those actors because I know exactly what to expect from them. Just tell them what you want to do; they do it. You don't have to waste time explaining the whole history of the characters to them.

Q : *Who's your favorite actor?*

A : Brigitte Bardot, no contest! [Laughing] Gary Cooper was a very good actor, much better than most people thought. Charlie Bronson could have been a great actor, but he's not aware of his own potential, and he missed his chance. It's also wonderful to work with Jack Palance. Burt Lancaster is a much better actor now than he was twenty-five years ago. He's fantastic in *Atlantic City,* but he could never have done that role twenty-five years ago. He's also excellent in *Ulzana's Raid* and in *Twilight's Last Gleaming.* He was quite good in *Bronco Apache* where the work he did was much harder than in *Vera Cruz.* That was an expensive film. He was the co-producer and a bit intimidated by Gary Cooper.

Q : *You don't seem to be comfortable with the structures of American cinema today. Brooks and Mankiewicz, for example, say they don't know any more what films to make.*

A: No, it's not that. We know what films to make, it's just a question of money. And it can be disastrous if you make the wrong decision. Making a film is not terribly expensive in itself. It's the cost of merchandising it that is unbelievably expensive. If you spend ten million dollars to make a film, you have to spend another twelve million to sell it to the public. It's easier for a producer to just turn down a project—that way he's sure not to be wrong and he won't make a mistake, but he also won't make any films.

Q: *Mankiewicz has said that films today ought to be made for twelve-year-olds, who only get excited over* Star Wars.
A: If you can do a film in twenty-five days, you can always find a television station to produce it. But Mankiewicz doesn't want to work in television.

Q: *American films today are less interesting than they were twenty years ago.*
A: Yes, but twenty years ago, no film brought in twenty million dollars.

Q: *But the big studios made huge profits!*
A: They earned a fortune. But two things have changed—the audiences now are much younger; and young people go see the same film four or five times. In the past, people only went to see a film a second time if it was exceptionally good. Now they go five or six times in two months.

Q: *Would you like to make films like* Star Wars *or* Blue Thunder?
A: I have no interest in making those kinds of films. I'm sure the people at Universal were quaking in their boots over *On Golden Pond* with Henry Fonda and Katharine Hepburn. But the public loved it and the film made lots of money.

Q: *The average cost of making a film is going up quickly. Your last film cost ten million dollars to make.*
A: Right, but *The Dirty Dozen* took five million to make. In today's dollars that would be twenty-five million. *Sodom and Gomorrah* cost three and a half million—again, that would be twenty-five million today. The problem now is that the filmmaker has to do everything—find a story and get the screenplay written, hire the actors, the screenwriter, the musicians, the photographer. No one tells you what musician or photographer to choose. After all that work, you have to sell "the package" to someone whose job to this point

has been to sit behind a desk. Unless you do all the work yourself, you'll end up with nothing. Franklin Schaffner, who by the way is a very fine filmmaker, has done practically nothing in ten years. And David Lean's only made one film in twelve years. You have to bring the whole "package" to the table.

Q: *Who are your favorite directors?*
A: Kazan. He was a great director—once upon a time. *Zapata, A Streetcar Named Desire* are wonderful films. John Ford was great—with certain Westerns. The Italians, Rossellini, De Sica are both sensational. I made three films with Milestone. He had a lot of taste as well as talent. He was a big influence on me. Joseph Losey wasn't very comfortable with "the establishment" and with how to treat a script, but he was terrific in dealing with the actors. Chaplin could have cared less about technique, but he had unbelievable energy. He could work fourteen hours non-stop. Everyone else would drop, but not him. You tend to borrow a little bit from everyone, even without knowing it. In the course of making a film, you might find the same solution to a problem that someone else had found before you. That's not plagiarism, it's adaptation.

Q: *And what do you think of Renoir?*
A: Enormously talented, but he wasn't used to working with Americans. And the technical guys in America aren't used to working with a European director. There were some misunderstandings when we made *The Southerner*, but his wife was wonderful and helped him a lot. Renoir was very gifted, very courageous and simply wonderful with the actors. I was a very hard worker and a great assistant but I'd never worked with a European before. Years later he directed a theatrical version of *The Big Knife* in Paris and he used the set from my film. He should have done something different. The next time we met, I joked with him about it. He was a really nice guy. He thanked me, so I didn't say anything else. By that time it was much too late to worry about it. Renoir was a truly great filmmaker, not so much for what he did with the camera, but for what he did with the actors. He sincerely liked them and he had confidence in them. It was fantastic to watch him spend so much time explaining exactly what he was looking for. I don't think he really cared where he put the camera, but still, he knew exactly what he wanted. In *The*

Southerner he cast a very ordinary actor, Zachary Scott, but he got a great performance out of him, the best performance of Scott's career.

Q: *What did you learn from working in Europe?*
A: In Italy I learned the importance of using two cameras. Hiring technical staff there isn't very expensive, but in the U.S. hiring two camera crews is a rare luxury—even though having two cameras adds a lot of possibilities during the editing process. Now I always use two cameras at the same time. Saves time and energy. But the cameramen don't like it. It complicates their lives.

Q: *Are you interested in editing?*
A: I always do the editing of my films. Once I finished filming, I can spend twenty weeks editing, if I have to.

Q: *Do you miss the time of the great studios, and the directors who worked under contract?*
A: The studios exploited the contract workers but they also taught them their craft and gave them a certain economic security. And when you asked for something, like a set, you got an answer in twenty-four hours—yes or no. Now it takes a year to get an answer. No one can make a decision. Someone can always tell you no, of course, but everyone's afraid to tell you yes.

Q: *Did you know Howard Hughes when he was head of RKO?*
A: I met him once when I was an assistant at RKO, after Hughes bought it back. One Sunday he ask for a production manager and an assistant to show him around the studios. I went and took notes while he checked out all the departments—music, sets, costumes. He never said a word. When the production manager asked him what he thought of it, Hughes just said, "Repaint the whole thing." That was the last time he ever stepped on a set. I was an assistant on the first film done at RKO when Hughes took control of *White Tower.* At the time, Lester Cole, the screenwriter—and a very good one—was suspected of being a Communist. So was the director. Both were fired and a new director and screenwriter were brought in. But they didn't fire the producer, Irving Allen. He had a 60 percent interest in the film. And it was a very good film. So he asked for 67 percent. But Hughes refused. Well . . . part of the film was supposed to be shot in Paris. So, night after night, we'd get ready to leave for Paris at midnight, on a TWA flight. Hughes owned TWA at the

time, and—night after night—he'd refuse to let us go. Finally Allen called
Hughes' associates to see what was going on. They told him they only
wanted to give him 25 percent of the film. Allen said he wanted 65 percent.
So they said, "OK, 65 percent of nothing, or 25 percent of the film." Allen
gave in and—that night—we left for Paris.

Q : *You seem to be more interested in your male characters, strong men like Burt
Lancaster in* Vera Cruz *or Lee Marvin in* The Dirty Dozen, *than in your female
characters.*
A : Not when it's Bette Davis! Most of my characters are cynics, very "sophis-
ticated." They don't give a damn about society in general. They're clever
guys but not very cuddly, or popular. Lee Marvin plays almost the same character in *The Dirty Dozen* as he does in *Emperor of the North Pole,* even though
the stories are completely different.

Q : *You have a reputation for working very fast.*
A : I try. When you're working on a film like *Emperor of the North Pole,* it's
hard to move fast. It takes a lot of time just to install the cameras on the
dollies, things like that. Not that you have to do things over and over, but
just setting the cameras up takes a while. I had forty-two days to do my last
film. I got behind schedule—it took me forty-six days. But that was because
I had to film a wrestling match outside, using five or six cameras. The attack
on the castle in *The Dirty Dozen* was also something I couldn't do quickly. If
I take a long time to shoot, it's not because I can't make up my mind or the
actors aren't ready. I rarely go over budget and I prepare my scripts carefully.
I was a little behind schedule on *The Dirty Dozen* because we kept changing
the script every day. When things aren't ready from the beginning, you're
forced to take more time—that can be very expensive. Joe Levine, the producer of *Sodom and Gomorrah,* made us start filming before we were really
ready. That cost him a bundle.

Q : *Frank DeVol has done most of the music for your films.*
A : Yes, I've done a lot of work with Frank because he almost always knows
and does exactly what I want. You speak English to some composers and
they answer in music. DeVol's a great musician—fast, inventive, and not very
expensive. I've worked with some other very talented musicians but they

weren't able to give me the kind of music I needed. The recording, dubbing and mixing processes cost much too much to allow you to redo them.

Q: *By way of conclusion, I'd like to ask you one final question: What would the people you've worked with say about you?*

A: They'd say: He's too set in his ways and he can be a pretty nasty guy, but if you understand how he works, he's easy to work with. If you make a mistake and tell him, there's no problem; but if he catches you in a lie, it's the devil to pay! One day I was working with the great director Bill Wellman and I made a huge mistake—really serious and very expensive. We were working on a war movie, about a patrol of seven men, called *The Story of G.I. Joe.* One night after we'd been filming with these seven guys all day, I realized that one of them had been killed in an earlier scene. Everything had to be done over. I admitted to Wellman that it was my fault—if I'd tried to lie to him he'd have killed me. And he'd have been right. But more important, if you let even one lie go by, your crew loses respect for you. You have to be patient with people who admit to their weaknesses and unforgiving with those who don't. Most of the time people think I'm a son of a bitch, but I know exactly what I'm doing, and I know my job—most of the time, but not all the time. . . .

INDEX

144; "The Doctor," 3, 14–15, 99, 144; "Four-
Star Playhouse," 100, 144; "Philco Play-
house," 99; "Playhouse 90," 99; "The Sun-
dance Kid," 100
Aldrich, William (son), 32, 168
Aldrich Company, 169
Aldrich Studio, xi, 29–30, 74, 75, 105, 144–45
Allen, Irving, 177–78
Altman, Robert, 104, 108, 123; *M*A*S*H*, x;
McCabe and Mrs. Miller, 108
American Broadcasting Company (ABC),
66, 68, 69, 71, 74, 82, 105
Archer, Eugene, 28
Associates and Aldrich (production com-
pany), 13, 17, 28, 45, 112, 165, 168–69
Attenborough, Richard, x, 33, 34
Attica State Prison, 110
Auden, W. H., 111

Bachmann, Lawrence, *The Phoenix* (novel),
15, 26
Baker, Herbert, 42; *So This Is New York*, 54
Bardot, Brigitte, 174
Battleship Potemkin, The (film), 168
Baum, Marty, 66
Begelman, David, 161
Bergman, Ingrid, 11
Berlin Film Festival, 5, 28
Bezzerides, A. I., 25, 45, 70, 130, 170
Biroc, Joseph, 32, 43, 45, 59, 60, 73, 106, 116,
165
Blake, Walter, 56
Blue Thunder (film), 175
Bogdanovich, Peter, viii, x, 122, 145–46; *The
Last Picture Show*, 79
Borgnine, Ernest, x, 31, 32, 33, 54, 67, 75, 78,
85, 120, 121, 173
Bowles, Paul, *The Sheltering Sky* (novel), 37
Boyer, Charles, 11
Briskin, Samuel, 64
Bronson, Charles, x, 164, 174
Brooks, Norman, *The Fragile Fox* (play), 6,
46, 103, 149

Brooks, Richard, 147, 157, 174; *Looking for Mr.
Goodbar*, 146
Brown, Jim, 103
Brown, Roscoe Lee, 85
Brynner, Yul, 70, 81
Brzezinski, Zbigniew, 115
Buono, Victor, 48–49
Burke, Mildred, 160
Butler, Hugo, 20, 46, 62, 63

Cahiers du cinéma, 24, 58
Caine, Michael, 78
Calendo, John, xiii
Canby, Vincent, 83, 122
Cannes Film Festival, 49
Carol, Martine, 25
Carradine, Keith, 78, 120–21
Carter, Jack, 95
Carter, Jimmy, 114–15, 118, 127
Cassavetes, John, x, 30, 61, 65; *A Child Is
Waiting*, 30; *Minnie and Moskowitz*, 65
Chabrol, Claude, 51, 58
Chaplin, Charles, vii, 28, 41, 56, 62, 137, 143,
154, 160, 165, 167–68, 169–70, 172, 176; *Lime-
light*, 56, 99, 144, 168
Chase, James Hadley, *No Orchids for Miss
Blandish* (novel), 79
Chicago Democratic Convention, 141
Christian Science Monitor, 83
Clay, Lucius, 114
Clément, Rene, 8; *Gervaise*, 7–8
Clouzot, Henri-Georges, 8; *Diabolique*, 8;
Wages of Fear, 8
Cobb, Lee J., 8, 35, 64, 104
Cohen, Ronald M., 114
Cohn, Harry, 14, 35, 47, 54, 58–59, 63, 102,
104, 131, 138, 159, 162, 166
Cole, Lester, 177
Columbia Pictures, 8, 13–14, 43, 47, 59, 104
Comfort, Madi, 62
Contrerez, Jaime, 73–74
Cooper, Gary, 24, 28, 174

CONVERSATIONS WITH FILMMAKERS SERIES

PETER BRUNETTE, GENERAL EDITOR

The collected interviews with notable modern directors, including

Pedro Almodóvar • Robert Altman • Theo Angelopolous • Bernardo Bertolucci • Jane Campion • George Cukor • Brian De Palma • Clint Eastwood • John Ford • Jean-Luc Godard • Peter Greenaway • Alfred Hitchcock • John Huston • Jim Jarmusch • Elia Kazan • Stanley Kubrick • Fritz Lang • Spike Lee • Mike Leigh • George Lucas • Michael Powell • Martin Ritt • Carlos Saura • John Sayles • Martin Scorsese • Steven Soderbergh • Steven Spielberg • Oliver Stone • Quentin Tarantino • Lars von Trier • Orson Welles • Billy Wilder • Zhang Yimou